D1568693

THE PITTSBURGH STEELERS

THE
PITTSBURGH STEELERS

THE OFFICIAL TEAM HISTORY

ABBY MENDELSON

TAYLOR PUBLISHING COMPANY, DALLAS, TEXAS

Published by Taylor Publishing Company
1550 West Mockingbird Lane
Dallas, Texas 75235

Book Design by
Bob Moon, SporTradition Publications
798 Linworth Rd. East
Columbus, Ohio 43235

Library of Congress Cataloging-in-Publication Data

Mendelson, Abby.
The Pittsburgh Steelers : the official team history / by Abby Mendelson.
p.   cm.
ISBN 0-87833-957-4
1. Pittsburgh Steelers (Football team)—History.   I. Title.
GV956.P57M45   1996
796.332'64'0974886—dc20   96-19075
CIP

Printed in the United States of America
10 9 8 7 6 5 4 3 2

PHOTOS (i-xv):

(i) The menacing stare of Mean Joe Greene. (ii-iii) Kordell "Slash" Stewart picks up one of his 30 first downs in 1995. Number 73 is Justin Strzelczyk. (vi-vii) Rod Woodson gets a grip on "Neon" Deion Sanders during Super Bowl XXX. (ix) Bloodied and bruised, the Louisiana Rifle, Terry Bradshaw, still outplayed the competition. (x) A proud tradition: Steelers memorabilia on display. (xi) Forget the blue, we'll go with Steeler gold! Terrible Towels at Super Bowl XXX, Phoenix, January 28, 1996. (xiii) Levon Kirkland levels a Patriot while fellow Sixty Minute Man Chad Brown, number 94, provides reinforcement. (xiv) With an offense based on passing to tough-guy Ernie Mills and handing off to resilient Bam Morris, number 33, the Steelers romped in the 1995 AFC Divisional Playoffs.

In memory of
Arthur J. Rooney
who made it all possible.

CONTENTS

ACKNOWLEDGMENTS

A project like this does not proceed as an individual undertaking, regardless of whose name is on the cover, and I could not possibly have completed my labors without the help of many devoted people. To them, I would like to express my profound gratitude.

A few names, *maestro*, please:

Dan Rooney, for inviting me to the party and then trusting me to get the story right. It is an honor to be a part, even in this fleeting way, of the outstanding organization he has built;

Art Rooney, Jr., invariably generous with both his time and spirit;

Joe Gordon, patron, advisor, guiding light. In the old days, he got mad at me twice—a truly fearsome thing: once when an editor had me ask an incredibly stupid question about the Chief, and another time when I wrote a flattering profile of him, who as the Steeler director of communications is the most visible invisible man I have ever known. With that in mind I will not risk his wrath, nor embarrass him further, except to say that he is the consummate professional;

Rob Boulware and Ron Miller, tireless in their efforts to track 'em down and bring 'em back alive for interviews;

Mike Fabus, the Ansel Adams of his age, a stellar shooter whose snaps helped shape this book's literal and figurative vision;

The current and former Steeler players, coaches, and personnel, who so freely gave of their time and their hearts. The former players, so rich in memory and gratitude, and the current crop, so fierce and bright about their mission, were invariably courteous and grateful (especially the ebullient Dwight White, who ended our time together by saying, "You're a great American." You could hear his laugh in Cleveland).

I would like to pretend that it is my brilliance and erudition as an interviewer that resulted in the wonderful stories you will read here, but it wasn't. These people are pros, on and off the field, and in most cases all I had to do was flip on the tape recorder and admire the view.

No writer works in a vacuum, at least not the good ones, and I would be remiss if I did not nod to those scriveners who have hit this sled before me.

Although the list is far too long to enumerate here, I must name a few whose earlier labors made mine far less strenuous: Pat Livingston, formerly of the *Pittsburgh Press*, Ed Bouchette (for whom I did indeed punch the button many years ago on a late-night Pirate story) of the *Pittsburgh Post-Gazette*, Roy Blount, and Jim O'Brien;

Larry Stone, friend and partner, and Taylor Allderdice, football coach, helped shape my thinking about Steeler teams past, present, and future.

I am also grateful to the many friends and colleagues who so solicitously asked how it was going (and were not offended when I growled, "Don't ask").

My children, Jesse, Elie (who so badly wanted a book, any book, with my name on it instead of somebody else's; it's hard to convince a twelve-year-old that ghosting can be a good payday), and Tova Chaya, for leaving me alone those many glamorous nights when I worked until my eyes crossed and fell asleep on my office floor.

Fran and Willie Newman, my incredibly supportive in-laws, who long ago stopped wondering when their eldest daughter's husband was going to have a normal career.

My parents, Annette Schiff and Ted Mendelson, who provided the framework and the chromosomes, and have remained my most vocal fans.

Despite the above, all the credit goes to my wife, Judy. Whatever gifts I have been given from heaven as a writer, researcher, and editor, they do not compare with the great gift of my wife, whose patience, kindness, and support make every endeavor possible. Whatever successes I have are hers and hers alone; the failures I will keep for myself.

Finally, my most profound thanks to old friend and former traveling buddy, radio ace Bill DiFabio, who put this project—and indeed my entire life—perfectly in perspective.

One afternoon, as I was leaving the Steeler offices, DiFabio drove by, stuck his head out the car window, and bellowed, "Get a job!"

Nice to know, after all these years, that I still retain the admiration and support of my colleagues.

Thanks, Bill.

FOREWORD

Last January, as the 1995 Steelers neared their Super Bowl confrontation with the Dallas Cowboys, more than one person expressed to me the guess that although Steelers fans were in a state of delirium, their excitement surely did not equal that which had existed in Pittsburgh in the 1970s, when the Steelers cut a path leading to not just one Super Bowl but four. I begged to differ. This time, as nearly as I could judge, the excitement was greater.

If so, why?

My best guess was that in this day, everything in pro football is greater—or larger. Media attention is larger. Adulation is larger—the adult who twenty years ago would ask for an autograph sheepishly, excusing himself by saying it was for little Jimmy, today makes no apologies and in many cases pays hard cash for the signature. Too, the business of sports is far larger—as are the distasteful transgressions of owners and players alike.

Welcome or unwelcome, everything is huge by comparison to the 1970s, so why should the excitement surrounding the Steelers' appearance in Super Bowl XXX have been an exception? It was not.

That said, the roads traveled by the Steelers since Art Rooney purchased a National Football League franchise in 1933, is the stuff of incredulity. Can it be that for more than six decades the Steelers, a near-worthless investment that lived to enchant a nation, have been governed by only two men—Art Rooney Sr. and his son Dan? The hurly-burly environment of pro sports has slapped tradition silly, but in Pittsburgh tradition survives.

The pages that follow are the Official Team History. "Official" histories, blessed by their subjects, normally mean many warts have been omitted. Indeed, author Abby Mendelson is frank to say in his Introduction that controversy is not on his menu.

"The offhand remarks, the middling tirades, fade quickly," he writes. We appreciate the highlights, the good times. The victories. There aren't many in life, and that makes them all the more enjoyable."

But know that in these pages, Mendelson does not grovel at the feet of his characters. He simply brings to life, skillfully and with humor, the annals of a football tradition that yields to none. He conveys the ongoing warmth that Steelers fans (when they are not hotly arguing a point or flat ripping their Steelers) harbor in their hearts for a team that is an institution.

I read the manuscript of this book in one sitting, taking a break only for lunch. If you are a Steeler nut, as I am, you may find yourself doing the same.

—Myron Cope

INTRODUCTION

"Now, after seventeen years."

Sidney Greenstreet
The Maltese Falcon

Pittsburgh is a city that shines today, with glittering towers, a spotless downtown, and tree-lined suburbs. But its corporate sheen rose from the muck of the earth, from the incessant grime of coal and steel, and from the dirt-stained hands and strong backs in the mines and mills.

The mills are long since silent, or nearly so, but that spirit of the town lives on. To survive you had to have spunk, character; as such, Pittsburgh grew to become singularly unpretentious: no glitz, no glory. Do the job, and get it done right. Don't brag, preen, parade, or pout. Just do it—clean, hard, and honest.

It was fitting, then, as heaven decides such things, that the football team be named the Steelers—nothing less would do. No animals, no flights of fancy, nothing but hard metal, ringing bright and true. Pittsburgh. Steelers.

Let us be honest about it. Pittsburgh is not—and has never been—a thrilling city. It's a big small town with strong-willed seasons, jagged terrain, and a great deal of charm.

Yet there is also the ineffable feeling that the world has inexorably passed it by. Like monuments of other fallen civilizations, the Colossus of Rhodes, the hanging gardens of Babylon, the Homestead works are all gone.

When the mills started to cut back and close and Pittsburgh lost one hundred thousand manufacturing jobs in the 1980s, it was only a matter of time before more and more of us moved away. The same hulking concrete highway that brought in people, goods, and services would take them out as well.

The population aged, sagged, and shrank. When pundits applauded the region's new manageable size, plain folk knew the truth and were dismayed. Where was everything going? Where were the good old days—when the now-closed Neville Island shipyard never stopped, and when you couldn't sleep for the noise and the soot, yet you liked them both because they meant money in your pocket and food on your table?

Pittsburgh slouched into the era of mergers, takeovers, and downsizing, with heartless, soulless, and faceless entities deciding the fate of thousands—and then skulking away.

Something was left—something we loved and by which the world knew us. A North Sider named Arthur Rooney and his son Dan, despite blandishments and big-buck offers, were loyal. They never complained, never blamed the fans for a blessed thing, never gave up. Because they love this place and these people, they never bad-mouthed Pittsburgh, never threatened, never moved away. They were always here. They were always ours. The fans understood that love and loyalty, and returned it. "This," sports aficionado, superfan, and saloonkeeper Steve "Froggy" Morris croaks, "is one of the best franchises in all of sports." Surely, it is so.

This, then, is the story of a football team and the people who love it. It is a story about character—in an owner, coaches, and players. The fact that the people who populate these pages have extraordinary physical abilities seems less important than the fact that they are extraordinary people. That's the part that really lasts—and that really matters more than the gleaming trophies, diamond rings, or fading yellow dish towels waved aloft on frigid Sunday afternoons. Character. Heart. Loyalty. So that when Bill Cowher said that his team won the 1995 AFC

> "The task at hand is clear and simple. What we must do is take the credibility and stability of the front office and the wealth of young and proven players. We're going to unite that. We'll bring back the pride and the tradition that's long been associated with the Pittsburgh Steelers—and more important, the great people of Pittsburgh."
>
> *Bill Cowher, upon being introduced as the Pittsburgh Steelers' head coach, January 21, 1992, exactly four years and one week before taking his team to its first Super Bowl in sixteen years.*

Trophy for you, the fans, he meant it. That is why it is there in the Steelers' lobby for you to see, along with the four Super Bowl trophies, the team photos, the Hall of Fame portraits—the Chief, Jack Splat, Mean Joe, the Emperor Chaz, and more. The door is open, walk in and enjoy.

I shouldn't admit this, but when I came to Pittsburgh in 1965 as a college freshman, I was not only a nominal New York Giants fan, but I didn't know that the Steelers existed. The Bears, yes. The Browns, certainly. The Packers, but of course. The Steelers? Never heard of 'em.

Things have happened since to change my perspective, of course, including the fact that a long time ago, during their heady days in the 1970s, I covered the Steelers for various publications. Then, as now, I was struck by the remarkable dedication, precision, and self-assurance of these fellows.

What makes their story all the more interesting is that many of the lads are not what the pros call "specimens." Many are undersized, by football standards at least, many are self-defined overachievers. Yet they succeed—largely because of heart, grit, and ultimately values. The athletes I knew in the 1970s have their plaques, rings, and trophies—but most of all they have a way of life built on dedication and courage.

When they came to Pittsburgh, they thought they were training for a brief career in professional football—how to play a grueling game for profit. To their surprise, they were really training to be men, to build a life. Their coach schooled them to block and tackle—and to get on with their life's work as men of character and pride.

Perhaps what most Steelers did with their opportunity was summed up best by former defensive back J.T. Thomas. Once upon a very bad time, growing up in the South in the 1950s and 1960s, he was not permitted to eat in certain fast-food restaurants because of something as simple and foolish as the color of his skin. Later, Thomas owned restaurants in the same chain. For those who are of an age, and who vividly remember such struggles, his story is a revelation.

Virtually every one of the Steelers is grateful for such opportunities, so much so that it is difficult to attend a charity event, community day, or sports banquet and not find a current or former player. These are people who give something back to the community; they remain rightfully proud of their accomplishments, and the special times are aging nicely in their memory.

Then, as now, the players, or most of them, were always polite gentlemen. They were also, individually and as a group, noticeably smart, gifted, and motivated. Indeed, Mr. Noll expected nothing less.

It's a part of the corporate culture, where the team owner's photo is conspicuously absent from official publications, that everyone gives credit to someone else. The Chief never grandstanded, and neither does his son Dan. Chuck Noll barely discusses his role in his successful creation, and certainly does not credit it. The Class of '71 bows to the Class of '74. The Class of '74 credits Joe Greene. Joe Greene credits Franco Harris. And so on.

Frankly, you would have to cover sports to know and appreciate how rare these men and the Rooneys are, and how fortunate Pittsburgh is to have them. Some franchises don't have the same owner for seven months, or even seven weeks. Some franchises are owned by screamers and substance abusers. The Rooneys have led the Steelers for nearly seventy years with no intention of relinquishing the reins. They neither boast nor berate; like our mountains and rivers, they simply are, and are so good at what they do, we tend to take them for granted. We shouldn't.

I once worked for one of the world's worst editors, a martinet who, by gum, was going to ferret out all of the planet's evils and expose them in his publication. (He didn't last too long, and neither did his journal, but that's another story.) One day he sent me to find the dirt on the Steelers—they were so successful they had to be crooked. I was told to see Dan Rooney and get to the bottom of this business of taking the reporters out to dinner the night before road games. Doesn't this influence coverage?

Rooney's look was one of piercing disgust. "If we can buy a guy for a dinner," he made a face, "we don't want him."

I last covered the Steelers during Super Bowl XIII—January 1979. Seventeen years later, I returned. When I left my sportswriting job, I wrote a letter to the organization saying good-bye, because of all the things I ever covered, the Steelers were my favorite. I enjoyed it all, even the player who threatened to make me into a knick-knack in the gift shop of the Denver Marriott—an incident about which my colleagues still needle me. It broke my heart to leave, in part because Mr. Rooney really was what people say he was: a kind man with a great gift of making everyone feel special. Chuck Noll, too, was brilliant, witty, incisive, and, at the right times, astonishingly personable.

At the time, I don't think anyone, not the players, writers, or fans, knew how great and rare the team's accomplishments were. It was all too new, and we took it for granted. "Don't it always seem to go," Joni Mitchell wrote in "Big Yellow Taxi," "that you don't know what you got 'til it's gone?" As time accumulates, we see more clearly. We see the greatness of the players, the organization, and the staff. At the time, none of us realized how truly good they were nor how much they meant to all of us.

Art Rooney, Jr., said that at a family funeral a priest remarked that the Rooney family is defined by humor and compassion. With that in mind, I have tried to write this book in their image. As they do with people they trust, the Steelers gave me free rein. I tried to capture the spectrum—funny stuff, characters, and kindness; hard work, values, and love. I hope you enjoy it.

It's a happy story—indeed, following the Steelers is not a painful duty, although some would make it appear so—and I wanted it to read that way. I eschewed controversy, not because I wanted a sanitized version of the story, but because I am genuinely not interested in controversy. The offhand remarks and middling tirades fade quickly. We appreciate the highlights, the good times, and the victories. There aren't that many in life, and that makes them all the more enjoyable.

This is the story of six decades of pride, loyalty, and tradition. A story of names like Noll and Cowher, Lambert and Swann, and Bradshaw and Greene. The story of a family named Rooney and a city called Pittsburgh.

We begin the book with Art Rooney, whose story, appropriately, is like so many Pittsburgh stories. The Chief was generous, as men of that era were: Before government hogged all the glory, he felt responsible for people. I know his story well. My wife's two grandfathers were roughly the same vintage. One, Reuben Levine, from Lithuania, had a small produce store in the Strip, and like the Chief, he ran it out of a little pocket notebook held together by rubber bands.

The family could never calculate the number of people he carried, the free loans he extended and never collected, nor the gifts he gave to down-and-outers. Her other grandfather, Nathan Newman, from Hungary, had a small dry goods store in Hazelwood hard by the Pennsylvania Railroad tracks. If you call Rege Cordic, now Hollywood's Golden Voice, he will tell you that it was Nathan Newman who carried his family and countless others through the Depression. That's the way people were back then. That was Reuben Levine and Nathan Newman—and Art Rooney.

This is where we begin, with a big-ticket horse player and small-potatoes sports promoter and a sooty, dirty city named Pittsburgh. It was in Pittsburgh that Rooney bought his $2,500 National Football League franchise in 1933, during the Depression, when people didn't have enough money for footwear, much less football. Let us return to the North Side, to the rough-and-tumble turn-of-the-century era in which Art Rooney was born.

Sixty years of family business: the Chief (left) and Dan Rooney with David Lawrence looking warily over his shoulder, 1987.

"My father always used to tell us boys," Art Rooney, Jr., recalls, "'Treat everybody the way you'd like to be treated. Give them the benefit of the doubt. But never let anyone mistake kindness for weakness.' He took the Golden Rule," Rooney smiles, "and put a little bit of the North Side into it."

That's where the story begins, on Pittsburgh's North Side in 1901, the horse-drawn era, adjacent to Exposition Park, where the National League champion Pittsburgh Pirates were the biggest thing in sports. Arthur J. Rooney, one of nine children, was the son of a saloonkeeper and a stern Irish matriarch who respected people and didn't stand for any nonsense from her children. He

CHAPTER 1

FATHER AND SON

Art and Dan Rooney

grew to manhood as a champion amateur boxer and prize fighter, football player, horseplayer *par excellence*, sore-armed baseball player, card player, and promoter who named his teams after anybody who'd pay—in cash or in kind. He won fortunes at the track. As a sports promoter in 1933, he invested $2,500 in the fledgling National Football League (NFL), renamed his semipro Majestics the Pittsburgh Pirates, and opened for business.

From such humble beginnings legends are grown.

To everyone he was simply the Chief, a name cribbed by his twin sons Pat and John from the popular *Superman* television series of the 1950s, leaked to the world, but never used to his face. This term of affection and respect fit him like a glove.

He rose, over succeeding decades, to become the most respected and beloved figure in Pittsburgh sports—if not Pittsburgh history. Kind, amiable, decent, humane, the same with king and commoner alike, Art Rooney was forever humble about

> "And remember, my sentimental friend, a heart is not judged by how much you love, but by how much you are loved by others."
>
> **Frank Morgan**
> *The Wizard of Oz*

The Steelers' legendary owner, Arthur J. Rooney, made his start from humble beginnings. He grew up above the family saloon on General Robinson Street on the North Side.

himself, and always treated everyone else like royalty— or at least like a member of the family.

In a business rife with cynicism and fast-buck artists, he stayed close to the earth, remaining loyal to his home town, family, neighborhood, and the Republican Party (the party of the turn-of-the-century Irish; he remained long after the GOP became unfashionable in Democratic Pittsburgh). He recognized the decency and humanity of all those around him—and was revered for it.

Rooney's trademark cigar and smile never left him. When he felt his team's losses, he suffered like a Pittsburgher—in silence.

He brought his five sons into the family sports businesses, and was succeeded at the Steelers by Dan, his eldest. In the early years, the Chief operated the Steelers out of a hotel office and a pocket notebook. He had a noticeable talent for tenacity, for hanging on when the more faint of heart would have long since folded.

The Chief had the great Irish pol's gift of knowing everyone's name, and using it. Well, he *worked* at it, especially in his later years. He waited until training camp thinned out a bit so that he would be able to memorize all the rookies' names from a glimpse on the practice field before going into the locker room to shake hands and say hello.

More than anything else, he demanded that his five sons be regular guys—never carrying on like big shots or considering themselves anything special. Putting on airs, like the lace-curtain Irish, was not for the Rooney boys.

It was fitting that a man so much larger than life got his own statue, in 1990, at Three Rivers Stadium's Gate D, just a few first downs from the spot where he had nearly drowned running a skiff through flooded Exposition Park. The Chief's there now, cigar in hand, spinning yarns, swapping stories with anybody who is within earshot, close to the ground, to the people.

He is where children can climb up on his lap and listen to tall tales of horse races, the time he boxed Luby DiMelio's ears right in the office, and that day in Saratoga, where he made enough money to put a new roof on Father Silas's orphanage.

The Chief loved to tell boxing stories—all stories, really. "He enjoyed talking to people," Art Rooney, Jr., recalls. "He always said if he hadn't made it as a promoter he would have liked to be a newspaperman."

Baseball player, football player, champion amateur boxer, and young man with a future: future pro football Hall of Famer Arthur J. Rooney.

The Rooney brothers were tough guys, athletes, and devout churchgoers. Dan eventually became Father Silas, priest and missionary.

Prizefighters, football players, anything for a buck: the Chief (second from right) shoulder to shoulder with champion boxer Billy Conn (right).

But stories were not his living. General Robinson Street was a rough-and-tumble area in the early years of this century. "One of the things that kept my father and his brothers on the straight and narrow was sports," Art Jr. says.

"Through sports he was able to interface with people a lot older than he," he adds. The youngster ran errands, learned to play the ponies and politics, later admitting that he didn't know until he was an adult that there was something wrong with casting another man's vote. ("Mr. Murphy's sick, son. Why don't you go and vote for him?")

Down in the Ward, Rooney quickly made a reputation as a tireless promoter and athlete, and the Chief retained an athlete's thick neck and broad shoulders all his life. At one time he considered boxing his way around the world, but thought better of it and came home.

In the days when Friday night meant a session of the sweet science, the Chief promoted the fights, punch-drunk palookas all the way to Brahmans like Billy Conn, Fritzie Zivic, and the world-ranked Ezzard Charles-Jersey Joe Walcott bout.

Then there were the ponies.

"My father was the best horse handicapper in the world," Art Jr. says matter-of-factly. "He still may be the best in the world." Rooney shakes his head. "It was a gift."

From the horse rooms on the North Side to tracks all around the Northeast, Rooney was the kind of fellow, his mother said, to whom money seemed attracted. By the time he was married in his late twenties, he was a wealthy man, and it was not uncommon for the Chief to go out with $10,000 in his pocket. By the mid-1930s, after a legendary two-day killing at Empire and Saratoga, he is said to have told his wife, Kathleen, that they would never have to be concerned with money again.

Although different amounts are discussed, the most conservative estimate is $250,000—in Depression dollars—which would be worth millions today. The story goes that the Chief hired a Brinks truck to haul it all back. Did he? Nobody knows anymore, but that's part of the lore and the charm.

Art Jr. remembers going to the track with the Chief after the era of legal bookies, when the odds were made early and held, marveling at his father's quick mind, how

The Chief charmed everyone he met. He had a knack for making people feel special.

he could figure out the percentages in his head. The Chief would get tips from people, sure, but he'd watch the tote board, see where the money was going, and how fast. The Chief would follow the betting—and win.

Andy Russell tells of the time the Chief took him and Ray Mansfield to Belmont to look at a horse with a shot at the Triple Crown. The Chief was treated like royalty, which was amusing because, as he confided to Russell, "At one time I was asked to leave this racetrack, because I was going to break it."

The Chief was a card player, too, with his fingernails always manicured, in the pro's way. "Every three weeks he'd get a haircut," Art Jr. remembers, "because that's what card players did. And he was a real serious card player." He even had a big table in his North Side house where they'd play pinochle, and his wife would serve sandwiches.

When the Steelers had first-floor offices in the old Fort Pitt Hotel, the office doubled as the home of a seemingly endless poker game. When the contests recessed at dawn, the fellas would exit discreetly through the window so as not to disturb the more genteel folk in the lobby.

Then there were the Steelers.

Then, as now, Pittsburgh was a hotbed of football. Strategically placed between Latrobe and Canton, "the ground was fertile," Art Jr. recalls, for all sorts of teams, scholastic and semipro alike.

Rooney promoted them all: the James P. Rooneys (after a brother who was a state legislator), the Hope Harveys (one was a doctor who gave free services, the other

"Don't ever let anyone mistake kindness for weakness." For Pittsburgh Steelers Chairman of the Board
Arthur J. Rooney these were words to live by.

TERRY AND THE CHIEF

Perhaps the Chief got along so well with Terry Bradshaw (he got along well with everybody, but Bradshaw was a special case) because the Chief saw in Bradshaw a refection of himself, of a gifted athlete who enjoyed himself, who played like the Chief boxed—because he liked it. No pretense, no smokescreen (despite the thick-as-a-brick cigar haze), and no carrying on like a big shot.

No, Brad was a regular guy, one of his boys, who liked a good story, had a great sense of humor, and enjoyed a good cigar—especially if they were one of the Chief's. Who could ask for anything more?

Bradshaw frequently dined with Rooney, or watched Monday Night Football with him, or visited the horse farm. They'd swap yarns, sometimes long into the night, the Chief telling him boxing stories and treating him like a son. The Chief even let him come into the office unfettered to rummage for cigars.

And he never let the young fellow's spirits sag. "Even when things were bad," Bradshaw remembers, "he always told me how great I was, how much he thought of me. I think he felt sorry for me." When he was on the road, the Chief kept up the special relationship, sending postcards to Bradshaw from Ireland and Europe. Bradshaw still has them.

"I'll never forget after Super Bowl IX," Bradshaw says. "He was up on the podium getting the Vince Lombardi Award, and there was a lump in all of our throats." Bradshaw pauses, "he was such a great man."

Terry Bradshaw once said he thought the Chief felt sorry for him. Their relationship was certainly one of the closest in the club.

reputation, and the blue laws, which at the time prohibited Sunday games. In any event, at age thirty-two he was an owner. (In fact, Rooney would have liked to buy the Pirates, too, but in the squeaky clean days after the Black Sox Scandal, his gambling background would have prevented it. "He wasn't kosher enough," Art Jr. says. He kept a hand in baseball, though, helping out Hill District numbers baron Gus Greenlee with his championship Crawfords. At the end of the year, owing Rooney some $5,000, Gus opted for a party. What about Art? someone would ask. Oh, he loves a party, the answer came. He wouldn't mind.)

"One of the things you have to remember about my father," Art Jr. says, "is that when he started the club during the Depression, in 1933, everybody was on the breadline. He kept the Steelers going. The genius was to keep them in business—not to win or lose, but to stay in business. The logical thing was to stay in business by winning, but that wasn't always the truth. You stayed in business by keeping your payroll in shape.

"Forty years of losers, and he hated to lose," Art Jr. continues. "He was the greatest horseplayer of his time, and he knew how to win. And he was no fool in the business of football. But the big thing was to survive. You traded guys to lighten the payroll. He became a master at that.

the firehouse where they changed), the Rooney Reds (when no one else would pay), the Majestics (after radio sponsors).

Naturally, Pittsburgh fell under the eye of the new National Football League, who wanted the area for their own. A team franchise cost $2,500 in those days, but Rooney probably could have gotten it for free—given his

Commissioner Pete Rozelle presents the Chief his first of four Super Bowl trophies in January 1975.

"Before TV, he didn't have the money to compete," Art Jr. explains. "In fact, some guys said he should get out, because he couldn't afford to win. But he hung on."

The Chief kept his cronies, too, hiring Irish Catholics or St. Bonaventure grads. "He hired guys under the wrong premise," Art Jr. recalls, "but he loved the game and loved the relationships. Football also gave him credibility. He loved the environment, the players, and the camaraderie with the other owners. That was his life, and it was a labor of love. He wasn't just a guy who bet the horses. He owned the Steelers."

But he never lost touch with the street. One day, the Chief and coach Luby DiMelio got in an argument over fighting versus football. The Chief maintained that although, yes, football players might be conditioned, they were not practiced pugilists. Luby took exception. The Chief called down for two pairs of gloves, and there in the office, with the furniture moved back, he proceeded to give Mr. DiMelio some instruction. "He beat the hell out of him," is how Art Jr. remembers it.

Another time, an owner got in a fight with a player on the field. The owner got his clock cleaned, too. Although most of the football world bemoaned the spectacle of an owner having a dust-up with one of his employees, the Chief took a different tack. He wrote his fellow owner a letter saying that if he were going to represent the ruling class in fights with players, that he might be advised to pick a guy he could beat.

The Chief was a strict Irish Catholic, Art Jr. recalls. "You just didn't think about doing certain things," he says. "Like missing mass.

"He was a guy who came up in a rough, tough world," Art Jr. continues, "but he never became a part of it. For tough guys, he and his brothers were really into their religion." The Chief's brother Dan became Father Silas, a missionary in China. One time, when his mother Margaret took sick, Rooney went to church at seven in the morning and stayed until eight at night, praying for her. She recovered.

"The Catholic Church was the real defining thing in his life," Art Jr. says. "Sports was the conduit, the vehicle he used.

"Everybody always thinks of my dad as a nice old guy," he continues. "And he was. You couldn't walk through the airport with him. He'd never get to the plane because he'd talk to everybody in the place. He was that way; he

One of the proudest moments of the Chief's life was his induction as an honorary member of the Three Rivers Stadium grounds crew. The legendary Steve "Dirt" DiNardo sits to the Chief's right.

liked people. But with his own kids, he was very strict. He'd dispense corporal punishment."

Like the time he belted son Tim in the head for some loose lip at Shamrock Farms, their Maryland horse haven.

One day, in the Steelers' kitchen, Steeler broadcaster Myron Cope was holding forth to the press about the hot topic of the hour—a streaker who had, er, exposed Three Rivers Stadium to his unique talents. Myron, a fellow with a taste for the absurd, was decrying security efforts to hustle the chap off the premises.

That's when the Chief opened up. He felt the streaker was not only immoral, but could incite a riot. Then he berated Myron for encouraging that kind of behavior.

The Chief's stormy departure was met with shocked silence. No one had ever heard him speak that way to anyone—except his son.

"Gee, Myron, you arrived today," Art Jr. said.

"How so?" asked the stunned Myron.

"He treated you like a member of the family," Art Jr. shot back. "He gave you hell in public."

But to everyone else, the Chief was invariably friendly. "The Chief had time for everybody," Art Jr. recalls. "He made time for everybody. He was a folk hero, and he worked at it. And the secret was, he didn't let you know he was working at it."

"His real thing was dealing with people," son Dan remembers. "He dealt with people like no one I've ever seen. He made you feel as if the most important thing he had to do was to talk to you. He made you feel as if you were a friend. It wasn't planned, and it wasn't calculated.

"He did it with all of our players," Dan recalls. "He talked with them before the games, as individuals. He wouldn't give them a pep talk. He talked to them about their families. He would remember if they had sickness or some problems.

"His biggest thing to me and my brothers," Dan adds, "as far as giving us advice, was people. He would really get upset with us if we ever talked badly about someone or said something prejudiced. He would really come on strong, and say, 'That's not going to do you or that person any good, talking like that.'"

FREEDOM OF SPEECH RARELY EXTENDS TO EMPLOYEES

Although the Constitution of the United States of America guarantees all citizens the right of free speech, no one ever pretended that it applied to employees, who had better mind their *p*'s and *q*'s lest they be found unfit to serve.

As true as this is in corporate life, it is even more true in sports, where loose lips are tantamount to bad sales—and early banishment.

Considering that, the Steelers are all the more remarkable. As Steeler broadcaster Myron Cope says, "There aren't too many football owners who would have sat still for some of the things I've said about the Steelers. When they're good, I enjoy it. But when they stink, I say it. They have never tried to censor or put a muzzle on me."

Once, when the Steelers made preseason games mandatory in season-ticket purchases, "I really hammered them," Cope recalls. Dan Rooney was plenty angry. On a road trip, Rooney suggested a private dinner, and Cope agreed.

"All through the meal we argued whether they were right or wrong to charge for those preseason games," Cope says. "We had it out, but there was no bad blood—just two guys with a different point of view. He never said, 'We're taking you off the air.' That's the last thing this outfit would ever think about."

Art Jr. remembers the time he made the mistake of being curt with a flight attendant—and his father silenced him. "Do not treat people like that," he said. "You be pleasant to them."

One time at the Rooneys' Yonkers racetrack, Tim's secretary got out of line, and Tim berated her. As soon as she was gone, the Chief told his son he wouldn't work for him. "How do you keep anybody around here?" he asked.

The Chief knew how to work with people. For example, when the ground crew changed the stadium from baseball to football, they sometimes had to work through the night. Those times, the Chief came down with food and drinks. "He would take care of them," assistant coach Dick Hoak recalls, "and they would do anything for him."

As a self-made, self-sufficient man, the Chief "never wanted to be beholden to people," Art Jr. recalls. He never borrowed money and always paid in cash. The first time he ever had to use a bank was to raise money to buy the family racetracks. "He was troubled by that," Art Jr. recalls.

But borrow he did, for Vermont's Green Mountain, Cleveland's Randall Park, Philadelphia's Liberty Bell, all of which the family has since sold. However, New York's Yonkers and Florida's Palm Beach Kennel Club are still retained by the family.

"Rather than give us money," Art Jr. says, "he made it possible for his boys to have a job, which was much better. We had our self-respect."

For a gent with boxer's mitts, the Chief was the softest touch in the world. One time at the track, for example, a woman approached him and said she had lost one hundred dollars that she desperately needed. The Chief peeled off a couple of the fifties he always carried and gave them to her.

"You've just been taken," his companion said, "she works every well-dressed guy here."

"Oh," the Chief said, "I know she's pulling a fast one. But what if I'm wrong? What if she's honest? I can afford the dough. But I couldn't stand the idea of some poor lady needing it."

"My father was a very charitable person," Dan Rooney recalls. "Money meant nothing to him. Values were important." Indeed, although the Steelers lost money in every decade, the Chief always gave money at the end of the year to charities. One time, as he was about to give a large donation to several of his favorite philanthropies, Dan objected, saying that they had lost money that year and couldn't afford it.

The Chief shook his head. "I don't give money for a tax deduction. I give money because these people need it."

The people who worked for him knew that, too.

"He was the finest man I've ever known," says retired trainer Ralph Berlin. "He was down to earth, sincere, and cared about people. He always had a smile on his face

The Chief and his son, Dan Rooney, in 1962. The senior Rooney started training Dan early to participate in the family business.

and never thought he was too big to talk to people. He knew the players by name, and the players loved him.

"When we won the first Super Bowl," Berlin adds, "none of Mr. Rooney's sons came into the locker room. They stayed out on purpose, because this was the Chief's day. The players hollered, 'Chief! Chief! Chief!' and gave him the game ball. Then NFL Commissioner Pete Rozelle presented to him the Super Bowl trophy. There wasn't a dry eye in the place. Only after that did Dan and Art come in—that's the tremendous respect they had for their dad."

Simply stated, the Chief received respect because he gave it first. Case in point is the 1974 NFL players' strike. The rookies were on the field, but the vets were picketing, holding signs that said, "No Freedom, No Football."

One evening, Rocky Bleier's roommate told him that Mr. Rooney had called that day and would call back that night. Bleier wondered—why would he call me? In 1974, the Rock was not a star, not even a starter. He was just another vet trying to make the team.

THE TALE OF A TIMEPIECE

This is a story of the respect and reverence even the most cynical had for Art Rooney, a man who could melt even the hardest newsie's heart.

It was 1975, the era of Watergate, when the press was trying to come as clean as a hound's tooth. They tried not to accept anything from anyone that could compromise their integrity, including benefits from the sports teams they covered.

Until then, it had been a different story. Many franchises had more or less carried reporters, providing them meals, transportation, accommodations, and so on—and had pointedly called in the favors when they felt coverage was lacking.

The Steelers were generous, of course, but had never reminded a reporter of what he should or should not print. That wasn't Art Rooney's style, nor his son Dan's.

After the team won its first Super Bowl—its first championship in forty years—the Steeler personnel received the customary rings, and the press were given commemorative watches.

After a few nervous coughs, one fellow said to then-publicity director Ed Kiely that he could not accept the watch. Conflict of interest and all, the man said, swallowing hard. Paper would never stand for it.

"That watch," Kiely said stiffly, "is a personal gift from Mr. Rooney. If you don't want it, or feel you can't accept it, then you give it back to him yourself."

None of the watches was ever returned.

Finally, the phone rang. "Hey, Rock, sorry to bother you at home," the Chief said. It seems he had heard someone on a talk show berating the players—especially Bleier—about loyalty, because of what the Steelers and the Rooneys had done for him. "Listen, Rock," the Chief said. "I just want you to know that what I did for you, I would have done for any one of my boys. And you paid us back, on and off the field, more than we could ever have asked.

So if you believe in this strike, I want you guys to be out there tomorrow. Hopefully, we can get it settled and go on to play some football. So I just wanted to call and tell you not to worry about what's happening."

"I said, 'Thank you very much,'" Bleier recalls, "and amazed, I hung up. That is the kind of person the Chief was."

Tunch Ilkin remembers the time he and two other prospects came in for their rookie physical. As the trio was sitting in the lobby, out wandered the Chief, who started to straighten up the brochures lying around. "Hello, young men," the Chief smiled at them, "how are you doing?"

"Are you the janitor?" one asked.

"Oh," the Chief beamed, "I do a little bit of everything around here. Rooney's the name."

"That just tickled him," Ilkin recalls, "that he would be thought of as a regular guy."

As player rep, Ilkin had an experience similar to Bleier's. During a 1987 labor dispute, Ilkin was able to talk freely and honestly with the Chief about what they both believed was best for football. "I never felt that I would get cut because I was the player rep," he says.

"You talk about a true monarch," Mel Blount says. "The thing that is still amazing about that man is that he didn't care if you were Joe Greene or the guy who'd never get in the game, he treated you the same. It was contagious to all of us."

For his part, Franco Harris was captivated by the Chief's stories about the beginning. "It really made you feel good about how he helped mold and build the NFL," Harris says. "He always had good things to say, encouraging words and a pat on the back. It was really wonderful, because leadership is everything. You can tell an organization by how the people conduct themselves at the top."

Dick Hoak agrees. "Mr. Rooney was the greatest man I ever met. He was always fair with everybody, and his players came first." Case in point, when the team had a lousy season in 1968, going 2–11–1, Hoak had a terrific

The Brothers Rooney (left to right), Dan, John, Art Jr., Pat, and Tim. The Chief didn't give his sons money; instead, he provided them with a way of making a living.

one, rushing for 858 yards, then the third-highest all-time Steeler total. One day, as Hoak went in to pick up his check, the Chief asked him to sit down. At this time Hoak was making about $17,000. The Chief said, "We're not having a very good year." Hoak nodded. "But you're having a great year," the Chief continued, "and I want to thank you." Having said that, the Chief gave Hoak a check for $10,000. Hoak protested, "Mr. Rooney, you don't have to do that." The Chief countered, "Yes, I do."

In the last game of the year, Hoak separated his shoulder. The next day, he went to see the team doctor, right across the street from the team offices. Afterward, he figured he'd stop in the Roosevelt Hotel office and say hello. This time, Dan asked to speak with him. Praising his performance, Dan gave him another check for $10,000. Hoak again protested, explaining that Dan's father had already given him a check. Dan nodded. "I know," he said. "My father told me to give you this one, too."

Joe Greene has a similar story. In 1969, his rookie season, Greene held out for more money. Finally, he came

Hey diddle diddle, Rogel up the middle. In the early fifties, the Steelers' offense was so predictable, the fans would chant the plays. The Chief got so fed up watching back Fran Rogel, he actually sent in a play—once.

to the Roosevelt Hotel for talks. Training camp had opened, but Dan Rooney was holding firm—at a $10,000 distance, in those days a great deal of money. Dan said, "Let's go talk to my father."

Greene went in to see the Chief, who gave him a cigar. ("He warmed me over right there," Greene recalls.) Dan leaned over and whispered something to the Chief, who just said, "Well, okay, give it to him." Negotiations were over, and Dan drove him to camp.

"I always looked upon him as a special person," Greene adds. "That was the edge we had as a football team. The Cowboys, the Raiders, all of those people were equal to us in terms of talent. The edge that we had was Mr. Rooney. We did it for the Chief."

As a kid growing up in Chicago, Mike Wagner wanted to be a pro football player. But he didn't want to be booed; he wanted to leave when he could no longer perform. In 1980, after ten seasons on the best defensive unit in football history, Wagner was in constant pain—his shoulder, ankle, and hip were so bad that he had to sleep with a heating pad taped to his shoulder, while keeping his foot in an ice bucket. He was no longer an All-Pro. It was time to go.

When the Chief heard about Wagner's decision, he called him into the office. Couldn't he give it one more season? Wagner demurred. A week later, the Chief called Wagner back in for a talk. Wagner came, but said he wasn't going to play. "Well," the Chief said. "Why don't you sign this three-year contract anyway, and take this bonus check?"

"You don't have to do that," Wagner said. "I'm not going to play."

"We know you're not going to play," the Chief said. "Just sign the contract and take the check."

"It was a nice good-bye," Wagner says.

Mike Merriweather fondly remembers the Chief coming around the locker room. "How you doin', Mike?" he would beam. "How's everything going? That's a good Irish name, Michael." (Merriweather, of course, is African-American.)

Andy Russell recalls his rookie year, when the team lost the 1963 division championship to the Giants on the last day of the season on an icy field in Yankee Stadium. The Steelers' cleats couldn't get any traction, and the Giants donned sneakers and won. The team was about as low as it could get, but the Chief came around to every player in the locker room, thanked them all personally

JON KOLB'S ART ROONEY STORY

Before the 1969 draft, Oklahoma State offensive lineman Jon Kolb was personally contacted by a number of football teams, but not the Steelers. So he naturally assumed it was the one team that would not draft him.

Wrong. After Kolb was taken in the third round, right after Joe Greene and Terry Hanratty, the Chief called to congratulate him. Only trouble was, Kolb didn't know he'd been drafted—and had never heard of anyone named Rooney.

So when a Mr. Rooney was on the phone saying he had been drafted, Kolb didn't believe him. "I thought it was one of my friends," Kolb remembers. Although he was not as high-spirited as collegians can be, he was somewhat blunt.

"Are you excited?" the Chief asked.

"No," Kolb deadpanned.

"Well, we are," the Chief continued blithely. "We'll be looking forward to seeing you."

And so on, the Chief talking, Kolb giving one-word answers.

That night, Kolb watched TV.

Oops.

The kicker is that although Kolb apologized to the Chief many times over, the Chief invariably said he did not remember the incident—highly unlikely, to Kolb's way of thinking.

"That's the kind of man he was," Kolb says.

for a great season, told each one how much he appreciated his efforts, hoped he would have a wonderful off-season, and looked forward to seeing him the following year. "I was so impressed," Russell says. "I always loved him for that, and for coming to practice, rain or shine, to look at his boys."

But times changed, and after that season, the Chief's eldest son Dan took on an increasingly important role in the franchise. Named president ten years later, Dan is the man most responsible for the Steelers' financial and organizational successes of the last three decades. Currently, he serves as a wise and moderate voice of decency, calm rationality, and fiscal restraint to NFL leadership councils. A quiet, modest man, he built the franchise, encouraged Coaches Noll and Cowher, yet left them alone.

"It was not assumed that I would go into the family business," Dan says. "It was not a guarantee. My father thought that I had enough wherewithal to make it elsewhere. Because in the 1950s, he wasn't too sure the Steelers were the world's greatest business."

But it's all Dan wanted—all he ever wanted. Indeed, one of his earliest memories is of going to training camp at St. Francis College when he was five years old in the

mid-1930s. As little Dan observed the practice from the sidelines, a player suddenly swept him up in his arms as the play ran right over his spot. By his teens, having been to Steeler camp in Hershey, and Waukesha, Wisconsin, when the team combined with the Chicago Cardinals, he was a grizzled veteran.

A moment of high anxiety occurred when the Chief, having sold part of the team to Bert Bell, called Dan at home. Dan asked, "What's going on with the football team?"

"Don't worry," the Chief said, "it's going to be okay."

But he was still a boy and he needed a home. "In the early years, while my father went to sporting events, my mother kept our house and our family and tended to what we needed as children. She was the one who was there when he was traveling. She was the one we went to with problems, the one who made sure we got to school, who carried the importance of our faith, our home, our meals."

"She would go to our games," Dan recalls, "not the Steeler games. She showed us the importance of us. That was a big factor when you had a very famous father."

Along the way, Dan learned from his mother, but he learned a lot of the football business on his own. The Chief, he recalls, "wasn't a doting father, by any means. He would take me to training camp and leave me, and go about his business. I would loaf with the players, the equipment men, and the trainers." Young Danny fooled around enough to get his nose broken, to engage in some underage driving for Jock Sutherland, and to become camp manager by age eighteen.

"I learned more about this business from coaches than I did from anyone else," Dan says. Getting players, signing players, handling the budget, making sure travel was taken care of—"I learned all this at quite an early age."

Still, the Chief wasn't so sure. He had Dan work in the construction business. He asked if Dan wanted to run the racing business. The answer was always the same. Football.

Once Dan chose, there was no doubt. After graduating from North Catholic and Duquesne, where he quarterbacked both varsity squads, he was with the Steelers full-time. At his first league meeting by 1957, the Chief encouraged him to speak his mind. By 1960 he was making up the league schedule.

At this time, Rooney *père et fils* had a coach named Buddy Parker, a good coach with a bad habit of trading draft picks and prospects, talent and promise, for little or nothing. By 1964, when the Chief tapped Dan to head up day-to-day operations, Dan requested that Mr. Parker reconsider his ill-advised ways. Mr. Parker balked.

Lest it be forgotten, Mr. Dan Rooney is Irish, and although the Irish may be many things, they are not door-mats. So when Mr. Parker threatened to absent his services, Dan assumed control of the club.

Ironically, Dan was just about his father's age when the Chief bought the franchise, and just about the age of both Chuck Noll and Bill Cowher when they came to run the on-field operations.

Along the way, Dan's been his father's son, but he's also been his own man. After the 1968 season, for example, Andy Russell went to his first Pro Bowl. There, he discovered that other linebackers were making two to three times what he was. Russell returned to Pittsburgh set to renegotiate his contract. But Dan Rooney was ready for him. "I can't be held responsible for the mistakes of other owners," Rooney sniffed. "Besides, those players play for winners."

One year, Russell broke his thumb and could not play like an All-Pro, so he asked for a pay cut. Dan Rooney refused, and gave him a ten-percent raise instead. "That was pressure," Russell laughs.

When Chuck Noll released shot-up Vietnam vet Rocky Bleier in 1970, Dan Rooney was the first one to call. "We want to put you on the unable-to-perform list," he said, "and we want our doctors to take a look at you. Hopefully, you can make the team and help us."

"He gave me that extra shot," Bleier remembers. "That was the character of the man. Here was a kid, former altar boy, Notre Dame halfback, who was called into service,

"We'll bring back the pride and the tradition that's long been associated with the Pittsburgh Steelers." This was Bill Cowher's commitment as the Steelers' new head coach. Here Dan Rooney welcomes him aboard on January 21, 1992.

got wounded, and came back. All heart, with not a whole lot of talent. They gave me a second—and third—chance. That's the way of the Rooneys—that's the way Art was, and that's the way Dan is."

"Dan's very bright," adds former Steeler player and scout Jack Butler, "and has a good way with people. He's like the Chief. They treat people like they're human beings—not possessions or assets. The Chief was a very fine man. So's Danny."

"Dan is much more quiet than the Chief," Tunch Ilkin adds. "I really respect him for what he's done with this organization. He's a leader who doesn't want to be a leader. He never promotes himself, and would rather not be in the forefront."

"Dan Rooney is a remarkable guy," Bill Cowher agrees. "He's probably the best friend I have here—and the easiest guy to talk to. He does things with family in mind. It's nice to come to work at a place where they have the same values I have."

"Dan's never received the credit for what's happened here," Tom Donahoe says. "Not only has he lived in the shadow of his father, but he's lived in the shadow of Coach Noll. But it's a team effort. If you don't have a good solid owner, a guy who has a vision and direction, it doesn't make any difference what else you have. If you don't have a solid person at the top of the organization, you're never going to be successful."

It's a Steeler question, asked of players, coaches, owners: How do you succeed a legend? "I had my father for a long time," Dan says. "I'm not saying that both of our egos didn't get in the way once in awhile. I argued with him every day, and every day we'd get in a battle about something. His line was, 'Okay, do it your way. Just don't make any mistakes.' He gave me great support.

"It was really something to go in and talk with him. I didn't always want to, I didn't always agree with what he had to say, but it was tremendous to be able and go in to talk to him. He had great values, a great feel—he had great intuition about things. It was good for me, and it was good for him. It gave me a feeling of being on solid ground.

"So I never really tried to be him. I don't know that anyone has his ability to relate to people. Human relations—that was his forte. He was the best. I have to work at it. It's a different time now. You need to have your people functioning on the basis of what you have to do. In his day they could react.

"I always said I'm going to be me, I'm not going to try to emulate him. So I try to run this business a little differently than he did. I don't try to act like him. I don't think I should. I don't think I can.

"I do hope I have values similar to his, though. I'm proud to be a Catholic, but he practiced his faith where it counts—love for his neighbor. I feel that's important and I try to carry it out as much as possible."

The Chief's days are gone. Back then, he'd give more privately, off the cuff, out of the vest pocket, to anybody with a Roman collar, a hard-luck story, or both. Today, Dan is more public. In the old days, it was corned beef and cabbage in Owney McManus's back room.

Now, it's banquets in the Hyatt or Hilton with ruffles and flourishes, the TV stations in attendance, and film at eleven. Today much of Dan's charitable work is public, more United Way and Ireland Fund, less peeling off a few bills from the wad for a down-and-outer with a good story.

Such is change.

Or perhaps not. Life has brought Dan Rooney full circle. His own children aged and grown, he has moved back into his parents' Lincoln Place house, the North Side home he grew up in. "I just felt that it was a good house," he said, denying more grandiose parallels. "It's a short walk from the Stadium, and I can make it to anywhere in town within fifteen minutes. It's a handy place."

As the Chief aged, more business accrued to Dan and his brothers, attorneys, accountants, and assistants. As horse playing was no longer what it used to be, the Chief was semirctired, amiable, and astonishingly friendly. On August 25, 1988, the world became a poorer place for losing him.

The Chief was a tough guy, but he could be gentle, open, and caring with people. Maybe that's why, to this day, so many of the current and former players speak so highly of him—and speak so softly.

"He never wanted you to be a big shot," Art Jr. remembers, "or anything special. Just a regular guy. He kept preaching that."

Everywhere Art Jr. goes, it seems somebody knew his father—in airports, gas stations, you name it. Some years back, Art Jr. was in Coronado, California, and visited a drug store. "Oh," the clerk smiled. "Your dad was in here the other day." "It was like the North Side," Art Jr. shakes his head.

Another time, he stopped in a local department store to buy some ties. When he gave his credit card to the clerk, she brought a friend over. "Oooh," she cooed, "you're a biggie."

Art Jr. just shook his head. "No, lady, I'm not a biggie. My dad's a biggie. I'm just the son of a biggie."

The Chief's secret was to be larger than life, but never act like it.

"Never carry on like a big shot," the Chief used to say. And his sons don't, still.

"My mother always said," Art Jr. smiles, "that her ambition for us boys was that we stayed out of the clink."

A fitting tribute to a living legend: the Chief in bronze, Gate D at Three Rivers Stadium.

BYRON 'WHIZZER' WHITE
~ HALFBACK
PITTSBURGH PIRATE
FOOTBALL CLUB

·· FORBES FIELD 1938 SCHEDULE ··
SEPT. 11TH ··· NEW YORK GIANTS ····
OCT. 16TH ··· CLEVELAND RAMS ····
OCT. 19TH ··· BROOKLYN DODGERS ·· (NIGHT)
NOV. 6TH ··· WASHINGTON REDSKINS ·
NOV. 20TH ·· PHILADELPHIA EAGLES

**The Chief's premier attempt at respectability, All-American running back Byron "Whizzer"
White led the league in salary and rushing yards, 1938.**

Depression Pittsburgh was something to see. Before smoke control, which would not clear the skies until after World War II, a man wore two clean shirts every day, and soot covered everything. But it was good soot, good clean dirt, all over the chairs and the carpets, because it meant money.

When the mills were turning shifts and the sulfur stung like hell itself, people were happy because food was on the table and the kids had clothes.

CHAPTER 2

"I ALWAYS HATED TO LOSE"

The Early Years

In 1933, when Pittsburgh entered the National Football League, the Point was a tangle of railroads and warehouses—Gateway Center was nearly twenty years in the future—and whole sections of the North Side were little more than shanties. They were rough neighborhoods, too, and even churchgoers like Art Rooney and his brother Dan learned to use their fists before they learned their catechism.

The dark-haired, handsome, jovial team owner was a thirty-two-year-old given to suits and cigars, and he enjoyed joining an elite club that counted as members Tim Mara (a bookmaker, albeit then a legal pursuit), George Halas, and George Preston Marshall.

They liked him, too, this Rooney. He was a promoter—you find the contest, he'd sell the tickets. Tout, card player, and college man, too, he hired college grads for his teams—it was worth

> "It ain't too exciting, but it's mostly legal."
>
> **Robert Earl Jones**
> *The Sting*

As head coach, world-class carouser and Hall of Famer, Johnny "Blood" McNally made a good half-back. In 1937, he led with ten pass receptions, but the club finished a dismal 4-7.

a couple of extra bucks to get back on the gridiron and get your face pushed in.

His boys played at Forbes Field, which, given Pennsylvania's autumnal rains, was generally a quagmire—when it wasn't iced over. He had offices in hotels, first the Fort Pitt, later the Roosevelt, but he ran the club out of a little book he kept in his jacket pocket, held together with rubber bands. He called them the Pirates, like the baseball team.

In the old days, the days of Apple Marys and breadlines, ticket sales were total revenues—there was no TV money, no merchandizing, no civic tax breaks, no corporate bailouts, no interest-free loans—nothing. Derided for years for being too cheap to pay good talent, the truth was that more years than not, the Chief shored up the sagging Steelers gate with money he won at the track. He was a world-class horse player, too—he knew how to win, and he hated to lose.

Also-rans—and ran-overs—the Depression Steelers were what one former club official called "small potatoes, a hustle." Bought on a day that will live in . . . obscurity, the Depression team was semipro at best, little more than a succession of sandlot teams, cronies, locals, and college boys back before getting on with their life's work. The names are largely forgettable, except for one William Shakespeare, late of Notre Dame, the club's all-time number-one draft choice, who had the good sense not to play.

The Steelers came of age in the days when helmets were little more than leather caps with ear flaps, cleats were metal spikes screwed into shoes, and pads were an unsightly bulge at the shoulders and knees. In those old days, when no one had heard of facemasks, the sure signs of being a football player were battle scars and a broken nose (usually the result of plowing the south forty with your kisser while some gorilla sat on the back of your neck).

On an afternoon, a lineman could earn as much as one hundred dollars—not a bad payday when a good wage was forty dollars a week. Two and a half weeks' work on a Sunday — and if the price was a busted proboscis, or a sliced-up calf, so be it. With rare exception, players left

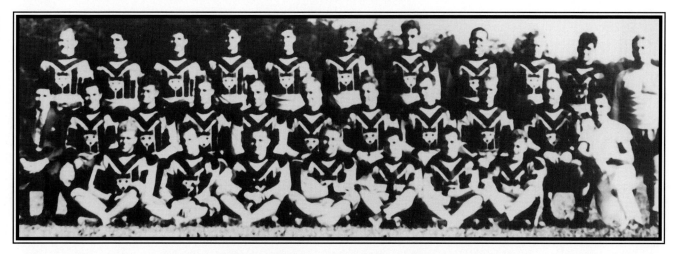

The members of the club's first squad, established in 1933, were little more than semipros, and their uniforms were a shameless tug at civic pride. Note the youthful Art Rooney (second row, left) and the first black player, Ray Kemp (upper row, fourth from right).

quickly, as soon as they found better-paying jobs, ones that didn't require stitches or liniment when the whistle blew at five o'clock.

The Chief confided to friends that he considered the Steelers a hobby—but not much more. Why not? There wasn't much money in it—football could hardly be considered a growth industry during the Depression—and besides, he made his dough elsewhere. Like many hobbies, this was sometimes expensive, but he enjoyed it. So early on, the Chief made the decision that the coaches would handle the players and football operations, not the owner (who more often than not preferred playing cards with his cronies or placing a bet on the sixth at Belmont). Oh, over the years he gathered together some good people—Hall of Famer Johnny Blood played and coached, Hall of Famer Bert Bell joined forces and coached, and Hall of Famer Walt Kiesling coached and coached and coached—but by and large, the policy was a disaster.

All births are difficult, and in the Steelers' case, the first game nearly went unplayed. Pennsylvania's blue laws were in effect, including a ban on Sunday football that had not yet been repealed, and a ministerial society had obtained an injunction against the team. But the wily Rooney had heard about the efforts and had invited the constable charged with serving the injunction to the game. The religious group couldn't find the fellow—and the

papers weren't served. ("Serve them after the game," the Chief reportedly told the constable.)

On the smoky days of autumn, the Steelers were a motley crew. Certainly they had some good players, but never all in one place at one time, and never working in concert. Although the memorable 1933-edition uniforms had the city seal on them—a shameless tug at civic pride— the players inside were ultimately forgettable; Corwan Artman, Angelo Brovelli, Elmer Schwartz, the names trail off into obscurity. The coach was Forrest "Jap" Douds, and with a 3-6-2 record he lasted but one season.

Coaching, like playing, was a part-time job. Strategy often meant little more than outfitting eleven guys a game—they were the real Sixty-Minute Men back then, playing both ways—and letting them knock heads. Whoever was left standing at the end of a long, muddy hour usually won.

For the first three years, the Steelers were truly dreadful. Then, under Joe Bach in 1936, they peeked out from under the rock to finish 6-6. But when the club lost the season finale to the Boston Redskins, the Chief fired Bach.

Although he later admitted his mistake—he rehired Bach in the 1950s, but by then the thrill was gone—the Chief replaced him with the irrepressible Johnny Blood, a man who exemplified the adage that rules are made to be broken. To that, Blood added his own corollary: As

Hall of Famer, player, and the Chief's three-time designated head coach, Walt Kiesling models the latest in fashionable gridiron headgear.

In the thirties when the Steelers were semipro at best, kicker Armand Niccolai was an exception. He played with the Steelers from 1934 to 1942 and led the club in scoring four times.

early and often as possible, including the one against playing pro ball as an undergraduate. You see, on Saturday, he was John McNally, Notre Dame collegian. On Sunday, he was Johnny Blood, NFL star, the name pinched from the Rudolph Valentino groaner *Blood and Sand*.

Charter Hall of Fame halfback John "Blood" McNally set the standard when football was populated largely by men small of stature but large of character. Joining the team for a season in 1934, he came back from 1937-39 as a player and coach. This was the era of the running game, when the pass was seen as somehow unmanly and used as sparingly as Scrooge's last dime. Little wonder, then, that in 1937 Blood led the team in completions with ten for 168 yards and four touchdowns. The hell-for-leather halfback scored five TDs as well.

The Chief must have liked Blood, who was as rowdy and roustabout as they come. He was an entertaining fellow, knew his way around the ladies, and could take a drink. Indeed, Blood's off-field antics are legendary—

and largely unprintable. As a head coach, Blood made a terrific halfback, and the team continued to flounder. Blood coached nearly three full seasons but won only a whopping six games.

Old friend Walt Kiesling took over from Blood in 1939. In fact, he took multiple turns as coach: 1939-40, 1941-44, and 1954-56. From all accounts Kiesling was a decent football man with all of the smarts—but none of the temperament to make much of a difference. Overall, his record was a sorry 30-55-5.

For a while in 1938 the Chief must've thought he had something. To complement the quick and crazy Blood, he bought one of America's greatest gridiron stars—Byron "Whizzer" White. An All-American out of Colorado, White had accepted a Rhodes Scholarship to study at Oxford. But before taking the boat, he squeezed in one season for the Steelers—for the unheard-of price of $15,000. Although the team went 2-9, White did his job. His 567 yards led the team—and the league. The club scored ten touchdowns all year, and White had four of them. At the end of the season, White was off for his studies—and a future seat on the United States Supreme Court.

Although White lasted but one campaign, some star Steelers stuck around longer. Wilbur Sortet, an end out of West Virginia, miraculously played the entire decade. (History does not record how the Chief repaid him for his long and devoted service to the cause.) Rookie tailback Hugh McCullough passed for 443 yards in 1939, and tackle/placekicker Armand Niccolai led the club four years in scoring, but nobody much noticed.

The Depression was also the time when Pittsburgh began a time-honored, thirty-year tradition of blowing the draft. In 1939, for example, the club traded their number-one pick to Chicago. The Steelers got journeyman end Edgar "Eggs" Manske, who played only one season, and the Bears took Sid Luckman and became the Monsters of the Midway.

All told, it was semipro barnstorming, not much more.

But at least it was. Some franchises folded (Brooklyn, for example) or moved (the 'Skins from Boston to Washington). The Steelers stayed.

continued on page 29

THE RACE FACTOR

Not that anybody's counting, but now that the Steelers are a predominantly black football team, it's hard to imagine a time when the team had no black players at all.

Although the Steelers' first squad in 1933 was integrated, by Ray Kemp, a tackle from Duquesne, for the next twenty years the squad remained all white. "You didn't have an abundance of black guys playing in the white universities where the NFL recruited," explains Bill Nunn, former Steelers scout and sportswriter for the *Pittsburgh Courier*. Black players played in black schools, and the pros didn't scout there.

Dan Rooney remembers that it was a struggle to get black players into the league. In 1952, for example, the Steelers drafted a running back from Alcorn A&M named Jack Spinks. As Rooney recalls it, "One man said, 'We can't have Spinks. He doesn't even have a coat.' My Uncle Jim said, 'He can have my coat,'" and took his coat off and gave it to Spinks."

By the mid '50s, and certainly by the '60s, with the advent of the rival American Football League and the ensuing wars for talent, things had changed.

Teams like the Steelers had such star black players as John Henry

RAY KEMP

Unlike most NFL teams, the first Steeler squad was integrated. Tackle Ray Kemp joined the club in 1933.

Johnson and Gene "Big Daddy" Lipscomb Still, it took effort to send scouts to the small, largely Southern, black colleges where the talent could be found.

As a sportswriter, Nunn traveled extensively, covering the Black College Game of the Week, publishing his annual Black College All-America Team.

By 1967, Dan Rooney asked Nunn to scout for the Steelers, which became one of the first clubs to send someone specifically to black colleges. "There's no doubt it gave us an edge," Nunn says.

Linemen Chuck Hinton and Ben McGee were both on Nunn's Black College All-America team, as were Ernie Holmes, Joe Gilliam, John Stallworth, Mel Blount, and Donnie Shell. These were all players, Nunn asserts, "who didn't get any recognition anywhere other than the black press."

Further, Nunn would often get information that other teams didn't have. In Stallworth's case, for example, the wide receiver from the relatively unknown Alabama A&M had been timed—but on a bad field. Nunn took him to better ground— and got a better time that only the Steelers had.

When Jack Spinks came as the Steelers' second black player in 1952, there were still many who felt that African-Americans had no place in pro football. The Rooneys would have none of such prejudice.

Even the dark ages had glimmers of light: star center, and later coach, Chuck Cherundolo saw service from the forties to the sixties.

1940-1945: SALES, MERGERS, AND THE SECOND WORLD WAR

As the winds of war blew across the globe and Pittsburgh industry geared up for its last great push, the Steelers looked like they were taking their last breath. Nineteen forty was another rebuilding year, and it ended disastrously—2-7-2. The Chief tried to stop the bleeding by hiring Pitt legend Jock Sutherland as his coach, but early talks went nowhere.

At the end of 1940, the Chief sold the team—a celebrated but largely paper move—to cosmetics heir Alexis Thompson. A three-way deal, the Steelers officially moved to Philadelphia, Bert Bell's Eagles came to Pittsburgh, and players got mixed and matched like a draft. The Steelers finally got some firepower—Joe Coomer, John Woudenberg, Dick Riffle, and center Chuck Cherundolo, a 1941 Penn State grad, who stayed twenty years as a player and coach. The club's first working-class hero, Cherundolo was not the brainy, patrician Whizzer White, but a rugged, square-jawed, gravel-voiced digger from outside Wilkes-Barre. White went to Oxford; Cherundolo became team captain and played both ways, center and linebacker.

The shakeup meant a new club—again—and always with an eye for promotion, the Chief decreed a contest for a new name. (Could be that the baseball Pirates couldn't draw flies either, but no matter.) Legend has it that Margaret Carr, wife of ticketmeister and long-time Rooney aide-de-camp Joe Carr, proposed the new name in the spring of 1941.

Quickly enough, the name caught on. In 1941 the Chief marched his boys, new name and new uniforms, to training camp in Hershey, Pennsylvania. A fellow passed a comment that he liked the snappy duds. "Yeah," the Chief groused, "but they look like the same old Steelers to me."

After the Chief tapped his old friend Bert Bell to coach, the new-look Steelers employed that new-fangled, man-in-motion T-formation so favored by Chicago. But what was magic on the Midway was a disaster by the Mon. The Same Old Steelers lost three straight and the Chief hired

---

PROGRAMS, PART I

In 1940 a Steelers program set you back fifteen cents, but it was well worth the price to read such rapturous riffs touting the product as, "football, the soul-sating pleasure of youth, the inhibition-releasing pastime of middle age, the mental relaxation and physical stimulus of the elders. Football, the bringer of great crowds, the equalizer of audiences."

Say that three times fast!

These were different times. Eddie Edwards offered union-made, two-trouser suits for $19.75—$24.75 if you were a real sport.

We are told in a full-page ad that the Steelers drink Knox gelatine. We are also enjoined to see Henry Fonda in *The Return of Frank James* at the Alvin Theatre. By mid-October the feature changed to the more topical *Knute Rockne, All American*, starring Pat O'Brien and a mildly talented B-actor by the name of Ronald Reagan.

Restaurants? We got Ella's Hotel on East Ohio Street, the Fontana Crystal Bar, and for the smart set, the Boogie Woogie Nut Club on Saw Mill Run Boulevard. (You can only imagine.)

Want to go on the road? A room with a bath at Washington, D.C.'s, Hotel Annapolis would set you back two dollars.

Take in the game? Half a buck, or thereabouts, would get you in—general admission went for fifty-five cents or $1.10, a reserve seat was $2.20, and an upper box $3.30.

America *Needs* Roosevelt

Vote Straight Democratic

He'd take an ad from any scoundrel, that Art Rooney.

---

yet another new coach—Aldo "Buff" Donelli, a chap who coached the Steelers in the morning and the Duquesne Dukes in the afternoon. He, too, lasted less than a season.

A pattern was definitely emerging, and it's clear where the buck stops. The Chief, a man with a nose for a good

AND YOU THOUGHT THE WHOLE SEASON WAS GOING TO BE A WASH

Nineteen forty-one's sole victory was a classic Steeler win—and as odd and ugly as they get. On a raw November day, the Brooklyn Dodgers were in town for what was supposed to be a laugher.

Brooklyn, coached by Pitt legend Jock Sutherland, was heavily favored. But the Steelers, coached by Walt Kiesling, whom fans wanted out in '39 (and, so stout was his record, every other year as well), battled all the way. It was a typical Steelers game, nasty, brutish, and fruitless. Finally, late in the game, with the score tied 7-7, Art Jones, a running back out of Richmond, came around the end toward the sidelines. A Brooklyn tackle got an arm on him, but Jones broke free and raced forty yards for the touchdown.

When the mud finally turned to ice, the Steelers had their lone victory. Final score: 14-7.

horse and the heart for a hard-luck story, governed more with soul than sense. He tended to hire people he knew and trusted, friends rather than fellas who could get the job done. They were not cronies, necessarily, just men, like Walt Kiesling, with whom the Chief felt particularly comfortable. Although Kiesling made the Hall of Fame, largely on longevity, he made a better friend than a coach. When the dust settled in 1941, with America at war, the Steelers had had three head coaches and one lone victory.

World War II was a dark time for the Republic, and even darker for professional sports. Travel restrictions, commodities rationing, and the draft (Uncle Sam's kind) decimated rosters, schedules, and accounts receivable. Anybody who was able-bodied went in the service—which meant the

pickings were mighty slim when it came to the gridiron. Aside from the 4-F club, one way to staff the Steelers was with men working in vital defense industries. Indeed, tackle Ted Doyle pulled Neville Island shifts—turning out ocean-going landing craft for the Navy—when he wasn't pulling down opposing defenders.

Soon, Doyle even had someone worth blocking for. In 1942 the Steelers drafted halfback Bill Dudley, 172 pounds soaking wet, out of Virginia. The brightest star of the club's first twenty years, Dudley announced a new era in Steeler football during the season opener against the Eagles. First, he ran the kickoff back to the Philadelphia thirty-five; then, two plays later, he raced in for a touchdown. The following week, Dudley returned the 'Skins' second-half kickoff for a touchdown. Suitably ignited, the Steelers went seven for nine in the ending weeks of the season to finish a respectable 7-4, good for second place and their then-all-time best. All told, the Bluefield Bullet's 696 yards led the NFL in rushing, and his 438 yards passing and six TDs led the team.

"He did everything wrong," Dan Rooney recalls. "He couldn't throw. He was not fast. He was not big. He couldn't kick. But he led the league in ground gained—and in interceptions [in 1946]. He was one of those play-

To conserve wartime resources, not the least of which was money, the Steelers and Eagles combined to play as the Steagles in 1943, a team full of 4-Fs and defense workers.

Hall of Famer, co-owner, servant to the National Football League, and, for part of a season, head coach, the ever-svelte Bert Bell.

The single greatest Steeler in the club's first two decades, Bill "The Bluefield Bullet" Dudley caught, ran, and threw with the best of them in 1942, 1945, and 1946.

ers—Dudley was intelligent and explosive. He was a winner."

Dudley was all-everything, all right, but he was quickly lost to the war. To survive, the Steelers merged with Philadelphia in 1943 to form the Steagles, and with the Chicago Cardinals in 1944 to form the Card-Pitts. Players, coaches, and all manner of personnel were tossed together, and with Walt Kiesling teamed first with Earl "Greasy" Neale, then Phil Handler as head coaches, it was Pearl Harbor all over again.

The two-year record: 5-14-1.

By 1945, with the war over, the Bluefield Bullet returned to a postwar boom—no Depression, no war, and Jim Leonard was at the helm. Dudley led the team in scoring, but the Same Old Steelers went 2-8 anyway.

1946-1956: THE SEARCH FOR RESPECTABILITY

Dr. John Bain "Jock" Sutherland was a man born to be either a Scottish chieftain or a football coach. A dentist hailing from the old country, he was a fabled Pitt player and coach who had quit in a huff and gone to New York. Bringing him back to town was nothing short of the Chief's biggest public relations coup since signing Whizzer White in 1938.

Indeed, for the two years Sutherland coached, 1946-'47, Forbes Field was sold out and the Steelers actually won more than they lost. Ultimately, his untimely postseason death from a brain tumor, much like the Penguins' Badger Bob Johnson some forty-five years later, robbed the club of its first great coach.

Indeed, Sutherland was the new breed—a coach who made a science out of football with playbooks, game films, classroom sessions, and a chalkboard on the sidelines where he could diagram plays. He even came with his own scouting system, culled from years of chatting up college coaches and long-time contacts.

This was a professional coach: scientific, precise, and demanding. Like Chuck Noll twenty years later, he had a system, a vision for what he wanted. The Steelers had never seen anything like it.

... BUT WHEN THEY WERE BAD, THEY WERE HORRID

How bad were the bad old days? Bad enough that the team's leading rusher quit before the season closer.

In 1944, when the Steelers merged with the Chicago Cardinals to play as the Card-Pitts and the rushing title was on the line at the season finale, the Bears came to town on a frigid December morning. Only trouble was, Carnegie Tech had played at Forbes Field the day before, and rain had turned the plowed-up field into ice. Leading rusher Johnny Grigas took one look—and handed in his resignation letter. "No honor is worth the present risk," he said sententiously. "The spirit is willing, I assure you, but this poor battered man's flesh is weak.

"P.S. Don't call me, I'll call you."

P.P.S. The Bears trounced the Card-Pitts, 49-7.

P.P.P.S. The Card-Pitts went 0-10 for the season.

No doubt about it, Jock Sutherland was an institution—he knew it and acted the part. A stickler for details, he wanted things his way and only his way. Predictably, the rigid Scotsman had words with the high-flying Dudley. "This is the way things are going to be," the exasperated Sutherland finally told his recalcitrant star. "No deviations." Dudley deviated. After the 1946 campaign, when the team went 5-5-1 and never gave up more than two touchdowns in any game, Dudley was traded.

Too bad, because in '47 the Steelers could have used him. In '46, Dudley had led the club in scoring and the NFL in both rushing (604 yards) and interceptions (ten, a team record tied by Howard Hartley in '51 that stood for nearly thirty years, until Mel Blount hauled in eleven in '75). But in 1947 Sutherland felt certain his talent was up to the task: Johnny "Zero" Clement (the moniker for his uniform number, not his candlepower) became a triple-threat tailback, passer, and defensive back (he led the team with 670 yards rushing, and passed for 1,004 more); tight end Elbie Nickel finished his career as the club's fourth-ranked all-time receiver; and Val Jansante

The sudden death of Scotsman, scholar, and gentleman Jock Sutherland deprived the Steelers of their first winning coach and one of only four to date.

hauled 'em in at a furious clip, leading the club in receptions five years running. At midseason, the Steelers ran off a string of six straight wins and finished 8-4, the club's best up to that time. Tied for the Eastern Division lead, they faced the Eagles in a one-game playoff.

Looked good, right? Wrong. In November, the Bears crushed the Steelers, 49-7, in the process kayoing Zero and back-up quarterback Ray Evans for the season. Then the Eagles trounced 'em 21-zip before the club regrouped with a season-ending win against Boston. So by the time the Steelers faced the Eagles in the late-December playoff, it would have been nice to see Bill Dudley in the lineup. The crippled, decimated Steelers limped home after a second 21-0 loss to Philadelphia.

Like his future counterpart, Sutherland left his successors a number of legacies, including his belief in building the team through the draft. Indeed, the '48 flavor was the best of its era, bringing such talent as Jerry Nuzum, Bill McPeak, and Pete Barbolak. They were complemented by defensive back Tony Compagno, who led the NFL with seven interceptions in '48 (returning three for touchdowns), and Jerry Shipkey, a three-time Pro Bowl linebacker. Slowly, the Steelers began to establish a reputation for having a core of good players, men who did well individually even if, for one reason or another, they could not put together the team initiative to win.

After Sutherland's passing, the Steelers again settled into mediocrity. Although run by decent men and decent coaches, the team had no vision, no system, no real will

The Steelers' first scientific coach, Dr. John Bain "Jock" Sutherland led the team, 1946-47.

After Jock Sutherland's untimely death, head coach John Michelosen's efforts in 1948-49 resulted in more losing seasons.

or way to win. Sutherland assistant John Michelosen held the reins from 1948 to 1951, a term marked by the team's insistence on using Sutherland's antiquated single-wing formation. As the league shifted to the more versatile T-formation, Michelosen sailed four-square into the past. All told, Michelosen's best season was '49, with the club winning its first four out of five, before stumbling to a 6-5-1 finish. The highlight film would surely include Bobby Gage's ninety-seven-yard run against the Bears, and Joe Geri's eighty-two-yard punt—once again, flashes of skill, but nothing sustained. Michelosen's four-year record: a pitiful 20-26-2.

If you can't go home again, as Thomas Wolfe said, perhaps you can visit. The Chief brought back Joe Bach for the 1952-53 campaigns, and the club responded by winning eleven games and losing thirteen. Rebuilding—again—the Bach Steelers floundered, and the Chief brought

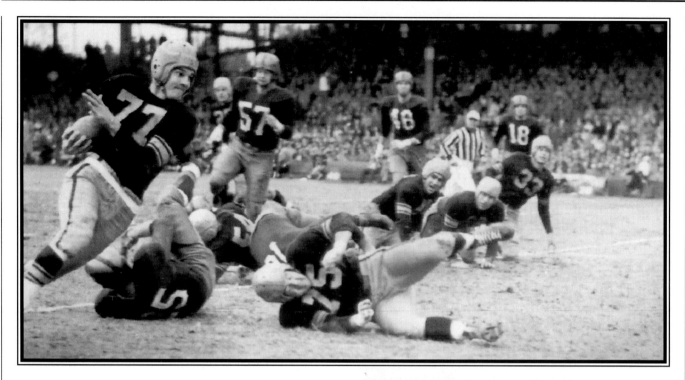

Bob Gage, number 77, races around the Redskins. Although Steeler squads were mediocre, there were always flashes of greatness. Gage recorded the longest touchdown run in team history, ninety-seven yards, on December 4, 1949, versus the Bears in Chicago.

back Walt Kiesling—again—for his third and last stand. Always innovators, the Steelers became the last team in the league to switch to the T.

Once again, the club boasted a few standouts. In '52, for example, Jim Finks threw for 2,307 yards, and a league-leading twenty touchdowns, and Elbie Nickel scrambled for 884 yards on fifty-five receptions—but the club finished below .500 again.

Then there was the defense, led by Hall-of-Famer tackle Ernie Stautner and should-be Hall-of-Famer defensive back Jack Butler. As one lifer, a season ticket holder from the Forbes Field era, recalls it, "Winning was not a concern of ours. It was how hard they played. Ernie Stautner, Jack Butler—those incredible defensive hits made your week."

Stautner, the first truly dominant defensive Steeler, was the last Steeler star to play both ways—although he didn't have to. One game, for example, he sacked the Giants quarterback three straight plays. "He was 100 percent

Joe Geri, number 35, avoids a charging Cleveland Brown. Geri's three-year career (1949-51) included the longest punt in Steeler history, eighty-two yards, on October 20, 1949, versus the Green Bay Packers.

football player," teammate Butler recalls. "He was strong, relentless, and never gave up. He just beat the hell out of the offensive tackles. He loved the game and played it to the hilt."

Butler was no slouch, either: nine years an All-Pro, 1951-59, fifty-two interceptions, including four in one

Lynn Chandnois made his debut in 1950, then provided the Steelers their best all-around offensive threat for seven seasons. He was a running back, receiver, kick returner, punt returner, and occasional passer.

As the club struggled for respectability in the post-Sutherland years, Elbie Nickel was a bright spot, leading in receiving two years and notching more than two hundred yards in a single game.

game, which remains a Steeler record. "Jack was one guy who could have played with the teams of the '70s," Dan Rooney recalls. "He was fast, smart, and tough."

"I was a thinker," allows Butler, "I had an advantage because I got to know the players. I loved the game. I enjoyed practice. I enjoyed everything about it. I had no complaints."

He also had no illusions about the '50s Steelers. "In order to win big," Butler says, "and be big time, you've got to have it all. We had some good ballplayers. We could play games. We could win games. But we didn't have enough."

Nevertheless, although the club didn't do it very often, on any given Sunday the Steelers were capable of beat-

ing even the best. In November 1952, for example, they romped 63-7 over the Giants. For openers, running back Lynn Chandnois took the Giants' kickoff at the Steelers nine—and never looked back. (He repeated the compliment the following year as well.) Quarterback Jim Finks was nearly perfect that day, firing with abandon and dead-

The fifties were a decade marked by futility, indecision, and marching quarterbacks. Ted Marchibroda held the job in 1953, 1955, and 1956.

ly accuracy, completing twelve of twenty-four for 254 yards and four touchdowns. The defense stuffed 'em—and snagged 'em, too, intercepting seven passes. For the record, the lone Giants tally came with a bit of the old razzle-dazzle, when the third-string quarterback, a skinny fella by the name of Tom Landry, hit Bill Stribling from the Giants thirty. Stribling lateraled to Joe Scott, who got hit on the Steelers thirty and lateraled back to Stribling, who ran in for the score.

As payback, Ernie Stautner knocked Landry out of the game with one of his patented eighteen-wheel tackles. (Landry, a most forgiving sort, later hired Stautner as a Dallas assistant coach.)

At the game's close, the 15,140 freezing fans tore down the Forbes Field goalposts—a Steeler first—and Joe Bach invited them into the clubhouse, such as it was.

And there was more gold amid the black. Tackle Frank Varrichione went to five Pro Bowls. Quarterback Ted Marchibroda took the snaps for a few years, linebacker Marv Matuszak snuffed the run, and punter Pat Brady

led the league in 1953-54, with a career average of 44.5 yards per boot. Guard Dale Dodrill was a four-time Pro Bowler, and Fran Rogel, playing from 1950 to 1951, rushed for 3,271 yards, good for eighth on the all-time list, leading in rushing four straight years, 1953-56.

For a time, things started to look up. With Walt Kiesling back in charge, 1954-56, '54 began as a campaign for the ages. The team broke fast from the blocks, winning four of five, including a 55-27 whipping of the champion Browns. Ray Matthews scored four touchdowns in that one, and the defense ran 147 yards on interceptions.

In the annual Forbes Field dust-up against the Eagles, which drew forty-two thousand (to a park that held only thirty-five thousand), the game was scoreless until the Steelers went up 3-0 on a third-quarter field goal. The final: 17-7 Steelers, thanks in part to a Finks fake to Rogel and a subsequent pass to Nickel. The club was tied for first.

Fade to black. The team went on to lose six of its last seven games to finish a dismal 5-7.

continued on page 42

You never knew what you'd see at a Steeler game; pressed into service as a quarterback, Jim Finks performed brilliantly and led the squad for the next five seasons, 1951-55.

QUARTERBACK CARROUSEL

After Jim Finks and before Terry Bradshaw, there was, of course, Bobby Layne, who directed the Steeler offense during the Buddy Parker era. But a variety of other quarterbacks also passed in, and through, Pittsburgh during the years between 1955 and 1970. And while the Steelers remained mostly a non-playoff, sub-.500 franchise, several signal callers moved on to championship teams elsewhere. These four can make the same claim: They got their start wearing the black and gold of the Pittsburgh Steelers.

Bill Nelsen (above) led Pittsburgh in passing in 1965, then directed the Browns to Eastern Conference championships in 1968 and '69.

John Unitas (right) was cut prior to the 1955 season opener. He resurfaced to lead the Colts to NFL titles in 1958 and '59 on his way to the Hall of Fame.

Buddy Parker's penchant for veterans led to Earl Morrall's acquisition in 1957, leaving rookies Jack Kemp (above) and Len Dawson (left) on the bench. Both moved on to the American Football League. Kemp won AFL titles with the Bills in '64 and '65. Dawson led the '62 Dallas Texans and the '66 Chiefs to crowns, then directed the Chiefs to victory in Super Bowl IV.

With 223 punts, Pat Brady was one of the Steelers' stars of the early 1950s.

1957–1968: THE DAYS OF WINE AND ROSES

The ailing Walt Kiesling had done his bit for king, country, and the Chief, and was replaced in 1957 by the Steelers' second great coach, Buddy Parker. A two-time winner in Detroit, and a chap with a taste for the gargle and a penchant for trading draft choices for cast-offs and clowns, Parker and his patchwork teams from 1957 to 1964 notched some of the club's greatest successes in the pre-Noll era.

Indeed, Raymond "Buddy" Parker joined the elite club of Chuck Noll, Bill Cowher, and Jock Sutherland as one of only four coaches ever to compile a winning record with the Steelers, 51-48-6.

"Parker was a very able coach," Dan Rooney explains. His major fault, though, is that he did not teach and he did not build. "Mistakes are what beat you," Rooney recalls Parker saying, "and you beat yourself. He didn't want rookies who made a lot of mistakes." With aging veterans, Parker had no long-term game plan, and insured no longevity. The scheme was little better than year-to-year—see who showed up and trade draft choices to cover the bare spots.

When Parker arrived he quickly established the main weapon of his eight-year regime—the arbitrary, unconditional, and totally capricious player cut. After Walt Kiesling advised the newcomer to do something drastic to take control of the team, Parker responded by impulsively cutting star Lynn Chandnois. Later, in a more reflective (or more sober) moment, Parker admitted, "as I went over the game films, it came to me what a great run-

Buddy Parker's first squad, the 1957 Steelers trained in South Park, played in Forbes Field, and went 6-6.

Buddy Parker hated the suits, the front office, and the league—and the feeling was mutual.

THE PLAY THAT
CHANGED THE RULES

Once upon a time, in the 1950s, game officials were assigned regionally. And the Steelers had trouble getting good—or at least fair—calls on the West Coast.

In Los Angeles in 1955, with the Steelers leading 26-24 and just seconds left on the clock, Steeler defensive back Richie McCabe was called for unnecessary roughness—a questionable pinch at best. The penalty was declined, but the stoppage gave the Rams the chance to bring on their field-goal team.

The kick is up . . . and it's good!

The Rams win 27-26.

Coach Walt Kiesling was so enraged that he had to be restrained by coliseum security guards from attacking the officials.

The Steelers lodged an official protest, and the following season the NFL assigned officials without regard to region.

Final score: Steelers 1, Left Coast 0.

ner Lynn Chandnois was. If I had known that, I never would have let him go."

This pattern was to continue. The Steelers lost; Parker became enraged; and players were cut willy-nilly. One year, after a preseason loss to Cleveland, he cut six players on the spot.

Ray Mansfield remembers the big 1964 17-14 season-ending loss in Dallas. On the way home, Parker, weaving drunkenly up the aisle on the plane, came looking for the guys who made mistakes, for guys to cut. "There was no security," the Old Ranger recalls. "Guys would literally hide. One guy hid in the men's room all the way back."

Still, there were good players on the field, like tackle Big Daddy Lipscomb (whose name, aggressiveness, and flamboyance captured the fans' imaginations—and

whose death from a drug overdose broke their hearts), tight end Buddy Dial, running back Tom Tracy, tackle Ernie Stautner, and more. "A pretty good team," Rooney says, "but the thing that the Steelers lacked was depth. When they got hurt—and you get hurt in this game—it would be a disastrous blow."

Sharing star billing was Hall-of-Fame running back John Henry Johnson, "a great football player," Jack Butler remembers. "He could do everything. He was tough, he was strong, he could run, he could block, he could catch. He did it all."

Dan Rooney recalls the time Johnson ran for more than two hundred yards against Cleveland, giving the club two one-thousand-yard seasons. "It was the end of the line," he says, "but he was still an explosive, power back."

Then there was quarterback Bobby Layne, whom Parker acquired in 1958. Dan Rooney remembers the day he picked up Layne at the airport and drove him to the team

Trading draft choices for has-beens and never-weres finally cost Raymond "Buddy" Parker his job. Even so, he was the Steelers' second great head coach.

One of Buddy Parker's first moves was to trade star running back Lynn Chandnois.

Head coach Buddy Parker and his assistants at training camp in 1958. So far everything looks great—no one's hurt and no games are lost. That's Walt Kiesling kneeling at the far right.

BOBBY LAYNE, PART I: THE POWER OF DEMON RUM

There is the curse of demon rum. And then there was Bobby Layne.

One night, Layne stayed 'til the wee hours at the Brentwood Hotel, leading a jazz band and generally having a good time.

A few hours later, December 13, 1958, fresh as the proverbial daisy, Layne set the all-time Steeler passing record—409 yards.

Then there was the street car . . .

Back when running back Tom "the Bomb" Tracy worked for a Detroit car dealership, he'd head home on his day off, then drive back in a new car and try to sell it to one of his fellow players.

One Saturday night, Layne borrowed Tracy's latest, spent the evening on the town, as was his wont, and finished by plowing into a streetcar, knocking it clean off its tracks.

Ernie Stautner, sleeping in the back seat, woke with a start, and said groggily, "nice move, Bobby, but the hall closed."

training facilities, then in South Park. On the way, Layne peppered Rooney with questions about the team, and when they arrived Layne went directly to practice. "When he went on the field," Rooney recalls, "Bobby Layne was in charge. In charge. There was no question of that from the first minute."

Layne, a two-time Hall of Famer (for football and carousing) gave Pittsburgh a potent offense and immediate respectability—and a 7-4-1 record his first year. "We had never had anybody like Bobby Layne," Jack Butler remembers. "He was one hundred percent competitive. He would throw the ball early. He was a smart ballplayer. Win at all costs. There was no in between, no gray area. He played one way—all out."

By 1962, the Steelers were respectable. With the strong backfield of John Henry Johnson, Joe Womack, Dick Hoak, and Bobby Layne, they finished second with a 9-5 record. But it was not enough for Parker, who forcibly retired Layne, later admitting, as in the Chandnois cut,

In 1962 the second-place Steelers were tapped to play the runner-up bowl in Miami. On New Year's Eve, with a nine o'clock meeting facing them, running back Dick Hoak headed off to bed—only to be snagged by Bobby Layne. Seems that Layne was about to play cards with some of the boys, Charlie Bradshaw and John Henry Johnson, and wanted Hoak along for good luck.

For the next four hours, Layne kept falling asleep, and Hoak would wake him to bet. Finally, at 5:30, Hoak stumbled off to bed, leaving Layne at the card table. Three and a half hours later, Hoak dragged himself into the meeting—only to see Layne stroll in, bright-eyed, bushy-tailed, showered, and shaved. "He looked like he'd had ten hours of sleep," Hoak shakes his head.

Jimmy Orr, who led the club in receptions, 1958-59.

that it had been a mistake. Later, Parker said his hasty move cost them the '63 championship, when the club was 7-4-3 and could have used a good field marshall against the Giants in the final game of the season. As Sutherland had with Bill Dudley sixteen seasons earlier, the team dumped a star one year too soon.

No, the Steelers were not great, but they had their moments. In 1964 defensive end Big John Baker, six-foot-six, 270 pounds, knocked Y.A. Tittle out of the second game. (*Post-Gazette* photographer Morris Berman's classic photo of the bloody Tittle kneeling in Pitt Stadium made *Life*

The last great Steeler who could stay out all night and play brilliantly the next day, Hall of Famer Bobby Layne scrambles in Pitt Stadium.

For decades, the club had excellent players but could never put them together to win. One such standout was powerhouse tackle Joe Krupa, who protected Bobby Layne and others, 1956-64.

Defensive back Jack Butler also played end on offense (above), then later became a top-notch scout. Butler was a four-time Pro Bowl selection in his nine-year NFL career (1951-59).

Steeler fans adored Big Daddy and he never disappointed. Here, in 1962, Mr. Eugene Lipscomb was out to do some damage to Cowboy quarterback Eddie LeBaron.

magazine.) Running back Brady Keys played well, and so did offensive tackle Charlie Bradshaw, but individual showings were not sufficient. In the mid-1960s, with football talent being gobbled up in a recruiting war with the then-rival American Football League (AFL) and the Chief in his sixties and slowing down, Dan Rooney stepped to the fore demanding sense over style, preferring plan and purpose to Parker's more typical panic and petulance.

Parker could go to the eighth round before having a draft choice, as they did in 1959 and 1963. In '61, for ex-

ample, Penn State running back Dick Hoak came in the seventh round, but was only the second Steeler pick. But the has-beens and never-weres were no longer enough; they needed new blood.

Clearly, things had to change, and Dan Rooney said so.

Buddy Parker took offense and laid into young Dan, but Dan, being a Rooney, wouldn't back down. We are not going to continue to do this, he said. It all came to a head one day after an exhibition game in Rhode Island,

continued on page 53

Although the team wasn't celebrating many victories, solid performances from players like defensive great Ernie Stautner helped the Steelers get by.

BUDDY'S OLD BUDDIES

Before George Allen assembled the "Over the Hill Gang" for his 1972 Super Bowl Washington Redskins, there was Buddy Parker's earlier version of the same idea: Simply recruit seasoned veterans from other NFL champions and before long the Steelers would be playoff-bound as well. Although the Steelers did enjoy four winning records in Parker's eight seasons, the club's only trip to the post season was to the 1962 Playoff Bowl, a battle of second-place finishers, since scrapped by the league.

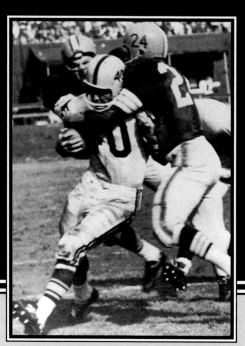

Running back John Henry Johnson (above) led the 1957 NFL champion Lions in rushing.

Quarterback Ed Brown (above right) led the offense of the 1956 Western Conference champion Bears. Kicker-defensive end Lou Michaels (above left) came over from the Rams.

Running back-receiver Preston Carpenter (number 40, left), played for the 1957 Eastern Conference champion Browns.

Five NFL titles are represented here. Quarterback Bobby Layne (above left) won three with the Lions (1952, '53 and '57), while defensive tackle Gene "Big Daddy" Lipscomb (above right) and center Buzz Nutter (left) played for the 1958 and '59 champion Colts.

John Henry Johnson gains a few more. It took more than mere mortals to drag him down.

BOBBY LAYNE, PART III: YOU GO LONG

When Bobby Layne took the Steeler snaps, they played on grass, largely on the dirt infields of Forbes Field, Cleveland Municipal Stadium, and Yankee Stadium.

Things weren't working? Layne would make up plays in the huddle, drop to one knee, and draw them in the dirt, like a schoolboy.

"It was different then," Dick Hoak smiles. "It was a lot of fun. But it wasn't fun when you lost so much."

when Parker called with one of his impetuous trades. Rooney demurred, saying he'd talk to Parker the following morning. Parker threatened. Rooney said this is the way it's going to be. Parker resigned.

"That's when I started to be the person you had to deal with in this organization," Rooney says. "It wasn't difficult because it was a very, very important change."

Parker assistant Mike Nixon got the nod in '65, and Bill Austin took over from 1966 to 1968. Today Dan Rooney admits that they hired Austin too quickly. He had made a good impression in his interviews, and Vince Lombardi had given him a great recommendation. With

The Steelers were short on victories, but never short on effort. John Baker, number 78, Gene Breen, number 52, and Ken Kortas, number 75, take their best shot at Jim Brown in 1965.

that information in hand, the Steelers ended the search. "The procedure was a mistake," Rooney says.

"There was never anything accomplished," Dick Hoak adds. "Every year we were rebuilding. It was a struggle."

So was the booze.

Running back Rocky Bleier remembers being introduced to the culture of drinking as a Bill Austin rookie in 1968. One day, the vets dragged him to The 19th Hole, a popular Latrobe pub. Bill Saul, an enormous linebacker, sat across from Bleier and challenged him to a chugging contest. To make it easy on the little fellow, Saul said, he wouldn't use his hands. He didn't—Saul simply clamped his entire mouth around the rim of his glass, tilted his head back, and bolted his brewski in a single gulp. Bleier, barely past the first sip, grinned weakly.

"How 'bout another one, Rook?" Saul prodded.

Bleier had thirteen beers that day and came home blitzed. Bill Austin was only amused.

"Drinking was a big part of that team," center Ray Mansfield recalls. "I don't remember ever running a wind sprint."

THE MAKING OF A MAJOR-LEAGUE COACH

From 1961 to 1970, Dick Hoak was a Steeler running back. Since 1972 he has been an assistant coach, a longer tenure than any other coach in team history. This may be the reason:

"I was the last of a dying breed," Hoak recalls. "A slow white running back. I didn't have all the talent in the world, so I had to get every edge that I could. I had to study the game. I had to know what everyone else was doing on the field. When I was in high school and college and the pros, I studied what other people did. I knew what the quarterback was supposed to do. I knew what the defense was supposed to do.

"When I was a kid I wanted to be a coach. You have to want to coach—not just in the last two years of your career. You have to study what other people do."

Running back Dick Hoak struggles to break one open in 1963. Joining Pittsburgh in '61, Hoak would go on to log more time with the Steelers, as player and coach, than anyone other than Art and Dan Rooney.

Wide receiver Roy Jefferson made his home with the Steelers 1965-69. He led the team in receptions twice, logging more than one thousand yards each time, and led in scoring once.

Mansfield, who came to the Steelers against his will in a 1964 trade from Philadelphia ("I did not want to come to Pittsburgh," he explains. "They were the joke ·of the National Football League"), was astounded to find a team "so pitifully out of shape. The theory was that you played yourself into shape. But we were so out of shape that we couldn't play."

Conditions were worse. The team practiced in South Park, in an old house. The upper floors were the meeting and coaches' rooms, and the basement was the locker room. Hooks served as lockers, only three showers worked, and rain invariably flooded the floor.

Although Austin knew talent, he was not emotionally equipped to be a head coach. He berated players publicly, did not enforce his own rules, and engaged in fruitless clashes of will. Linebacker Andy Russell sums it up: "It was crazy."

It wasn't much better on the gridiron. Austin won eleven games in three years, losing twenty-eight and tying three.

"Our mistakes from 1965-68 helped," Dan Rooney says, "because I could see the fallacy in how we were doing things."

As 1968 drew to its dreary close, with a 2-11-1 record, that was just about enough. It had been thirty-six long years, and the Steelers had just eight winning seasons to show for it. Bill Austin didn't seem to be getting any better—no, he'd never improve. That was it. It was time to change, time to get a new coach.

No one knew it at the time, but teammates Ray Mansfield, Andy Russell, Rocky Bleier, guard Sam Davis, and punter Bobby Walden would all survive, prosper, and make it to the team's first Super Bowl in 1974. But that was light-years away.

First, they had to find a man named Chuck Noll.

The Cowboy Cheerleaders they weren't, but for a brief, shining moment in 1968, the Steelerettes shook the pom-poms.

Punter Bobby Walden, who played for Pittsburgh from 1968 to 1977, was one of only five players who moved from the sad sixties to the super seventies. His 716 boots are a team record.

His moves on the field were better than this: attorney Paul Martha masquerades as a Steeler defensive back, 1964-69.

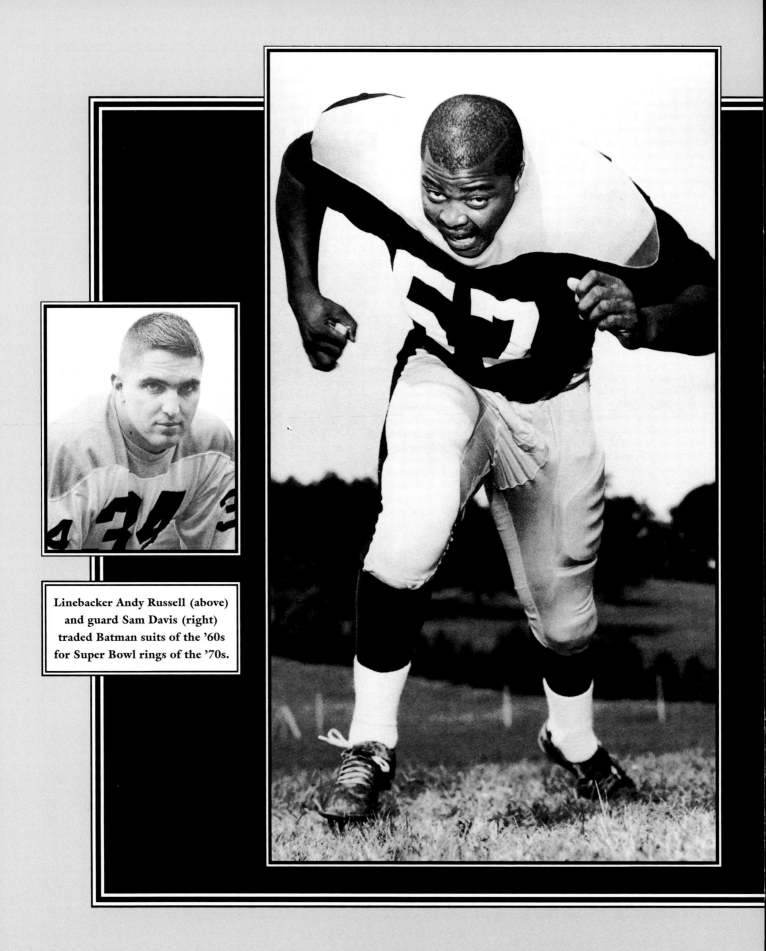

Linebacker Andy Russell (above)
and guard Sam Davis (right)
traded Batman suits of the '60s
for Super Bowl rings of the '70s.

CAPED CRUSADERS

The Steelers experimented with a variety of jersey styles in the 1960s, the most memorable—or forgetable—of which was the "golden shoulder" look, featuring a V-shaped neckline that, from various angles, made players resemble Batman, the popular television hero of the era. However, there wasn't nearly enough *biff!*, *bam!*, and *pow!* in those jerseys to keep the Steelers from losing. New uniforms and a new coach would soon follow. A superhero look would be replaced by Super Steelers.

(Above) Out of the Bat Cave and onto the field: the 1966 Steelers.

(Left) Robin, meet Brady Keys.

CHAPTER 3

DRIVEN TO SUCCEED

Chuck Noll and Bill Cowher

They are indeed men of vision and precision, of drafts and motivation. They are gentlemen, smart and savvy. In a sport where shouting often substitutes for sense, both are astonishingly bright, canny, and insightful. They would be successful in any field.

More than just men of great intellect, they were men of emotion. No one could ever forget Chuck Noll's steely eyed, thin-lipped fury or Bill Cowher's Wagnerian outbursts—fuel that powered the club.

They are tough, but fair. Neither tolerates losing; both are driven to succeed.

Both were tough Midwestern players, both learned coaching from acknowledged masters. Both are family men who are definitely in control, but who understate their roles.

(Above) Bill Cowher celebrates an overtime win in Chicago, the Steelers' first-ever victory in the Windy City, 1995.

Success breeds success. The only four-time Super Bowl winner, member of the exclusive two-hundred-win club, the Emperor Chaz.

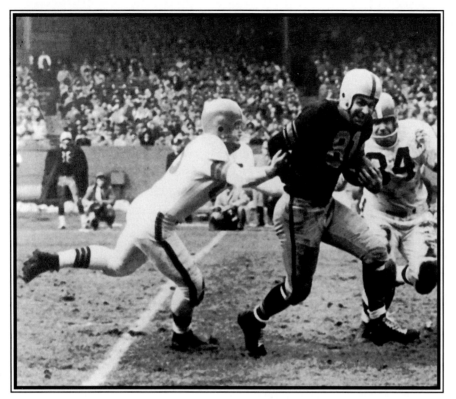

Paul Brown's undersized messenger guard, Chuck Noll (left), also played linebacker as a Cleveland Brown, here chasing the Steelers' Elbie Nickel in Cleveland Stadium.

Noll reigned for twenty-three years, 1969–1991, Cowher since 1992. Their personalities and visions have shaped champions.

Back in '69, Dan Rooney's first criterion for the coach who would succeed Bill Austin was that he would fit in Pittsburgh—a family man with good values. They didn't want a carpetbagger, a showboater. No big shot; no booze. These are the Pittsburgh Steelers, buster, and don't ever forget which name comes first.

So carefully following the procedures they had laid out, Rooney & Co. talked to a number of coaches a number of times. At one point Dan called Don Shula, then the head coach of the National Football League (NFL) champion Baltimore Colts, and asked permission to speak to a highly rated assistant, Chuck Noll. Shula said, not until after Super Bowl III, but he's definitely the guy you should talk to.

Rooney set the meeting for the Monday after the game, the day after Noll's Colts got whipped by Joe Namath's Jets. Although his team had just lost the Super Bowl, Noll spoke for two hours about the Steelers, he spoke with great familiarity—the players, his approach, the team's values. After the session, the Chief told Dan, "Don't let Noll's name get off the list."

Dan didn't need to be told. "The more I talked with him," he recalls, "Noll was the guy. His knowledge of the game and his intelligence were excellent. So was his commitment— the game itself meant so much to him. It was similar to what I felt. He was not just a guy who was in this for money or for what he could get out of it. The NFL and the game of football were very important to him. His values were right on. Now we had some disagreements right off the bat, which was good, because it showed he would speak up. But overall, I felt that he could come into the Steeler organization and be like us.

"Every time we talked after that, we gained more confidence that he was the guy." Dan smiles. "We finally did it right."

Charles Henry Noll was the Cleveland-born son of a working-class German Catholic family. For the first decades of his life he was all-Ohio, playing football at Benedictine High, the University of Dayton, and seven seasons with the Cleveland Browns as an undersized offensive guard and linebacker under Paul Brown. By age twenty-seven, Noll was a defensive coach in the brand-new American Football League (AFL), for Sid Gillman's Chargers, first in Los Angeles, then in San Diego. A three-year swing in Baltimore coaching under Don Shula completed his apprenticeship. As a player, Noll toiled on four conference champs, including two NFL title winners.

During his six years on the West Coast, the Chargers won five conference championships and one AFL crown

(1963). In 1968 the Colts took the NFL. Yes sir, Mr. Noll knew all about winning, knew it from the inside out. How to make it happen, how to work with an entirely new organization, or an established one, and how to build from the bottom and make it come out on top.

"I got some real training," Noll recalls. "It was great going to an organization that was starting from scratch. Brand new—brand new players and a brand new coaching staff. It was a great learning experience for me.

"I had some good teachers," he continues. "People who were good technicians. There's the *what* to do—but they were very helpful in *how* to do it. That carried over into my coaching, and it's been a part of my football learning and teaching. The skill—that's the real motivator. People think motivation is yelling at somebody. It's not. It's knowing *how* to do something—because if you know how to do something, you *want* to do it because you're successful at it. Success breeds wanting to do more and to have more success.

"Plus," Noll adds, "football was very interesting to me. Not only is it helping an individual perform or the makeup of a team, but it's also the strategy that's involved and how a team works together.

"Now when the Steelers called, that was a tough time—right after we had just lost the Super Bowl. I wasn't in a

great frame of mind. But after talking with Dan and meeting the family, I knew they wanted to go in the right direction. They were willing to do whatever I wanted. There was no request that was turned down."

Bottom line: Noll may have liked what he saw, but he didn't come to the club to be anybody's friend—not Dan's, not the Chief's, not the players', and certainly not the press's. He was all business: He came to get the job done. He came to win.

The Rooneys liked him immensely; this self-controlled, measured, and thoughtful man expected the same of those around him. To ensure that the team would use his ideas, his methods, and his players, he would start fresh, taking only from the draft.

"You could tell there was a difference," says assistant coach Dick Hoak, then a Steeler running back. "Chuck knew what he wanted to do. He knew the type of player he wanted. He wasn't just going out and getting players to fill in for a year or two. He knew he wanted to build a team through the draft. He wanted guys who understood the game. He had a plan. You could see it.

"He was going to do it his way," Hoak adds. "He was going to be his own person. Some guys, they've coached for so-and-so, so they try to be like so-and-so. Chuck wasn't like that."

"Chuck didn't want cast-offs or trades," former assistant coach George Perles recalls. "He didn't want to hear players say, 'We used to.' Chuck wanted his program, done his way. The less experience they had with other situations, the better he felt."

Like Perles, virtually all of Noll's new assistants were college—not professional—coaches, for good reason. "He wanted teachers," Perles says. "He wanted things taught, and he wanted them taught his way because it was almost impossible to find a coach who knew as much about offense and defense as Chuck did," Perles adds. "He had a background that was second to none."

And he had a plan. "I came with things that I felt were basic," Noll says. "We went from there. Our first year I found that we needed some weapons, some people who were dedicated and could focus on a particular goal. Having been on championship teams, I had a pretty good idea

Champion blocker Ray "The Old Ranger" Mansfield is backed by Bruce Van Dyke and Larry Gagner, 1969.

of what I wanted. So we were trying to bring people, and we wanted them to be themselves. And we wanted to tie it together."

Tall order, but the players were excited—or they were gone. Linebacker Andy Russell, for example, got a call from the new coach in the off-season. "He was an extremely impressive guy," Russell recalls. "Very bright." Noll said that Russell had to improve—and Russell agreed, winding up the season in his first Pro Bowl.

"When Chuck came," center Ray Mansfield adds, "what a difference." Mansfield was one of many who received an off-season letter outlining his conditioning program—and the tests he would take during the upcoming training camp.

"You guys wonder why you can't win in Pittsburgh," Noll said that summer. "The reason you can't win in Pittsburgh is that we don't have enough good football players. Making this team will depend on you. We're going to work hard. Some of you will make it, and some of you won't."

"He was very methodical," Mansfield says. "Very well thought out in everything he said. He never said anything off the cuff. He never said anything in anger. We had a great training camp—best one I ever had. We worked hard, but it didn't seem like we were working hard."

Practices were regular; the players knew when and what was going to happen. Noll did not punish them if things did not go well. "All of a sudden you have a track to run on," Mansfield says. "You know what to expect from this guy."

Then the '69 season began. The Same Old Steelers won their first game—then lost thirteen straight, and three more in 1970. "The fans booed, and you booed yourself because you hadn't gotten it done," Andy Russell remembers. "Everyone agonized about getting beat.

'Am I fundamentally a loser?' we asked. Noll told us, 'No, you're not losers. We just don't have enough good players. I'll take care of that.' And he did."

"A miserable season," Ray Mansfield adds. "We were pathetic, but Chuck never lost his cool. He went right back to his plan."

"Mr. Rooney summed it up one night in the office," George Perles remembers. "He'd come back in the evening when we were working late. 'You know when I knew we had a coach?' he said. 'When we won one game and lost thirteen—but he never lost the team.'"

"I had been associated with championship teams in Cleveland, Los Angeles, San Diego, and Baltimore," Noll explains. "So the stuff that I believed in had been successful in a lot of places. It was all good stuff—and you don't change it overnight. It was just a question of execution. You have to have people to do that, and that takes some time.

"At the heart of anything you do," he continues, "there are basics and fundamentals. This was drilled home to me very early: In football, if you're fundamentally sound, if you know the basics—and the basics are blocking and tackling—you can succeed. At the Steelers, our whole idea was that to stay healthy, for your survival, it's better to give than to receive. It's better to hit than to be hit.

"You not only have to know that," Noll points out, "you have to work on that. Because hitting's not a natural thing. You have to learn how to run into people and survive. So that's something we worked on very hard. If you're not in position to deliver the blow, you're going

The Coach and the Chief.

He was a strategian, but first he was a teacher. Chuck Noll conducts a master class at training camp at St. Vincent's College, Latrobe.

JON KOLB'S CHUCK NOLL STORIES, PART III: THE LONG GOOD-BYE

JON KOLB'S CHUCK NOLL STORIES, PART III: THE LONG GOOD-BYE

Jon Kolb's tenure with the Steelers lasted exactly as long as Chuck Noll's. Coming in as an offensive tackle in 1969, Noll's first draft, Kolb graduated to assistant coach in '82, and departed with the Master after '91.

Never one for emotional speeches or heart-to-heart talks, Noll stayed in character right through the end.

When he was about to resign, Noll called Kolb. "It's over," Noll said.

Along the same lines, when center Mike Webster, who played for Noll for fifteen years, was asked how it was first getting acquainted with Noll, he shrugged. "I'm not sure," he shook his head. "I'm still not acquainted with him."

to take it. Then you're going to get injured, and you're not going to survive. It's as simple as that.

"So when we did well," Noll continues, "we expected to do well. You prepare hard, and you expect to be successful. When you are, it's a matter of fact. To play well, you have to have that state of mind. It has to be there. So that when you go out on the field you just execute." Noll does not smile. "It worked very well that way."

"It was the system," center Mike Webster agrees. "You just did it. You didn't have likes or dislikes, you just did it."

"Noll was an individual who really had it," admires former Steeler defensive back and scout Jack Butler. "He ruled with an iron hand. 'This is the way we do things,' he said. 'If you don't like it, you find some other place to do it.' You did it his way or there was no other way.

"The name of the game is people," Butler adds. "And if you know exactly what you want for each position, and you can fit people into your system, you're going to be a winner."

Noll had that great coach's gift—knowing when to pour it on, when to let up. "Chuck didn't over-coach," Dick Hoak says. "You can have great players, but if you over-coach them, and you don't let them be themselves, you end up not very successful. He knew the players he had, how to teach them, and how to handle them."

"I have the utmost respect for Chuck Noll," adds defensive back Mike Wagner. "The job of a coach is to push players. Chuck was able to pull together the talent of the team and of the players, and let us do our thing. Some people say Chuck was lucky, but I don't think so. I think he was able to do three things—bring talent, put it together in a package, and let everybody play football. And it worked. It absolutely worked."

Indeed, most players responded extremely well. "I consider myself very fortunate to have played most of

Steely-eyed, thin-lipped fury: never one to show a great deal of emotion, Chuck Noll was a Hall of Fame nonverbal communicator.

my career for Chuck," says kicker Gary Anderson, with 1,343 points the team's all-time scorer. "I really responded to a guy like that. He had very high expectations; he never felt it necessary to stroke players. If you showed up for work in the morning, he assumed you were professional enough to get the job done.

"He was very even-keeled," Anderson adds. "If you had a bad game, he wasn't in your face. If you had a good game, he never said you were the world's greatest. I always enjoyed that about him, that quiet and confident understanding. He respected and admired the job I did. And he left me alone."

That was Noll's style—simple, quiet, and understated. No screaming, no arms flailing, no standing on the burning deck. "Chuck Noll made one speech before every game," recalls retired trainer Ralph Berlin. "He made the same speech for the Super Bowl as he gave before the first preseason game. It was a business speech. 'You've got this job to do,' Chuck'd say. 'You've got that job to do.' He never said, 'Let's win this one for Mr. Rooney,' or 'Let's win it for the city of Pittsburgh.' It was 'Play for yourself and have fun.'"

"Chuck was the smartest guy in the world," recalls quarterback Terry Bradshaw, "because Chuck didn't have

Coach Noll tries to persuade an official. Bubby Brister, number 6, and Donnie Shell, number 31, back him up.

to give pep talks. He drafted people who were self-starters. People who couldn't stand to lose. People who rallied at Tuesday meetings and were angry all week long because we lost. Those were the people Chuck had, and they made his job easy."

Sometimes, recalls defensive back J.T. Thomas, Noll didn't have to say a word. "Chuck was the best nonverbal communicator in the world," he says. "He had a way of telling you that you were the best—or that you would not be here next year—just with a look. If you weren't into nonverbal communication, you missed Chuck Noll. Because he'd never come up and say, 'You're my guy,' or 'I think you're great.' In his nonverbal way, it was there."

Adds defensive end Dwight White, "We had a lot of strong personalities and a lot of strong-willed people on that team. And he was able to keep everybody focused. He made us believe in the strategy, in the game plan. He put the muzzle on after the game and took it off at one o'clock the next week."

"We could have gotten by without some players,' adds Hall of Fame linebacker Jack Ham, "but we didn't win championships without Chuck Noll. You can say anything you want about the great players we had, but if we didn't have Chuck, we wouldn't have been successful.

He was able to make players believe that we had a championship football team. Guys with great ability just cared about winning football games—Chuck was able to instill that in all those players."

"Chuck was never one to get emotional," Joe Greene says. "He was always straight ahead and focused. He wouldn't let us feel too good about ourselves or feel too bad about ourselves. We were professionals."

"By the time we got to the Super Bowl," Ray Mansfield recalls, "we were ready, physically and mentally. He called upon you to look inside yourself and see what you want to be and how you want to prepare yourself. It runs through Chuck's career: If a team is prepared they can beat a better team that is not prepared."

"I stressed that the team has to be the most important thing if you're going to be successful," Noll nods. "We had a slogan, 'whatever it takes.' That was our definition of teamwork. It was not fifty-fifty. If you stand back and say, 'I'm going to match his performance,' then the game's over. Because there are times when people are unable to perform to their capabilities, and you may have to reach down and give a little more. You do whatever you have to do. You may have to dominate. Our guys picked that up pretty well."

They also picked up Noll's values, and many consider him the great secondary formative influence in their lives. Indeed, offensive lineman Larry Brown could speak for the rest of his teammates when he says that the importance of the Dynasty years was not on the football field, but off the field, in the values he learned from Noll: self-respect, self-motivation, dealing with adversity, and how to succeed.

Cornerback Mel Blount works with troubled teens in his rural Washington County Youth Home. "There's not a day that goes by that I don't use or think about some of the things that Chuck taught us," he says. "As the kids say, 'He's got it going on.' Chuck probably doesn't know or realize this, but he's influenced a lot of young men. He inspired us to go on to bigger, better, and greater things. I can't think of where he was offtrack—he was consistent across the board, in his teaching, in the way he carried himself, and in the way he treated his people. He was

A conductor and master orchestrator of talent, Charles Henry Noll takes the baton at the Pittsburgh Symphony Orchestra.

more of a father figure than he realized. I have the utmost respect for him. He really did a good job with us."

Former running back Rocky Bleier now makes his living giving motivational speeches. "So much of what I talk about," he says, "so much of what I believe in, comes from Chuck, from his philosophy of how you achieve, how you become a success."

For his part, Noll characteristically shifts the credit aside. "It's all something I learned from the people I played for, something that I passed on. I wish I could say it's all original with me, but it's not. It comes back to basics. Aside from the basic in how to hit and how to tackle, there's a basic attitude—'whatever it takes' is an *attitude*. What we were trying to pass on is a winning attitude. All these things add up to just that.

"You learn through the difficult times," Noll adds, "that losing is a greater learning experience than winning. You have to be able to handle success, but you have to be able to overcome failure. It's not a sin to fail. The thing that separates football players—that thing that separates people—is not their basic physical ability, but their attitude."

By the 1980s, Noll got his first prolonged taste of failure, as the team wallowed in mediocrity for most of the decade. "The great frustration was that we couldn't get any consistency," recalls director of football operations Tom Donahoe, who joined the Steelers in 1986. "This was a great frustration for Chuck. Toward the end you got the feeling that Chuck was tired of the whole process. He gave it a great effort, but you got the feeling this was wearing him out."

After the 1991 season, after thirty-nine years in professional football, after 209 wins and four Super Bowl rings, Noll retired. "It was time to go," he says. "No question about it. As I look back on it, my deepest satisfaction was watching young men grow and develop the skills to play professional football."

The Hall of Fame? He was pleased to be inducted, of course, but "that was not the goal," he says. "Or anything like that. It was frosting."

But saying good-bye was not easy. "Chuck's a very sensitive individual," wide receiver John Stallworth says.

CHUCK NOLL ON FAIR PLAY

"**T**his game is rough enough, tough enough, and physical enough. It has rules for good reason. You don't want to win by hurting somebody. That's something we never wanted. You play fundamentally sound football by the rules and if victory comes, it'll be well deserved. But you don't try to hurt somebody and get him out of the game so you can win. I don't think there's any room for that. That's not the way I was brought up."

"I think that a lot of things that went on affected him, but his way of handling it was not displaying that emotion but keeping it all inside."

After the 1987 season, for example, the retiring Stallworth and defensive back Donnie Shell were given a farewell party at the Allegheny Club. Posing for pictures, Noll turned to Stallworth and said very quietly, "John, I feel like crying." Then the Noll iron. "But that wouldn't be appropriate, would it?"

Defensive back Carnell Lake is one of a select group who have played—and played well—for both Chuck Noll and Bill Cowher. He likes them both, but for different reasons. "Coach Noll was a very good teacher," Lake says. "When I came, I thought I knew the right technique, but he taught me a better one, and I still use it.

"He taught me that football is a game of leverage," Lake says. "One way to protect yourself and combat a bigger person is to get low, use leverage, then explode at the point of contact. That took my technique to the next level. So instead of getting out of a lineman's way, I was hitting him and knocking him back."

As much as players admired and respected Coach Noll, they didn't necessarily feel close to him. "I always wanted to get to know Coach Noll more on a personal level," Lake adds, "but he didn't allow that. Keeping his distance allowed him to be more effective. Still, my biggest regret is that I didn't get to know him better before he left."

Bill Cowher's a whole different matter.

"Change is very difficult for everybody," Lake considers, "especially if you're comfortable and making progress. But Coach Cowher came in very motivated, very personable, and that helped alleviate any anxieties that I had at the time. I wondered, 'Is he going to come in and slash and burn, or is he going to come in and see what kind of talent he has here?' He came and saw—and instilled a greater sense of team unity."

In addition, Cowher invited Lake into his office to express "my wishes and desires about where this team might be headed," Lake says. "In three years I never once was in Coach Noll's office. It was a totally different setting and environment, and a very comfortable one. I felt I could express my individuality, yet be a part of something special, a team concept of winning.

"Coach Cowher understands that communication is very important," Lake continues. "If you open up the channels of communication, you can eliminate small differences before they become major obstacles. We were able to sit down as coaches and players and go over a game plan. Everyone had input, so everyone felt like they were part of something special."

"The most important thing as a player is to concentrate on progressing as a player," Cowher told Lake, "and everything else will fall into place. Concentrate on winning and doing your job."

Dick Hoak, who played and coached for Noll, and now coaches for Cowher, knows them both as well as anyone. "You can talk to Bill," Hoak says. "Chuck didn't do that. If he had something to say to you, he'd call

you in and talk to you. He wasn't going to invite you to dinner at his house. Sure, Chuck's door was always open," Hoak allows, "but you wouldn't go in to talk to Chuck about some things. Bill's more like one of the guys."

No question, Cowher is looser, livelier, and more aggressive than Noll—perhaps because Cowher came of age in the feel-good '70s, not Noll's gray-flannel '50s.

Bill Cowher, both the man and his methods, gets high points from cornerback Rod Woodson as well. "He's done an outstanding job," Woodson says. "He inherited a team that had a lot of talent, and he molded that talent into his own team. Everybody says he's a player's coach—because he talks to players and has an open line of communication. He also respects every player on the football team and gives each one an opportunity to prove himself—even if they do wrong. He gives them a lot of respect, and they play a lot harder for themselves and the team."

Right from the start, Cowher announced he was his own man, Woodson recalls, bringing his own assistants, evaluating every player—no matter who you were—verticals, shuttle runs, forties, the works. Anyone who couldn't measure up, even (and especially) big names like Huey Richardson, the '91 first-round draft choice, was sent packing. "It sent a message that we were keeping only the best players," Cowher says. "How they got here wasn't important. What was important was what they did when they got here. That speaks volumes instead of giving lip service."

Only after the trials, tests, and cuts did he write the famed—and feared—Steeler attack defense. "He made a system fit the players," Woodson nods, "instead of making the players fit the system. When Coach Cowher did that he provided the opportunity for the players to blossom."

Case in point is All-Pro linebacker Greg Lloyd. In '92 Cowher asked Lloyd to move from outside linebacker to inside—where, in a 3-4 defense, the 225-pound Lloyd could easily get crushed.

Outside, Lloyd could move faster, get open, and motor. Lloyd acceded to his coach's wishes and tried inside—and was profoundly unhappy. When Lloyd let his displeasure be known he was moved back outside. Said

After thirty-nine years, Chuck Noll retired in January 1992.

There is no more emotionally involved person on the football field than Steelers coach Bill Cowher.

son who has the ability to teach and the ability to motivate the team." Perhaps above all, "a person who has an appreciation of Pittsburgh."

At thirty-four, Bill Cowher, a highly rated assistant in Kansas City, was the youngest man on the Steelers' short list. Joe Greene, then a Noll assistant, was there, too, but while Greene had leadership and that legendary intensity going for him, he was deemed not ready. The club needed a fresh face, a new approach.

Right away, they liked what they saw in Cowher—his enthusiasm, intensity, and ability to communicate. "He was a very good communicator in the interviews," Donahoe recalls. "He was well organized, had a plan for what he wanted to do, and could articulate that plan. He was also extremely enthusiastic. That's the way he is—a very aggressive personality.

"What's more," Donahoe adds, "he didn't try to imitate other coaches. Bill's himself, what you see is what you get. He's very consistent and confident. He knew at some point he would be a head coach in the National Football League. He was preparing for that opportunity."

"There was no doubt that he's one of us," Dan Rooney adds. "There was no question that he was going to fit in. He was almost an extension of Noll." Rooney pauses. "He's a Pittsburgher."

A Crafton native and '75 Carlynton High School grad, William Laird Cowher grew up in a house where the Steelers were religion, where the TV was draped in a Terrible Towel. As a scholastic linebacker, the wild and crazy kid's hero was—surprise!—Jack Lambert. Although Cowher wanted Penn State, North Carolina State wanted him, and south he went, to become defensive captain, team MVP, and squad leader in tackles. Picked up by the

Cowher, simply, "if a player doesn't believe something will work, it won't." That was that.

"He's a great coach," quarterback Kordell "Slash" Stewart agrees. "He's very motivating. Wants the best from us, and puts the best players out there. It's a matter of going out and showing what you can do."

Yes, wide receiver Ernie Mills allows, "Coach Cowher is very intense. Yet you can still talk to him. Off the field, he cares about you."

Get us a good one, Dan Rooney instructed Tom Donahoe when Chuck Noll stepped down, and Donahoe complied.

Rooney wanted nothing short of "a good person," he recalls, "a person with character and intelligence, a per-

BILL COWHER ON BECOMING A COACH

"**A**s a marginal player you've got to find the way to succeed. So you'll spend the extra time studying, working, or trying to find that little edge that'll get you up to the gifted guy. The work ethic, or the approach that you have to bring to the game as a marginal athlete, is one that you can take over to coaching. If you have communication skills and the understanding—and if you get the opportunity—you can be successful.

"Marty Schottenheimer is the backbone of my coaching career. He taught me the importance of being organized. Practices. What and how you present to the players. Dealing with each person, in adversity and success. He taught me to be consistent, but demanding, to motivate players and get the most out of them."

pros, he was a special teams player for Cleveland from 1980 to 1982 and for Philadelphia from 1983 to 1984 before a knee injury ended his career.

Cowher was at a crossroads with only a degree in education—until Marty Schottenheimer took Cowher as a defensive assistant in Cleveland, and later Kansas City, where Cowher gained attention as an excellent teacher, well organized, with strongly held beliefs. In '89 Cowher's KC defensive squad was ranked top in the league, and the following year they led in sacks, fumbles recovered, and tackles.

In Pittsburgh, Cowher paid immediate dividends, taking a talented club that Noll had built and putting it into overdrive—more aggressive defense, tighter workouts, more intense practices, and stricter fines. In the process, Cowher's tactics garnered much-needed respect, just as his trademark emotional outbursts pumped new energy into the squad. His 11-5 rookie season, the team's best since 1979, netted Cowher Associated Press and *The Sporting News* Coach of the Year kudos. (Just for good measure, he went back to Kansas City and waxed 'em, 27-3.)

One measure of how well Cowher does his job is his ability to recruit and sign free agents, a part of the foot-

ball landscape that essentially postdates Chuck Noll. In '92, for example, Cowher brought in former Ram guard Duval Love. The free agent could have gone anywhere, but came to Pittsburgh in part because Cowher took him to lunch, talked with him, and made him feel welcome and wanted. "Bill's involved," one man says, "and the players produce for him. That's the difference between doing a good job and great one."

Former linebacker Kevin Greene tells a similar story. "Coach Cowher took me to dinner and talked," he recalls. "We established a friendly, honest rapport right up front. I had a chance to feel him out, to find out how dedicated and committed he was to the program. His personality sold me on the team. Basically, I said I really want to play for this guy.

"He's a player's coach," Greene adds. "He's tuned in."

One reason, perhaps, is that Cowher's turn as a player was never easy. First, he had an agonizing summer, cut from the Eagles, before he made the Browns. Then, playing for two pro teams, he was never secure. "I was always that guy who had to sweat out the forty-seven-man roster to make the cut."

He knows what these men go through, and how difficult it is to choose the right berth for themselves. "The game has changed from what it was," he allows. "With free agency you're involved with recruiting players, with trying to keep them here. In my case, I went from playing to coaching in 1985, and I still felt like a player. It's a benefit to know what these guys are going through, what the demands are, and make decisions accordingly.

"After all," he adds, "recruiting is a people business. I want people to feel comfortable coming here. I think this is a great city, with a lot to offer. This is a special organization, and a very stable franchise. I tell them, 'It's hard work, but you're one of us. We're all in this together.' The more I can show that to people, the better I feel—even if the person says no. At least they had the opportunity to enter into it." Cowher shrugs. "Ultimately, who knows what touches the mechanism to make that decision to stay here?"

Is *here* a dream come true for Bill Cowher? "It's a very unique situation," he allows. "The chance to come

Bill Cowher wears his wet suit after the AFC Divisional Playoffs in 1994.

back, to have my parents experience this with me and for them to see their grandkids on a regular basis. Having grown up here, the opportunity to return to Pittsburgh is one of those things I didn't want to consider before it came true. Once it has, I've been very appreciative.

"I went to my twentieth high school class reunion," Cowher smiles. "That was kind of special, after twenty years, to come back, and be the head coach of the professional football team in the same city that you grew up in. That was pretty unique.

"So is Pittsburgh," he continues. "I've lived in New Jersey, Cleveland, and Kansas City, but Pittsburgh has a unique atmosphere—very family oriented. There are a lot of people who live here and never want to leave. It's special because people have a deep appreciation for their sports teams. Growing up here, playing well was okay, but winning was important. The Steelers were always a big part of being from this city—they gave you a sense of pride."

Chuck Noll was a great reason for that pride and tradition. Was it hard to succeed a legend? "I don't think so," Cowher shakes his head. "I never looked upon it from that standpoint. I had been coaching only for a relatively short period of time, and when this came along I just looked at the position—not at following Chuck Noll. It was a case of trying to seize a great opportunity. All the other things take care of themselves."

The team has been enormously successful in Cowher's four years—four years of playoffs, one Super Bowl. (Indeed, in his eleven years as a coach, Cowher has missed the playoffs only once.) A lot of men coach, and coach well, but why has Bill Cowher had this extraordinary degree of success?

"Assistant coaches have a lot to do with it," Cowher says, following the venerable Steeler tradition of giving credit to someone else. "So do the football players. We continually try to get the right kind of people that fit together. This is a such a group effort that I don't think any

At his first training camp, Cowher had the courage to cut a number-one draft pick.

Bill Cowher points the way to Tom Donahoe (left).

one individual should be accountable for the large degree of success or failure. It's an organizational attempt to win a championship. We're all in this thing together. That's the bottom line. We win as one, and we lose as one.

"In my case," he continues, "I wasn't coming to a team that didn't have good players or didn't know how to work. I was very fortunate to follow Coach Noll, for he left a great work ethic on this football team. It was the case of getting a couple of guys, and some assistants, and bringing them together to play as one.

"So when I bring guys here," Cowher nods, "I look for how they approach the game. I look for how guys prepare and how they work. How they show the game falls within their personality. It's important to be yourself. My personality, I don't hide it very well." Cowher smiles. "There's nothing wrong with being emotional."

Emotion isn't the only way the game has changed, for, as Cowher has discovered after four years as head coach, there is a great deal more mobility. His first free agent, Duval Love, whom Bill Cowher took to the Allegheny Club to convince that the Steelers were right for him, is gone. Offensive tackle Leon Searcy, Cowher's first draft pick, has opted for free agency, as has Kevin Greene. Cowher's first assistant coach, offensive coordinator Ron Erhardt, has gone to the Jets. And so on.

"None of those guys is here anymore," Cowher says. "You know what that does? It tells you that life goes on. It tells you that in this business you have to be able to make decisions. You can't let your heart overcome what you need to do."

Cowher is successful—no question. But a Super Bowl in four years? "Those were our expectations when we hired him," Tom Donahoe nods. "When we talked to Bill initially, once everybody got over the fact that he was so young, we felt that he had special qualities and was the right person for the job. It wasn't an easy situation coming in, because he was replacing someone who put Pittsburgh on the football map. But the success that he had gave him some instant credibility, and he's been able to build on that. The Super Bowl? I don't think we were surprised; we were pleased that what we thought was going to happen did happen."

As Cowher faces the second half of the decade and beyond, he seems the coach for the go-go '90s.

"It's an experience," Jerry Olsavsky admits. In the 1995 AFC Divisional playoff against Buffalo, for example, defensive end Ray Seals made a play that Cowher didn't like. When Seals came off the field, Cowher screamed you can't do that. Seals screamed back that yes, he could. In the ensuing melee they almost came to blows. Later, Cowher apologized, and Seals said he understood. "Bill acts like that every once in a while in a game," Olsavsky adds. "It's good for the players—keeps your emotions up. You always know he's behind you."

Coach started screaming one day, Rod Woodson remembers, just to keep the team in focus. "He's a good motivator," Woodson smiles. "He doesn't let you lose it."

Like another great Steeler. Like Joe Greene.

Bill Cowher holds a stopwatch to his multitalented rookie, Kordell Stewart, in 1995.

Joe Greene's sixty-six Steeler sacks rank second all-time.

Chuck Noll actually credits the press for this one. "In 1969," he says, "some of the newspaper people said, 'Wait'll you see your defensive line.' That's when we drafted Joe Greene. He was like a beacon. He set a different standard from the people that we had at the time."

Indeed.

Size and statistics aside, Joe Greene was a formidable player. No one so epitomized the transformation of the franchise—its desire to win, its willingness to do anything to succeed—as Joe Greene, Mean Joe Greene to his fans. Chuck Noll's number-one draft pick in his number-one draft, Greene announced when he arrived in training camp that he would tolerate nothing less than

CHAPTER 4

NOT TO BE DENIED

A Man Named Joe

a full effort—and success. A dynamo on the field, a gentleman off it, he played with a verve, strength, style, and fury that projected indomitable pride and power.

Arguably the single most important player in Steeler history, Greene was a leader among leaders, a man who defined and personified the Pittsburgh Steelers' proud tradition of excellence and achievement.

Andy Russell was a veteran linebacker when Joe Greene arrived, and he saw the difference immediately. "He had a devastating influence," Russell says. "He was just unrelenting. He refused to lose. And he made huge plays when they had to be made. He was just an awesome addition to our squad.

"Joe was a very emotional guy, very proud," Russell continues. "He was not out to impress anyone with his attitude, but he was not afraid to show his anger. He just hated to lose; he hated to get beat. And he just refused to accept that we were losers. He

> "When legend replaces fact, print the legend."
>
> **James Stewart**
> *The Man Who Shot Liberty Valance*

Joe Greene, number one draft choice from North Texas State, wearing his rookie number, 72.

AND A THANKFUL PARENT HEAVES A SIGH OF RELIEF

One standard training camp exercise is the aptly named gassers—running fifty yards across the field four times. In his rookie season, Greene was doing four gassers, meaning sixteen trips back and forth. By the middle of gasser number two, Greene recalls, "I'm sucking it pretty good."

The next thing he knew, a ten-year-old, from the seeming safety of the sidelines, started razzing him.

"C'mon, Number One," the leather-lunged laddie began to bellow. "You shoulda been in camp earlier. C'mon, you can do better than that, you big fiery fat hog."

Hmm.

"That kid was standing right in my path as I was making my turn," Greene recalls. "Something deep inside me said, 'Joe, don't run over this kid.' 'Cause I wanted to kill him. But I felt it was going to use up too much energy."

was unquestionably the player of the decade. There was no player who was more valuable to his team."

In 1969, everybody expected the Steelers' first pick to be Butler, Pennsylvania, native, Notre Dame All-American, pure-blood Irish quarterback Terry Hanratty. Hanratty was highly touted, to be sure, but he had undergone knee surgery and did not have a rifle arm. Hanratty could wait—second round would be good enough.

While an assistant coach for Don Shula in Baltimore, Chuck Noll had scouted Joe Greene three years running at North Texas State. Noll saw the quickness, speed, power, determination, focus, and attitude. He saw the first of the big linemen who could run, a six-foot-four, 275-pound defensive tackle who could turn a 4.8 forty. And, Noll says flatly, "I never saw him lose a battle."

An unknown player from an unknown school, Greene was just right—a superb athlete with a fierce desire to win.

The press asked, "Joe who?" but Noll knew.

Greene, for his part, wasn't so sure.

First, he doesn't recall Noll scouting him in college. Second, the Steelers never talked with him. (Philadelphia did.) Third, the Steelers didn't seem like such a hot idea.

"I didn't think it was a great day for me," Greene says. "All I could see was playing in those ugly uniforms that they had at the time." (Surely you remember: a black-and-gold jersey, gold on the shoulder pads and chest, with a V on the back. The entire effect was a fey Batman suit.) "Pittsburgh hadn't won any ball games. Pittsburgh wasn't one of the best football teams—if they weren't at the bottom, they were close, for a long, long, long time."

Greene shakes his head. "At North Texas, in my sophomore, junior, and senior years, we lost five ball games. I established an attitude of winning. Losing was not something that I tolerated. Coming to Pittsburgh, I didn't want to tolerate it. It was as simple as that. That was the reason for all my tirades and outbursts. Anybody who would listen—I'd tell them. And probably a lot of people who didn't want to listen."

There were a lot of players who didn't want to listen. But some did. More important, the coach and the owner wanted to listen very much.

Some saw Greene as Noll's alter ego: While Noll kept so much hidden, so much under control, Greene was very much out in front. "Joe was very vocal and wore his emotions on his sleeve," Noll nods. "There was no hiding anything. Joe was right out front."

"He was the best leader I've ever seen in my life," Dan Rooney adds.

Indeed, Greene established himself literally from the moment he arrived in training camp. Because he had held

out, camp had begun: There were nine defensive tackles, and he came in ninth.

Taken to the locker room, Greene suited up and hit the field for the famed and feared Oklahoma drill. Simply stated, the drill pits offensive and defensive lineman, full bore, head to head.

A few chuckled as the rookie hold-out challenged the Steelers' offensive line—a line with some pretty good talent, including Ray Mansfield, Sam Davis, Bruce Van Dyke, and others. "Chuck wanted to see what Joe Greene had," Ray Mansfield recalls. "Guard Bruce Van Dyke said, 'We'll show the rook now.'" Mansfield shakes his head.

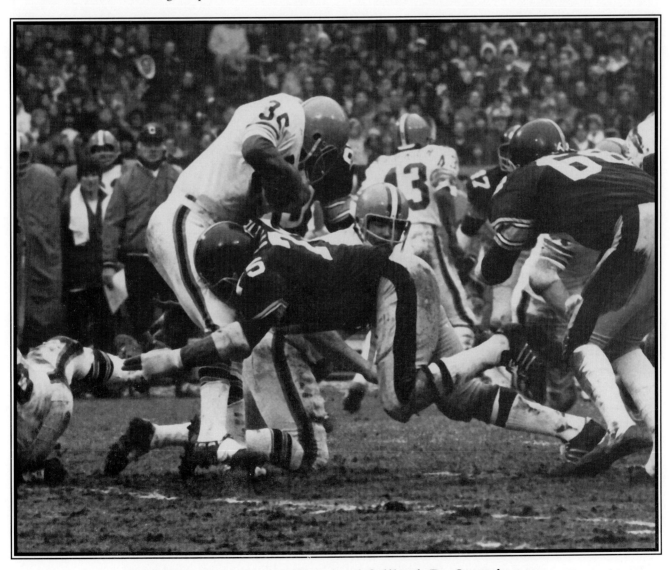

Mean Joe Greene cuts Cleveland fullback Bo Scott in two.

Joe Greene, having recovered a fumble and about to be hit, prepares to lateral the ball for a touchdown. Steel Curtain linemate Ernie Holmes trails the play.

"Joe beat us up so bad. He was so strong. And so quick. He'd hit you and—bang!—move on you. By the end of scrimmage we were trying to tackle him just to slow him down."

One by one, Greene dumped the entire offensive line. "None of those guys wanted to get up there," L.C. Greenwood smiles. "He just ran through them."

His success was more than physical. Why did Greene have such an attitude? It may be because he acted as a father to his younger brothers and sisters after his own father left home. It may be that Greene was immensely fair, even as a young man; he took care of people, and he hated it when people cheated or violated the rules. A serious, large, thoughtful man, he was a leader as a teenager. He picked up the "Mean" tag at North Texas State, where the team itself was called the Mean Green. In truth, he hated his nickname, and it took him years to make peace with it—and his image.

"Joe was from Texas," linemate L.C. Greenwood explains, "where everything and everybody is big. He had an attitude because he was coming to Pittsburgh. He came in and wanted to disrupt things. He wanted to have things go his way, to happen the way he wanted them to happen.

"Joe was the star," Greenwood adds. "He was the number-one draft choice."

"I had a belief in what I was doing," Greene says of his own fierceness, "in the people I was working with and working for, a love of what I was doing, and the place that I wanted to be."

That place was winning. Indeed, at the first team meeting, Chuck Noll said to the Same Old Steelers, "Our goal is to win the Super Bowl." Some players snickered. Greene didn't.

He would win—he would show them how. "Joe brought everything," wide receiver Lynn Swann says. "He had great physical skills, emotional intensity, and love for the game. He was an intelligent ballplayer, studying the game, doing the right things, and being prepared. Through his leadership he motivated the people around him to be better than they would normally have been.

"Joe Greene was going to be great no matter where he was," Swann adds. "He was going to be a Hall of Fame player. He was going to play at that level of intensity and dedication, and people around him would have to rise to his level, because he was not going to sink to theirs."

"He was the dominant factor," Mike Webster agrees. "He was one of the rare guys who could change the complexion of the game all by himself. Football is the ultimate team sport, but he could make the difference in a ball game." The offense blew it? "Joe would get upset. He could run through three or four guys and take the ball away. He was that dominant."

"There were games that Joe literally just took over," Tom Donahoe recalls. "They couldn't block him. He just disrupted everything that an offense wanted to do."

One example is the December 10, 1972, game in Houston. "We had to have that game to win the division," retired trainer Ralph Berlin recalls. "And we were having a tough time. The offense failed to convert, and as the

WHO'S THE BOSS? PART I

In the middle of one game, defensive tackle Ernie Holmes ran off the field, caught backup Steve Furness's eyes, and jerked a thumb.

Furness ran on the field.

Defensive coach George Perles asked Holmes why he came out of the game.

"Joe said to get off the field," Holmes said.

"What?" Perles asked, incredulous.

"Joe said to get off the field," Holmes repeated. "Joe said I was free-lancing, and if I'm not going to play the defense, to get off the field."

Perles was nearly apoplectic. "Get back on that field," he screamed.

But Holmes wouldn't budge—until Greene said it was all right for him to come back in the game.

defense went back on the field, defensive back John Rowser said, 'Damn it, here we go again.' Joe said, 'I'll be damned if we are.' And he sacked Dan Pastorini four straight downs.

"He was so quick, so strong, that offensive linemen couldn't block him," Berlin adds. "When he decided to come, it did not matter. People had never seen anything like Joe Greene."

"Joe was the best defensive lineman I've ever seen," running back and assistant coach Dick Hoak agrees.

"It was fun to watch him," Terry Hanratty recalls. "To this day there isn't a tackle that's any better. Joe always had two guys blocking him, sometimes three, and he still made a huge impact. His strength was incredible, and his quickness was second to none."

"Joe Greene was what that team was built on," center Ray Mansfield says. "His fierceness, his competitiveness, and his never-say-die attitude. I never saw anybody who could block Joe in his first five years. I couldn't block Joe—and he didn't even go full speed in practice.

"Joe Greene scared other people," Mansfield smiles. "When Joe Greene came to the Steelers nobody ever bothered us."

In 1974, Greene won over rookie defensive back Donnie Shell during a game at Cleveland. Greene went in on a rush, read the play, dropped back, intercepted a pass,

A tiger on the field, a pussy cat off it: the legendary Joe Greene, singing in the rain.

There is no more touching tableau in the Steelers' rich history than that of Joe Greene carrying stricken comrade Lynn Swann off the field in the 1975 AFC Championship Game.

Swann, who took his fair share of abuse as the Steelers' wide receiver of choice in the '70s, had been knocked cold and was lying supine on the Three Rivers Stadium turf.

Before play could be stopped, Greene ran out and picked up Swann. It was a heart-rending scene, and there wasn't a dry eye in the house.

"People always talk about that," Swann says, "saying that Joe must have cared about me a great deal. Joe didn't care about me that much," Swann shakes his head. "He just didn't want to waste a time out. Joe was always trying to figure out how to win a ball game."

Joe Greene carries the unconscious Lynn Swann off the field during the 1975 AFC Championship Game.

ran twenty-five yards upfield, got hit, and lateraled to defensive back J.T. Thomas, who ran the ball in for a touchdown. Shell was awestruck. "I'd never seen a lineman make that kind of play," he remembers. "I said, 'Hey, everything that's been written about this guy is true.'"

And more. Joe Greene was playing a kind of football no one had ever seen in Pittsburgh. A late hit against the Giants' Fran Tarkenton—Greene got the thumb. A fight with the Vikings' Jim Velone—out of game. And so on. "My first year," Greene says, "I was tossed out of six or seven ball games. I didn't like that."

He didn't much care for the '69 season—he didn't much care for losing anytime. During the last game of the '70 season, a 30-20 loser in Philadelphia, the Eagles drove to the Steeler one-yard line. The enraged Greene picked up the ball and hurled it into the stands. (For the uninitiated, an NFL football is as hard as a rock with two lethal points at the ends. Fortunately, Greene's outburst didn't maim—or kill—anyone.)

Then there was the time he punched a guy in the face and nearly started a riot. Or the time he broke Cleveland center Bob DeMarco's jaw. Seems that DeMarco threw an elbow under Greene's chin, then ran off to lead a screen-pass block. Greene started to steam, but let it go. In the second half, the Browns ran the same screen, and DeMarco again whacked Greene. This time, however, Greene chased DeMarco twenty yards and clotheslined him. As DeMarco was being carried off the field, Greene proceeded to the Cleveland bench and told them just who had done what—in case there was some lingering doubt about what had happened.

In 1976 someone missed a block—they still argue about who—and Cincinnati scored, depriving the team of what would have been its sixth shutout. Chairs flew in the clubhouse. "They had that pride," Ralph Berlin says. "You were not going to stop them.

"They held Joe," Berlin adds. "They leg-whipped him. One game, after about three times, one guy tried it again.

Up the middle there was no more fearsome combination ever: Joe Greene pulls down the San Diego Charger while Jack Lambert mashes him from above.

Greene jumped back, then jumped up and down on him. He got thrown out of that game, too."

One time in Chicago, Steeler running back Warren Bankston fumbled, and the Bears Ross Brupacher recovered and ran the ball back for a touchdown. Greene was so furious he flung his helmet at the goalpost. "The helmet disintegrated," Ralph Berlin says.

"Joe Greene did not know fear," Berlin adds. "One time he spit in Dick Butkus's face. Butkus had the presence of mind to walk away."

the game was over. Although you couldn't expect anybody to play with those emotions every game, he just dominated."

"I was the kind of guy who bumped on all the edges," Greene says. "At the time, I didn't let anybody's feelings or opinions get in the way of what I wanted to do, which was to win. I was a young kid, twenty-two or twenty-three years old, and I did a lot of things I'm not proud of. I know if I had gone someplace other than Pittsburgh, with someone different from Chuck who wouldn't approach me properly, that I wouldn't have had a career in football. But Chuck, Dan, and Mr. Rooney made it very easy to be a part of being there. They allowed me to develop and mature into a man. Some of the foolish things that I did they handled in a way that I could keep playing football. Some people would not have understood or appreciated some of my behavior, and probably would have handled the situation a lot differently."

How the opposition handled the situation was very carefully. Indeed, the word around the league was don't get Joe Greene angry. Talk to him. Ask about his family. Be nice to him. Help him up. Or he'd eat you alive.

Whatever you do, Viking coach Bud Grant said, *don't* hold him— because that makes him ballistic. When that happens, he's liable to hurt someone.

"There was one guy on the Giants," L.C. Greenwood says, "who kept talking to Joe. 'How are the wife and kids?' talking nice. Then he blocked Joe. Joe kept falling

Then there was the time in 1977 that Denver lineman Paul Howard was holding Greene. Tired of it and furious, Greene unleased a roundhouse to Howard's midsection. The belt heard 'round the world cost Greene his entire playoff check.

One time in Oakland, George Perles recalls, Greene said the Raiders had some sort of grease on their jerseys. The officials disagreed. "Joe exploded," Perles says, "and for it—he had gotten Joe so relaxed that Joe wasn't thinking about what was going on."

"When Joe warmed up," George Perles remembers, "the other team came by and said hello. Everybody in the league wanted to make sure they were on the good side of Joe."

One time in Cincinnati there was a slight pregame tussle about where the teams would warm up. The Bengals wouldn't budge—until Perles told quarterback Kenny Anderson that Joe wouldn't take kindly to all this palaver. The Bengals moved. "They knew," Perles says, "that if you wound Joe up it was all over. He could be a violent football player—within the rules.

"If you blocked him fairly that didn't bother him," Perles adds. "If you tried to take advantage of him, he got violent. And when he got violent, we'd win games. I was always looking for a reason to keep him violent—but you just can't expect a guy to play that way every week.

"He was as valuable in the locker room as he was on the football field," Perles continues. "He didn't want anyone acting up in the locker room. No one was interested in offending him because he was capable of handling everything."

"Joe Greene was the boss," Ralph Berlin adds. "Whenever I had a problem, I never went to Chuck Noll. I never went to Dan Rooney. I went to Joe."

One team rule, for example, was that the clubhouse stereo would be turned off twenty minutes before the game. One day, equipment manager Tony Parisi turned the stereo off. Ernie Holmes turned it back on. Joe Greene turned it off. Holmes turned it back on. Greene ended the dispute by pulling the wires out of the wall.

In training camp, rookies get taped first, then veterans. One year, a first-round draft choice came in late for taping, and Ralph Berlin demurred. The fellow said a few choice words and stormed out. Greene, who had overheard the outburst, told Berlin that he'd take care of it. Two days later, the rookie came back and apologized. "Joe said I was out of line," he said sheepishly.

"Joe Greene was something," cornerback Mel Blount recalls. "He was awesome. But he was also a good person, honest and fair. Joe didn't put up with a lot of foolishness, and you had to respect that. In the locker room, he was the kind of guy who not only demanded but commanded respect just by his presence."

"The aura of Joe Greene was so remarkable that it made you act in a certain way," receiver John Stallworth recalls. "As a younger player, in tough situations, I looked to him to let us know how to handle things."

"Off the field," remembers receiver Lynn Swann, "Joe was as playful and warm as he was intense in a game." Swann, who came five years after Greene, would punch him and run. If Greene could catch Swann, he'd stuff him in a laundry basket, tape him in, send him down the hall. And leave him there.

And Greene enjoyed the Tuesday card game, which ran for nearly ten years, as much as anyone. "He was a leader," Swann adds. "He worked hard, and people respected him."

Then the unthinkable happened. Warming up for a 1975 game, Greene slipped, pinching a nerve in his neck. In the short term, he saw extremely limited action in the AFC Championship Game and Super Bowl X. In the long term, it was the beginning of the end.

"After he got hurt," Ralph Berlin recalls, "he was a shell of his former self on the field. He still commanded the respect in the locker room—he was still the boss. But he was never the same player again."

Joe Greene injured? How could Joe Greene get injured?

"It bothered the heck out of me, too," Greene recalls. "It wasn't a good time. Going through the injury and not being out with your team was very painful. But it also let me know that there were parts of me that could enjoy watching my teammates' success. There was disappointment, but there was also joy and happiness." Greene pauses. "I'd hate to think about what would have happened if we hadn't won and I had not been there to help."

Overall, though, he believes the pinched nerve helped him to be a better player—and the successful coach he is today. "Until I got injured," Greene says, "I was reckless, and to some extent disrespectful. Once I experienced not being able to do what I wanted to do, then I had to learn how to play. It's probably the reason I'm coaching today. I started to understand more of the game because I had to look for ways to excel. Physically, I was no longer able to do it.

"Chuck was always teaching technique and fundamentals," Greene adds. "He was a 220-pound guard, and

he had to know them. Over time, I started to understand and believe in the details, too. You have to be able to think through the game a little more, too."

The problem was that by 1980 thinking wasn't enough. The team of the '70s all arrived together, and they all got old together. After the fourth Super Bowl, in January 1980, the team did not make the playoffs again until 1982. By that time, Joe Greene was gone.

"It was difficult at times because I couldn't perform the way I wanted to perform," Greene says. "The requirements for me to perform were still there—there was nobody else, and I couldn't defer it. It was the same for all of us, really.

"The disappointing thing is that it had to end someplace," he adds. "Being a competitor you think you could've

A limping, ailing Joe Greene swaps his uniform jersey to guzzle a Coke. Whatever this award-winning commercial did for the product, it made Greene an off-field star.

One game, defensive back Mike Wagner was limping around, saying his hip hurt, *really* hurt, and that he had to come out of the game.

"No, Mike," Greene said, "I want you in the game. Because you playing hurt is better than the next guy playing healthy."

Wagner played.

done better. But that was really the primary reason I decided to retire. I couldn't be a part of those championships anymore. I couldn't do it."

But all the leadership on the field and in the locker room helped make him a coach. Five seasons after Greene's retirement, Chuck Noll brought him behind the bench.

"I'm very grateful to the Steelers for allowing me to come back, and to Chuck for giving me the opportunity. I had never coached, but he gave me a position on his staff. Our relationship started off good, and it ended up great."

The team was wallowing—7-9 in '85, 6-10 in '86—and Greene brought his customary fire. "He made a good contribution," Noll allows.

Ray Mansfield recalls Greene and Noll talking together, almost like father and son, sitting on locker room stools. "The early screaming wasn't leadership," Mansfield shakes his head. "Joe learned through Chuck's handling to become a leader."

"There was no nonsense," linebacker Mike Merriweather adds. "It was pure football all the time."

"He was still very intense," says Tunch Ilkin, who played both with and for Coach Greene. "But he was very helpful, very encouraging. To have Joe Greene tell me I was doing well—what an encouragement! He became a teacher—like Chuck. A lot of Chuck rubbed off on Joe; I could see it." Sure, Coach Greene was still capable of his rages, "but he also had a very soft side," Ilkin says. "He was a very effective leader."

"He was a natural," adds Joe Walton, a Steeler assistant with Greene in 1990-91. "He's got a good feeling for people."

Jon Kolb, who both played and coached with Greene, found him a wise, warm, and supportive friend.

"He was very nice and calm off the field," offers defensive back Carnell Lake. "But once the game started, he didn't like anyone to relax. He would get highly emotional. I could see how he was as a player—very intense. He scared me as a coach, but we needed that fire set underneath us. We needed that emotional kind of coach. Maybe Chuck Noll liked having Joe Greene around because Joe had the emotions that Chuck couldn't show."

Rod Woodson remembers Coach Greene slamming down chairs and yelling to get the players' attention. "He was very intense. But I like Joe tremendously as a person. I used to call him Teddy Bear Greene. He didn't like that, and I used to run from him a lot."

"Joe expected a lot out of us," recalls linebacker Jerry Olsavsky, who as a Youngstown-area youngster played Joe Greene in schoolyard games. "He was great to be around. We would tease him all the time. It was like the little dogs picking on the big dog. You were all right until the big dog got mad.

"He was so intimidating," Olsavsky adds. "So emotional." That was the problem in '92, as Olsavksy sees it. With the highly emotional Bill Cowher as head coach, the Steelers did not need—and could not afford—two such men on the sidelines. Cowher had to be the emotional heart of the team, not Greene. "I'm gonna miss Joe," Olsavsky said. "But it's the best thing for the team."

Indeed, Greene had been in the running for head coach until the end. He knew it, of course, and would have stayed in any capacity. "It wasn't my choice to leave," Greene says. "I could not work there, so I was disappointed. Anytime you're trying to achieve something and it doesn't happen, you're disappointed. But it didn't last more than a day. I had to focus my attention on getting a job.

"They've had an awful lot of success," Greene allows. "Dan made the right choice. If I were Dan, I'd probably do the same thing. When Chuck retired, Dan invited me into the process. I hadn't thought about being a head coach up until that time. I said, 'Let me think about it.' Then I said, 'I could.' But I don't know if you hand over your head coaching job to someone who just started thinking about it. From the standpoint of experience, Bill had

The number one pick and the number one owner: Joe Greene (left) and the Chief in his office.

High-stepping to Canton: Mean Joe Greene demonstrates his Hall of Fame form.

The Player of the Decade, an honor richly deserved: Chuck Noll celebrates Joe Greene's induction into the Pro Football Hall of Fame in 1987.

more. He had been at it longer than me. So there was no bitterness on my part. I knew that Dan made his decision honestly. This is a man I had been involved with since 1969, and I trusted him. I wasn't going to argue or get belligerent with him."

Nevertheless, it was hard to say good-bye. "It was difficult," Tom Donahoe allows. "Joe's a special person, as a player and as a coach. Joe has a lot of qualities that we like and admire. But in our opinion he was not ready to be a head coach in the National Football League."

Today Joe Greene coaches in Phoenix and is enshrined in the Hall of Fame. "That was nice," Greene admits. "I was very happy about it, because it gave me an opportunity to reminisce about a game I cared for, and about people whose lives I touched and whose lives touched mine." He pauses. "I'm very proud that I was a part of that team. At least once a year, and it's been sixteen years since that time, I talk about it with someone. They bring up the pleasant memories and the fun. That's something that can never be taken away."

With Joe Greene anchoring the defense and rookie Franco Harris rushing for one thousand yards, the Steelers finally made the playoffs in 1972—and for the next eight seasons never looked back. The Immaculate Reception against Oakland gave the team mythic status—and turned Harris into an instant star. The Steelers now deserved respect, and they would not be denied.

The lineup bristled with outstanding players and future Hall of Famers—Harris, Jack Ham, Jack Lambert, Blount, Terry Bradshaw. The Steel Curtain alone—the defensive line of Joe Greene, L.C. Greenwood, Dwight White, and Ernie Holmes—was astonishing. With brilliant linebackers Ham, Lambert, and Andy

CHAPTER 5

DAWN OF A NEW ERA

The Steel Curtain, et al.

> "I don't feel I have to wipe out everyone, Tom. Just my enemies."
>
> **Al Pacino**
> ***The Godfather, Part II***

Russell and defensive backs Mike Wagner, Blount, J.T. Thomas, and Donnie Shell, the defense was the best in history.

Overall, the Team of the Decade's record is unmatched: After winning the AFC Central Division in 1972 and returning to the playoffs in 1973, the Steelers won six consecutive AFC titles, 1974-79, and won Super Bowls IX, X, XIII, and XIV.

COME UP THE YEARS

It is a truism of sports that playing with great players improves everyone's play. Certainly that was the case with the Team of the Decade. Winning four Super Bowls took constant refinement. Some claimed the team peaked in 1976, when the Steel Curtain slammed shut with five regular-season shutouts, while others argue they reached their apex in 1978, when the Blond Bomber's Aerial Circus brought a passing title and an unprecedented third Super Bowl victory.

Hall of Fame running back Franco Harris, credited by many teammates as being the player that made a good team great.

BUILDING BLOCKS: *1969 Draft*

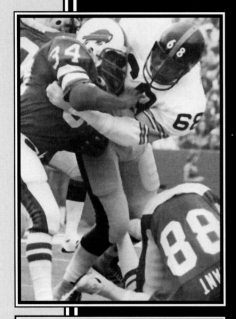

The most devastating defensive end on the most destructive defensive line of all time, L.C. Greenwood holds his ground.

The very mean, and very powerful, Mr. Joseph Greene.

Notre Dame All-American quarterback Terry Hanratty piloted the Steelers club—for a year.

Jon Kolb came as a third-round pick in '69 and stayed twenty-three years. Undersized and undervalued, he explains the moves to Dan Radakovich.

1969. Things look dark as the team wins one and loses thirteen. Bright spots: Chuck Noll's first draft includes top-three picks Joe Greene, Terry Hanratty, Jon Kolb, and in the tenth round, a fellow by the name of Greenwood from Arkansas.

1970. Drafting first, the Steelers take Terry Bradshaw and Mel Blount. Bradshaw is uneven, the team goes 5-9, and Chuck Noll continues to be unshakably patient.

Nothing shows yet, but those in the know knew. At the '71 Super Bowl, Vince Lombardi confided to friends that Noll would be the next great head coach.

Let us repeat: These were the 1-13, 5-9, soon-to-be 6-8 Steelers, but it was Lombardi, for heaven's sake, so nobody laughed. At least not in his face.

1971. The 6-8 record shows improvement, sure, but the real news is the draft, arguably the second-best in team history. Frank Lewis, Jack Ham, Steve Davis, Gerry Mullins, Dwight White, and Larry Brown are the first

six picks. Ernie Holmes came in the eighth round, Mike Wagner in the eleventh.

Are we beginning to see a pattern here? Suddenly, the Steeler drafts go from good to astounding. "A lot of our real good drafts happened when we were drafting early," Chuck Noll allows. "You get lucky sometimes, you really do. You almost have to. Greenwood and Wagner were both late picks—they were size and speed pick-ups, and we were lucky. Generally, what we'd like to do was to get good athletes, good football players, good people, and good team players. We really didn't have a measure for it at the time. So we had to get them together and work with them and see what happened. It's like getting married—you don't know until you live with them."

They looked for musculature, certainly, but most of what they looked for was above the eyebrows.

"We tried to draft intelligent people," Noll says. The club gave them twelve-minute intelligence tests, sent for

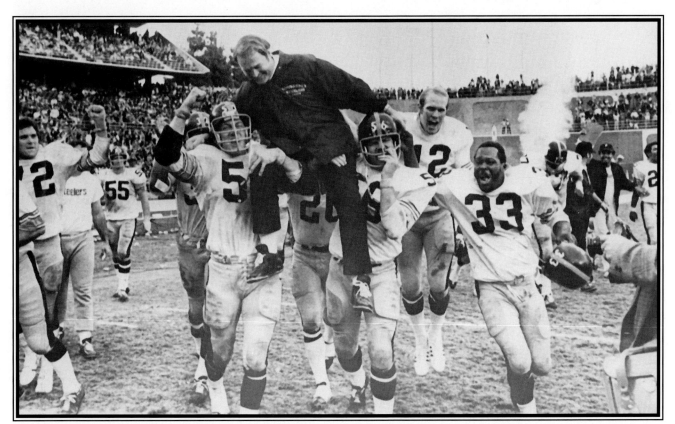

The Steelers celebrate their first divisional championship in San Diego in 1972. Chuck Noll is held aloft by number 56, Ray Mansfield, and is trailed by number 33, John "Frenchy" Fuqua, and number 12, Terry Bradshaw.

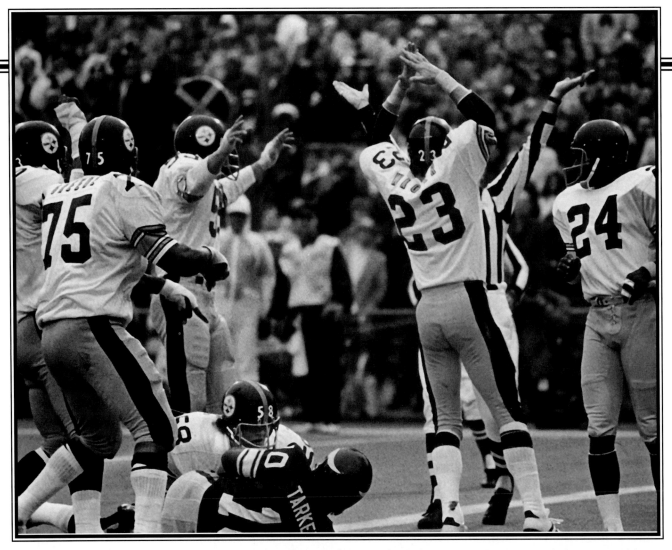

The score at the half was 2-0 after Jack Lambert set Minnesota Vikings' quarterback Fran Tarkenton on his end zone in Super Bowl IX.

transcripts, looked at the courses they took. "We thought that was important," Noll said, "very important."

1972. Franco Harris had played in the shadow of Lydell Mitchell at Penn State, but Noll liked his power, speed, and ability to read plays. Harris came as the number-one pick, rushed for one thousand yards, led the league with seven one-hundred-yard games, won Rookie-of-the-Year honors, and put the team over the top. The Steelers went 11-3, making the playoffs, winning something, *anything*, for the first time in forty years. His Immaculate Reception, in the last seconds of the AFC playoff against Oakland, "just gets bigger every year," Harris smiles.

To this day, many Steeler veterans feel they should have gone to the Super Bowl, but first they had to meet the Dolphins for the AFC title. Miami, having their extraordinary undefeated season, squeaked by the black-and-gold 21-17, a game that many Steelers believe they could have won.

1973. Nothing much happened in the draft. The team regrouped, going 10-4, before losing to Oakland in the AFC wild card playoff.

1974. By '74, they were ready—or were they? With training camp opening during a players' strike, it was mostly rookies on the field. But what a class, clearly the greatest in Steeler history, perhaps in NFL history. With Lynn Swann, Jack Lambert, John Stallworth, Jim Allen, and Mike Webster the first five picks, need we say more?

"That draft put us ahead of the league," Mel Blount says. "Those guys came in, made contributions, and had careers."

Lambert came early to study films and learn the system. With the veterans on the picket line, the rookies

Mel Blount snags another one at the Ice
Bowl during the AFC Championship
Game in 1979. The final score versus the
Houston Oilers was 34-5.

BUILDING BLOCKS:

1970 Draft

Terry Bradshaw spots his target against
the Browns in Cleveland. The Steelers
dominated the rivalry during Bradshaw's
career, winning every game in Three
Rivers Stadium, 1970-83.

BUILDING BLOCKS: *1971 Draft*

Offensive lineman Gerry "Moon" Mullins opens a hole for Rocky Bleier. Mullins played guard and tackle, 1971-79.

Defensive end Dwight White smokes Bengal Ken Anderson. White anchored the Steel Curtain front four, 1971-80.

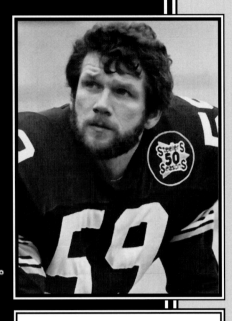

Hall of Fame linebacker Jack Ham (1971-82) played as if he had already seen the game film and was merely following a script.

Just call me Arrowhead: overshadowed by Greene, Greenwood, and White, Ernie Holmes bids for a new persona—and more press.

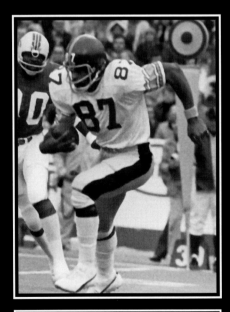

Tight end, offensive tackle, and all-around good guy, Larry Brown on the move. He was a Steeler from 1971 through 1984.

Safety Mike Wagner recorded thirty-six interceptions in his Steeler career (1971-80), including eight in '73, tied for the league high.

were able to make an impact almost immediately. And once Terry Bradshaw settled down . . .

Going 10-3-1, the Steelers again headed for the playoffs, first Buffalo, then Oakland. "It was never a question of whether we were going to win," Ralph Berlin recalls. "It was how much were we going to win by—and whether we would shut them out."

Before the AFC title game some dolt made the fatal mistake of saying that the "real" Super Bowl had been the Oakland-Miami playoff game, making the Oakland-Steelers face-off a mere formality. Getting the Steelers angry? Not a bright idea.

When Chuck Noll strode into the Tuesday meeting, he was already wearing his game face. "I want to tell you," he said, "the best team is sitting right here in this room."

"That's when I knew," Joe Greene says, "right there. It's the most special thing an athlete can feel. And the most beautiful thing about it is that it lasted two weeks. When he said that, there wasn't anything the Raiders could do to win that game."

At halftime, with the Raiders winning 10-7, John Stallworth caught the ball in the end zone—but it was ruled out of bounds. "In a big game like that," Greene says, "you need those points. If you don't get them, you're disappointed. That didn't happen to us. On that football team, we didn't care, we were still going to beat them. That was our attitude. They didn't have a chance.

"We had the desire and the will to win the biggest game in the history of the Steelers up to that time," Greene says. "I'm not underestimating the talent, but our attitude was so high. The zone is not a place that you visit very often. You're lucky if you get there once in your career. That's where we were that day as a team. It was a quiet confidence, and it lasted a long time."

"That game showed the true essence of the Steelers," Franco Harris agrees. "It made us believe we were a great football team. We felt we were the best. From that moment on we had the feeling that we were going to win."

They disposed of the Raiders 24-13, and by the time they got to Super Bowl IX, Greene adds, "we were happy—because it was going to be a win. It was also a new beginning." After all, they had lost to the Dolphins in their

BUILDING BLOCKS:
1972 Draft

Franco Harris arrived in 1972 and soon became Terry Bradshaw's favorite runner. When it worked, it was the prettiest ground game in football.

perfect season. And they had lost to the Raiders in '73. "That showed us we weren't ready for the big time," Greene says. "We could play the .500 ballclubs and win. So the Super Bowl was a very sweet victory."

It was a defensive gem. Halftime score: 2-0 Steelers on a safety. In their 16-6 loss, the Vikings gained 119 total yards, seventeen on the ground, and coughed up the ball five times. For his part, MVP Franco Harris romped for 158 yards on thirty-four carries with one touchdown. When Pete Rozelle gave the gleaming Lombardi Trophy to the Chief, there wasn't a dry eye in the place.

"What emerged was a team," Rocky Bleier says. "Guys who believed that we could do things. Success breeds success."

"We wore the championship hat pretty good," Greene says. "We had our cockiness and our swollen heads, but they were in check. I felt that we had become a pretty good football team and that we could be much better. But the only way we could realize our full potential was to play in the big games against good football teams. Because they brought out the best in us."

1975. "The toughest part of winning the Super Bowl," L.C. Greenwood recalls, "was that we had to go out the

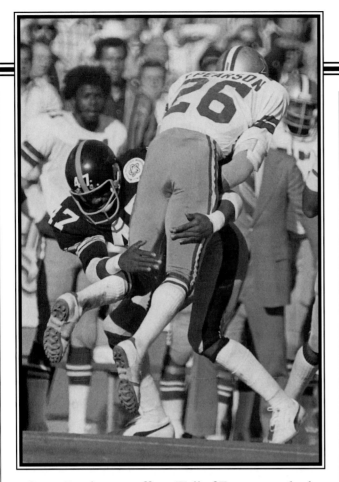

Super Bowl, super effort: Hall of Fame cornerback Mel Blount eats former Steeler Preston Pearson's lunch during Super Bowl X.

next year and play every game like it was the Super Bowl. Every Sunday, every team was after us. But that's how we surpassed a lot of teams at the time, how we were able to make it two years in a row."

Winning the opener by shutting out San Diego, the Steelers dropped game two, then peeled off eleven consecutive wins, only to drop a 10-3 squeaker in L.A. and lose the finale. Final record: 12-2.

"Once we got into it," Joe Greene says, "the offense started to get as good as the defense. Then we were the best team for the entire season. We were the team that everybody had to deal with. That was the year that nobody was going to get in our way."

The Colts and the Raiders didn't in the playoffs, and neither did the Cowboys in Super Bowl X, who lost 21-17.

How tough were they? With the Steelers leading 10-7 late in the second quarter, kicker Roy Gerela missed a field goal and was taunted by Cowboy safety Cliff Harris. Harris patted Gerela on the helmet. Lambert, enraged, picked up Harris and dumped him.

When we consider that game, however, we think of the Steelers' quintessential money receiver, Lynn Swann,

Most Valuable Catch: Lynn Swann's excellence, Super Bowl X.

BUILDING BLOCKS: *1974 Draft*

From Huntsville, Alabama, and Los Angeles, California, came John Stallworth (left) and Lynn Swann, the gold-plated receiver corps of the '70s.

Jack Lambert (below) bears down on the Polish Rifle, Philadelphia Eagle quarterback Ron Jaworski.

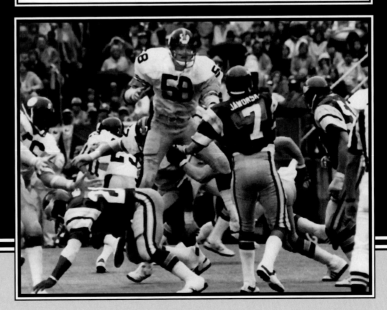

In one game, center Mike Webster dislocated three fingers, set them in the huddle, then taped them on the sidelines.

The game ball and his second Super Bowl trophy are presented to the Chief in January 1976; (left to right) Commissioner Pete Rozelle, the Chief, Chuck Noll, and broadcaster Charlie Jones.

whose four receptions and 161 yards (including a sixty-four-yard, game-winning touchdown catch and a leaping, arching Swann perfecto) netted him the Most Valuable Player trophy.

1976. Rocky Bleier has many coreligionists who share his belief that "this was probably the best team ever, except for the injuries."

Freshening the blood with tight end Bennie Cunningham, Gary Dunn, Ray Pinney, Mike Kruczek, and Jack "the Hydroplane" Deloplaine, the Steelers opened the season with perhaps a touch too much of the post-season bubbly, as the Steelers lost four of their first five. Then, at the end, injuries took their toll, notably to both Harris and Bleier, as they lost the AFC championship game, once again, to their despised rival Oakland.

In between, however, the 10-4 Steelers were perhaps the most magnificent team, with the greatest sustained defensive effort anyone has ever seen. Their nine straight victories, plus one against the Colts in the playoffs, included an astonishing five shutouts. "No one could move the sticks," Andy Russell shakes his head. "We won ten in a row. Five shutouts—and shutouts in the NFL are unheard of. No field goals?"

And not many points, either, until the Colts scored two touchdowns in the AFC playoff game. In those nine wins the Steelers gave up a total of twenty-eight points.

"If we would have been healthy," Franco Harris says, "it would have been a different story. We would have won three in a row."

1977. As the draft brought such solid performers as Robin Cole, Sidney Thornton,

Despite missing a third straight Super Bowl, some considered it the best team of all time: the Pittsburgh Steelers, Class of 1976.

Ted Petersen, Dennis Winston, and Cliff Stoudt, all of whom would play a role in the Steelers' future, the 9-5 season was a time of adjusting to a new passing game. The team would have all off-season to lick its wounds from the postseason loss to Denver.

1978. Then there are those who rate this flavor as the best of all time—not merely the Steelers' best but the all-time NFL best. It's hard to argue with them.

The team went 14-2 in the regular season, then crushed the Broncos in the playoffs, 33-10. The AFC championship game was played in a steady, freezing rain in Three Rivers Stadium. Slippin' and slidin', the Steelers slapped 'em silly, beating the hapless Oilers 34-5. Play of the year: flea flicker to Bennie Cunningham to clinch a 15-9 overtime victory over the Browns.

Bradshaw won it all that year—passing title, NFL Player of the Year, Super Bowl MVP—throwing 318 yards and four touchdowns, hitting everything that moved, including an all-timer, a seventy-five-yard touchdown pass to John Stallworth.

Super Bowl XII was a talent show all right: Blount intercepted, Harris ran, Swann snagged 'em—and the

IT AIN'T OVER 'CAUSE IT AIN'T OVER

The Scene: The locker room, Orange Bowl, Sunday, January 21, 1979. The team that many consider the best of all time has just completed a resounding drubbing of the Dallas Cowboys, winning an unprecedented third Super Bowl title in five years.

The Challenge: In his farewell address to his victorious troops, Chuck Noll, still steely eyed, growls, "This team hasn't peaked yet."

The Riposte: To that, sweat-soaked center Mike Webster, all-time Steeler iron man, drawls, "Way to put the pressure on, Coach."

Steelers were champions again with an unprecedented third win, 35-31 over Dallas.

1979. Although no one knew it at the time, this was the season to close both the decade and the Dynasty.

The team looked good, marching easily through a 12-4 season, playoffs against Miami and Houston, and finally on to Pasadena for Super Bowl XIV against the Rams.

Again it was Bradshaw, in the 31-19 win, who netted his second consecutive MVP honor. He threw for 309 yards, completing fourteen of twenty-one, including three to Stallworth for 131 yards, one of which was a seventy-three-yard, fourth-quarter touchdown pass that he caught over his back. Nine times out of ten, anybody would have dropped it, and no one would have blamed him. But this was Stallworth, and it was for all the marbles.

With the Rams charging and the crowd screaming "DEE-fense!" Jack Lambert, number 58, intercepted a Ram pass to stop 'em cold. Nobody ever did it better.

Four Super Bowls, fourteen of eighteen playoff games. Not a bad decade's work.

John Stallworth is making another of his patented tough grabs, this one against the Rams in Super Bowl XIV.

THE DEFENSE

When Ron Johnson came to play cornerback in '78, he looked up in the huddle one day and his jaw dropped. "You're all legends," he bubbled. "The Steel Curtain. *Legends!*"

"Aw, shut up, man," they all answered. "Just do your job."

"In the '70s," Dan Rooney says flatly, "the Pittsburgh Steelers played the best defense that has ever been played."

Although the intricacies are far too complex for our brief overview, what made the defense so good were the systems invented by Assistant Coaches Bud Carson and George Perles.

When most teams were playing man-to-man in the secondary, Carson came up with a new double zone defense, a system perfect for the Steelers—who specialized in strength and quickness. "We had that edge," Carson says. "We were doing something that people didn't understand."

On the line, George Perles invented the infamous stunt 4-3, working assiduously all season to take away every offensive edge the opposing team had. The result: Slanting Joe Greene to eat up two or three offensive linemen, L.C. Greenwood stuffing the tackle, and Jack Lambert rambling at will. "The stunt 4-3 freed Jack up," Carson recalls, "allowing him to play his game, to take advantage of his natural talents. The stunt 4-3 and the double zone turned Pittsburgh from a loser into a big winner."

"Until other teams found out what we were doing," Assistant Coach Dick Hoak adds, "it was tough for them to run the ball against us." In the '74 playoffs, for example, Buffalo's explosive ground game went a whopping thirty-seven yards, and Oakland ate up but twenty-one. In the Super Bowl, the Vikings picked up a measly seventeen. "They had no idea what was going on," Hoak adds. "Besides, we were tough—top players and intimidators."

"If you look at a psychological profile," says defensive back J.T. Thomas, "the ballclub was two parts, the left side and the right side. The left side was more quiet—

A quarterback's worst nightmare: one-on-one with Jack Lambert. From 1974 to 1984 no one was a more devastating middle linebacker.

Ham, Wagner, Greenwood, Thomas, and Greene. Naturally, when you got to Joe things got noisier. When you got to Lambert, a transition took place, a total change. You had a bunch of guys that were more emotional, more erratic. Lambert, he's bizarre, he's wild. Ernie Holmes—his motive was to hurt somebody. Dwight White was bitching for sixty minutes about something—something

He could cover it all. Run, pass, blitz, name it; Jack Ham stuffs the run.

was always bothering Dwight. Dwight talked the whole game. Everybody was holding Dwight. He was cursing everybody's parenthood on the field. What in the hell was Andy Russell doing over there with those guys? He was out of place. But all those personalities working together was the key.

"We were also innovative," Thomas adds. "Mel used to say, 'Why are we reading this playbook? We wrote this book. Why should we study it?' We put it in the back of our cars—because if we lost it, it'd be five hundred dollars. Basically, a lot of things we did were improvisational. Guys reacted to the situation like musicians—we were in the same key, but if there was a modulation, everyone knew where the change came. We'd come back to the sidelines, and the coach'd have his card there and say, 'What play is that?'

"When we left," Thomas smiles, "that playbook left with us. The way the trap was, the way Joe Greene did it, was based on talent, not based on the text."

The stunt 4-3 and the double zone turned a loser into a winner: defensive coach Bud Carson, 1972-77.

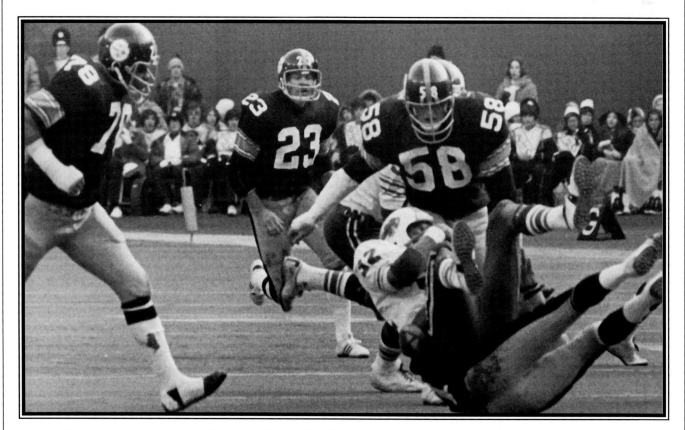

The Steel Curtain closes. Dwight White, Mike Wagner, and Jack Lambert converge to stop the run.

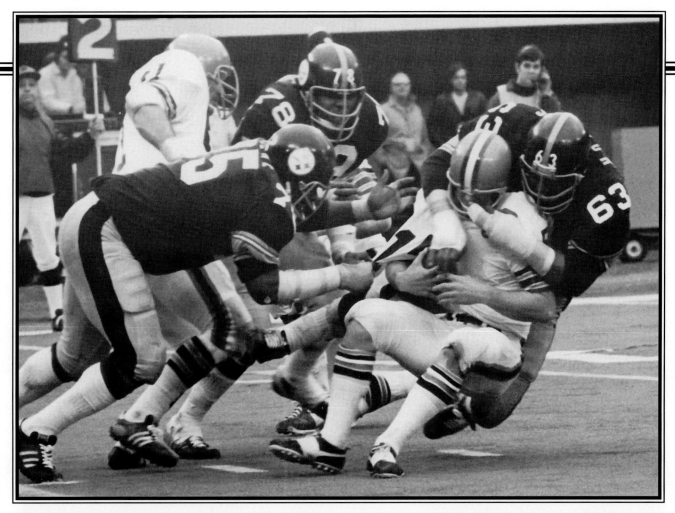

The Steel Curtain sacks another quarterback. Joe Greene (left) tries to cop Mike Phipps's jersey for his collection. That's Ernie Holmes trying to rip his nose off and Dwight White looking for somewhere to land.

THE DEFENSIVE LINE

The justly vaunted Steel Curtain—Hollywood Bags, Mean Joe, Fats, and Mad Dog—started and ended as pals.

"The four of us together had a great time," defensive end L.C. Greenwood says. "It wasn't like work. It wasn't stiff competition. It was like four guys shooting hoops—everybody's just making buckets. We didn't care who we played against. The better they were, the better we reacted against them.

"It was because we were in sync," Greenwood adds, "like a symphony. We enjoyed being with each other. On the football field we were friends. We just blended together. We didn't need a whole lot of coaching because we had goals and objectives. We knew what we wanted to do, and what we had to do."

"People brought us together," Joe Greene says. "Sometimes you get lucky."

It was more than that. "We wanted to win very badly," Greene adds, "especially when things were so difficult for us. We were out there growing up together, getting beat up, and kicked in the face. Experience was the best teacher for us. We were all very, very competitive. We were getting beat on a regular basis—and nobody liked it. Because of the direction of the organization, the only way to go was forward. That was the only way we wanted to go."

Much has been made of the fact that all four were black, were from Texas, or nearly so, and from modest roots. They all saw an enormous opportunity for themselves, wanting to use football as a springboard to a better life.

"We did most of our bonding during training camp," Joe Greene adds. "We'd go off together and talk and dream. We'd dream about winning."

George Perles arrived at the Steelers in 1972, inheriting what was quickly becoming the best defensive line in football history. The story goes that one day in camp

His one unfulfilled wish was to play one game without pain or injury. L.C. "Hollywood Bags" Greenwood a-baggin' it on the bench.

HOLLYWOOD BAGS'S UNFULFILLED WISH

"**W**hen I think about things that happened on the football field," defensive end L.C. Greenwood says, "my body starts aching. I can feel that pain. One thing I always wanted: to be able to play one game when I wasn't hurt, when there was nothing wrong with me. Because I never played a game that my ankle or my shoulder or my knee or my back or my hand wasn't hurt. I always wondered if I could play a complete game without injuries. Without that little edge of pain, what could I do? But it didn't happen."

the four were sitting together on tackling dummies. Chuck Noll cast his customary steely eye at his young charges and asked Perles what they were doing. Perles is said to have shrugged.

"We had a group that understood that we had to stop the running game," Perles recalls. Doing that, he adds, forced the offense into a passing situation—where the Steelers' devastating secondary would eat them alive.

Ernie Holmes's grandpappy gave him the name Fats, although he preferred Arrowhead after he shaved his hair in the shape of an arrow. Standing six-foot-three and 295 pounds, an eighth-rounder in '72, Holmes was cut. Later he came off the taxi squad. He struggled with his weight, but when that ball was snapped. . .

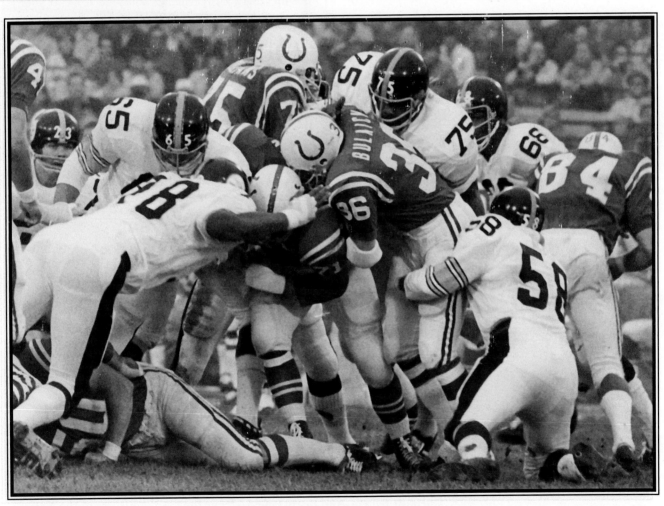

The Steel Curtain slams the door on the Baltimore Colts' Norm Bulaich: throughout the '70s, teams found it impossible to penetrate the feared stunt 4-3 defense.

L.C. Greenwood, a hunch pick in the tenth round of the '69 draft, was long and lean, six-foot-six and 220 pounds, floated like a butterfly and stung like a bee—hard enough to be the all-time Steeler sackmeister with 73.5. When he came from Arkansas A&M, Greenwood had no strength or technique to speak of, but he could run and he was determined. That's all it took. Hollywood Bags was born.

"Nicknames just stick with you," Greenwood chuckles. Assistant Coach Walt Hackett called him Greenbush, Greenbrier, and finally, Bag It—which became Bags. Then in 1970, a rumor circulated that Terry Hanratty and Greenwood would be traded to the Rams. "If we get traded," the Rat ribbed Bags, "you can become Hollywood Bags." Greenwood throws up his hands. "I can't live it down. I can't get rid of it." He even wears a bracelet with "Bags" inscribed on it. And while everyone else wore regulation black shoes, Greenwood preferred gold—size 13.

"We worked together extremely well," Greenwood recalls. "We got to a point where we knew each other, how we would react to certain situations on the football field. We'd line up and say, 'Meet you at the quarterback.' We did pretty much what we wanted but stayed within the framework of the team. We'd put in our own defenses, and the coaches never knew what was going on out there.

"I felt sometimes when we needed a big play," he adds, "I could take a chance—but those chances were pretty calculated. I could get out of the original defensive structure and make a play—because I knew where Joe, Lambert, and Ham would be.

"If we made a mistake," Greenwood shakes his head, "we could work it out on the football field. 'Man, you're screwing up. This guy's gettin' off on you.' We knew Ernie'd be there. Dwight would be talkin' plenty of stuff over there. Joe would be destroying things—

DWIGHT WHITE TELLS WHAT IT'S ALL ABOUT

"We were all team players and confident in each other. We all had that same intensity. We played a lot of games together in all types of conditions, and that's how you can tell what your teammates are made out of. Everybody's pretty good in September—they're not all beat up and banged up, and the weather's still nice and pretty, and you're fresh.

"But in late December, when it's cold and everybody's a little banged up, people are playing hurt, you look in the guy's face in the huddle, you see blood skeeting out of his nose, and he's all whipped, and this guy's telling you, 'C'mon, babe, suck it up,' that's really what it's all about. It makes your skin crawl.

"We were tough people—and we took great pride in being tough people. I took great pride from being from a smokey, dirty city. That was part of our personality. We're going to smoke your butt and dirty you up.

"We'd dominate the situation. And we would win."

The most feared—and justly famed—front four in the history of the National Football League: (left to right) Dwight "Mad Dog" White, Ernie "Fats" Holmes, Mean Joe Greene, L.C. "Hollywood Bags" Greenwood.

John Banaszak prevents a pass. A defensive end and tackle, he provided valuable reinforcement for the Steel Curtain's front four from 1975 through 1981.

Joe Greene consoles an uncharacteristically pensive Dwight White.

and I'd be runnin' till the whistle blew. We worked well together and just got at it.

"We were coming," he laughs. "If you weren't going to get moving, you'd get run over."

"There were some synergies there," Dwight White agrees, "good chemistry. We were confident in our own talents. And we executed very well together.

"That was our job," White adds, "shut 'em down. Winning was important, but we were just having fun. 'You come to Pittsburgh, don't even try it. You're going to lose the game, and we're going to dominate it.' It was almost arrogance, but as Dizzy Dean said, 'It ain't braggin' if you can do it.' And we did it."

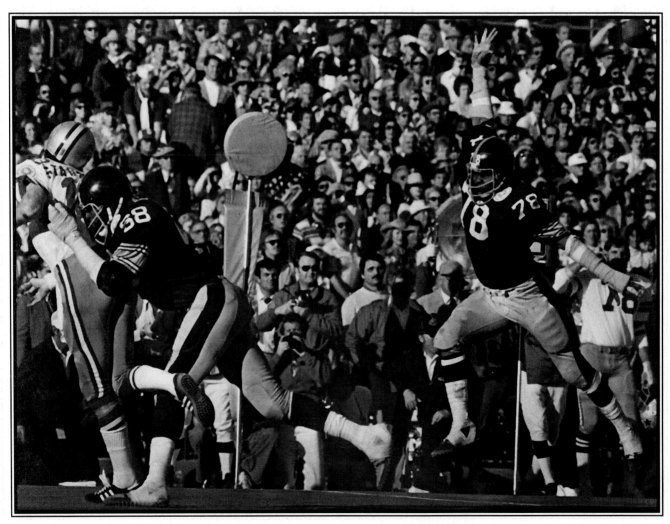

L.C. Greenwood recording one of his record 73.5 sacks, followed by Dwight White, performing his famed Peter Pan imitation against the Cowboys in Super Bowl X.

A study in contrasts, technique versus emotion: Andy Russell stops the run, while Dwight White prepares to rip the limbs from the man's body.

THE LINEBACKERS

"Andy Russell, Jack Ham, and Jack Lambert—our linebackers were all 220 pounds, ran 4.5 forties, and were smart as all get-out," Terry Bradshaw says. "Those are the kind of people Chuck wanted. Because smart people don't make mistakes. They may lack a little bit physically, but they make up for it. They're in the right position because they're so smart."

"Andy Russell?" Dan Rooney asks. "The ultimate intellectual."

Russell, a sixteenth-round choice in 1963, didn't care for hitting people when he came to the Steelers. "I had to force myself to do it," he recalls. "I really appreciated the technique. If I nailed somebody, I didn't feel any personal thing. It was all execution.

"I really wanted to be successful," Russell continues. "And since I lacked certain physical talents—strength, size, and speed—I had to make up for it some other way."

So Russell got information, studied formations and tendencies, and took game films home—and became perhaps the smartest player anyone had ever seen. "I prided myself in being able to know the opponents," Russell allows. "I knew what they were going to do before they did.

"By the end of my career," Russell smiles, "it became almost subliminal. It was almost embarrassing." Indeed, he'd call out opponents' plays before the ball was snapped, before the quarterback could audible. "I could see it in

"HE HAD NO BUSINESS PLAYING..."

So they get to New Orleans for Super Bowl IX, and Dwight White is in the hospital. For the duration, the docs say.

They practice backup Steve Furness at defensive end.

White calls George Perles every night and says he'll be there. Perles makes nice noises but does not believe for two seconds that White will be anywhere near the game.

Super Sunday, White arrives, dresses, and goes on the field.

Perles and Chuck Noll are on the sidelines. Suddenly, they hear "Boom! Boom! Boom!"

White and Joe Greene are banging heads.

Perles says White's sending a message that he's ready to play.

Furness says, let White start. Perles tells Noll he'll start White, let him go one series, then yank him. Noll agrees.

Out goes White, who proceeds to play the entire game—brilliantly, one might add. Minnesota picks up seventeen yards rushing.

White goes back to the hospital for another week.

"This is the kind of motivation Dwight had," Perles says. "He had no business playing. He wasn't strong enough to be playing. But he did."

"God takes care of fools and babies," White explains, "and I wasn't a baby. I had a lot of pride and made a big contribution that year. The bottom line—it was too big a game to miss."

the quarterback's eyes," Russell says. "That's one of the exciting things about professional football."

Two of the exciting things about professional football were Russell's linemates, Ham and Lambert, whom Russell simply calls surgeons. "Jack Ham was a brilliant player," Russell adds. "He didn't make any mistakes, knew the game, and anticipated well. Plus, he was an explosive talent, probably the fastest Steeler in five yards. Not in

"I knew what they were going to do before they did," said linebacker Andy Russell, who captained the all-time brightest Steeler team.

the forty, but he had an incredible explosion off the blocker. And he'd make it look easy. It was astounding how good he was," Russell shakes his head. "He was the best linebacker I ever saw—absolutely unbeatable."

"He's the best I ever saw for coverage," Bud Carson recalls. "There was nobody like him."

"Jack Ham was so good," Dick Hoak says, "that it got to the point that teams wouldn't throw the ball over there anymore."

Indeed, for many, Jack Ham was the best outside linebacker anyone ever saw—a man who played so well and so calmly that it seemed as if he had already seen that game's film and was merely following the script. Or as one observer put it, it was as if Ham was on real time and everyone else was on seven-second delay. On a team of noticeably smart players, Ham seemed to possess an uncanny sense

of where the play was going and where the ball was.

Yet in 1971, when he came as a second-round draft choice from Penn State, Ham was not happy. "The organization always played tough, hard football," he recalls, "but it did not win the games. It did not have that championship reputation."

At Penn State, the Nittany Lions lost three or four games in Ham's entire career. By midseason, the Steelers had equaled it.

Yet the Steelers were on their way, due in part to Ham. "I was a student of the game," he allows. "I saw what the teams' tendencies were. I anticipated, recognized what was coming, and got a jump on a play—that one step closer."

Yet Ham is quick to add that he was but one player in a larger defense—and all individual honors do not equal team successes. "I firmly believe that if I had played for the Tampa Bay Buccaneers I would not be in the Hall of Fame," he says. "The Hall of Fame is more a credit to our football team than it is to an individual. It's not that I don't enjoy that great honor," Ham adds, "but it's not close to winning championships."

A pair of Jacks, a contradiction in style—the cool, cerebral Ham, the emotional, hard-hitting Lambert. The Lambert whose legs shook before the snap, who'd point a finger in an opponent's face, who'd unceremoniously dump a guy who'd insulted a teammate, who'd scream at his teammates on the field. Yes, *that* Jack Lambert, also in the Hall of Fame.

"Lambert may have had the image of a wild man," Andy Russell says. "But he killed you with his precision. He was a great anticipator. Read his keys. Penetrator. Took angles away from blockers. Great technique. Never made a mistake. But what really sets him aside as a great mid-

The three canniest linebackers on the all-time great defensive team:
(left to right) Andy Russell, Jack Lambert, Jack Ham.

Hall of Fame coverage master, Jack Lambert, feasted on the pass, run, and quarterback.

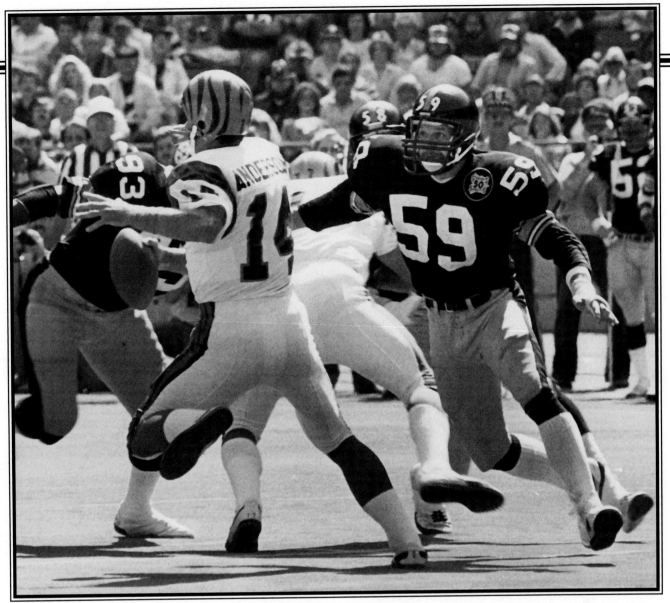

No one ever broke through coverage faster—or more accurately: Hall of Famer Jack Ham closes in on Bengal quarterback Kenny Anderson.

dle linebacker was his ability to cover the pass—he was dramatically better than anyone on the pass. He covered the tight end man-for-man. He covered the first back out—that's unheard of. Lambert did things never asked of a middle linebacker—and did them superbly."

"Jack was very smart," Ham agrees. "Oh, he made a tough hit on somebody, and people said, 'There's that crazy guy out there on the field,' but he was a very intelligent player, and in that sense we were kind of alike. We'd make sure we didn't make a mental error—because at that level it's not the physical things that will beat you. It's the mental breakdowns. In the big games, two or three plays will make the game for you."

"Lambert would get on anybody," George Perles recalls. "He was on the same page as Joe Greene wanting to win. He made adjustments and did audibles. He was an exceptionally smart middle linebacker."

"When you start talking about attitude and focus," offers Chuck Noll, "Jack is the epitome. He was the most focused individual I've ever had. He'd go on the practice field and there was no nonsense. It was get the job done. And he had the ability, at six-foot-four, to win the battle of hitting."

"Make no mistake about it," Tunch Ilkin adds, "Jack knew everything. He was mentally tuned to the game as much as Andy Russell or Jack Ham."

Perhaps because of the players' strike, which gave the rookies early run of training camp, or perhaps due to individual temperament, the Class of '74 was not like others. Case in point: one hot-tempered young fellow named Lambert.

It's a time-honored tradition that rookies are hazed in training camp. Although at one time things got a bit thick, nowadays it's as tame as singing your school fight song before the assembly in the cafeteria. When one foolhardy fellow prodded Jack Lambert, the emerging Number 58 would have none of it.

Lambert: "I don't !&#*&% sing," he snarled and strode out.

There was grumbling among the players as they decided how to handle this heresy.

"Hey, Joe," one player said to The Force, "what about it?"

Greene, who had taken a liking to the long, lean rookie's intensity, focus, and style, just smiled. "I guess Lambert doesn't sing," he said—and left it at that.

THE DEFENSIVE SECONDARY

To begin with, nobody expected oversized Hall of Fame cornerback Mel Blount to be as fast as he was. But Blount'd cover everything, and knock 'em out when he was finished. Safety Mike Wagner, did he ever play on anything other than guts? Safety Donnie Shell couldn't catch a cold when he strolled on a free agent. But he made the team on sheer will—and bone-fracturing hits. And J.T. Thomas at the other corner—he played so hard that if he gave up three touchdowns a season he considered it a failure.

That's what opponents faced if they made it to the backfield.

"Mel Blount was the greatest athlete I had ever seen," Ralph Berlin says. Bud Carson adds, "He's still the best ever to play the game. There's no one who comes close.

Jack Lambert and Mel Blount join forces to shut down the run.

With Blount's speed, anticipation, height, and reach, nobody could get away from him."

"Football is a team sport," Blount says. "You're no better than the people that surround you. I was fortunate to be surrounded by great athletes. Chuck Noll had a way of pointing out big plays. It was something I looked forward to in team meetings. It was always a motivating factor to me—to make that big interception or the big play. It made me want to go out and perform well."

So what about this size thing? Isn't lithe Rod Woodson more like a cornerback? "I was different," Blount allows. "But I did have speed—and there's no substitute for speed. That's not something you can coach. You can put a guy on weights and make him strong, but you can't make him fast. Speed is a God-given talent. You either have it or you don't."

It didn't hurt that Blount was a wide receiver before moving to corner, so he knew where the ball was going and how to catch it. (His fifty-seven interceptions are a Steeler all-time record.) "My biggest strength was one-on-one, man-to-man coverage," Blount says. "I had an advantage with my height and very long arms. I could be beat, but I could cover so well because my arms are long." He smiles. "It worked out."

It worked out for safety Mike Wagner, too, sometimes appearing to be the hardest hitter on a team of hired as-

The hardest hitter on a team of hired assassins, Mike Wagner pops Earl Campbell.

Cornerback Mel Blount's fifty-seven interceptions are the Steelers' all-time best.

On Retiring

"It wasn't hard for me to leave," Hall of Fame cornerback Mel Blount says. "I was always honest with myself. I knew that when I left it was time to go. I knew that I hadn't held anything back. I had given what I had to give."

After fourteen years, Blount had a year left on his contract, a year that would have paid him more than he had ever gotten from the Steelers. But he wasn't interested.

"I had never played for the money," Blount says. "I played because I enjoyed the game. I loved it. I could have hung around for another year, but I also knew that I couldn't perform on a level that would have been acceptable to me. So I left. And I never looked back."

Dan Rooney celebrates Mel Blount's induction into the Pro Football Hall of Fame in 1989.

sassins. "No one's trying to kill anybody out there," he allows, "but they're still trying to knock people out of the game. Not to injure them for next week but to get them off the field."

One time, on a safety blitz against the Bengals' Kenny Anderson, Wagner literally bent Anderson in two—from behind. "The situation wasn't just tackle him," Wagner says, "but hit him so hard that he'd give up the ball. Take that face mask and drive it as hard as I could right into him." Wagner pauses. "I thought, 'Oh, man, now that you've done that, now what? I have nothing to be proud of here because someone may be maimed.' The game is very physical, but those are the parts that I shake my head at."

Like the time in Super Bowl X when Wagner caught Cowboy receiver Drew Pearson in midair, carried him for a bit hoping someone would come and knock the ball loose, and finally dumped him. Pearson's ribs were cracked, but he held onto the ball. "It's football," Wagner shrugs, "and it's serious business."

Wagner took it, too, including three cracked neck vertebrae in Cleveland in 1976. Trying to prevent fullback Cleo Miller from getting a first down, Wagner buzzed around the end, bore down on Miller, ducked his head, and whack! Miller clubbed him with a forearm. Wagner was out cold, and the season was over.

"That's the give-and-take of football," he says. "If you're trying to hit somebody very hard, they're going to try to hit you very hard, anyway they can."

Another time, Bengal running back Boobie Clark clotheslined him, "Just about tore my arm out of my shoulder."

Then there was the time Wagner snagged one and headed upfield, cut here, cut there, doing just fine until some enormous offensive lineman belted him. "I thought he tore my head off," Wagner remembers. "They could hear me scream in the upper deck. After that, if I intercepted a pass, I went straight line for the sidelines. If I got in the end zone, great. Otherwise, let Lynn Swann wow the crowd."

The other safety was Donnie Shell, a smart, tough, self-motivated walk-on who came in 1974 and retired a mere fourteen years later. "We had some guys who could play back there," Shell allows. "We were very physical, but I always stayed in great condition. I only missed four games—it was a blessing."

The thing that cornerback J.T. Thomas most remembers is not the technique but the confidence. "Chuck would come in and say, 'Let's go out there and play ball and get this thing over with.' His presentation to us was like the game had already been won—we had only to go through this formality. There was no doubt that we were going to get it done. Even in the Super Bowl."

At Super Bowl X, for example, down in the runway before the game, the Cowboys offense and Steelers defense stood face mask to face mask. While the Steelers were loose, the Cowboys were glassy-eyed. Dwight White turned to Thomas and jerked a thumb. "'We got 'em now,' White laughed. That was *before* the introduction," Thomas says. "We knew then. That was our confidence. We thought we were better than anybody."

Donnie Shell, whose fifty-one interceptions lead all Steeler safeties, was a free agent in 1974.

After the Dynasty, the Steeler defenders were perennial Pro Bowl participants. Class of '77: (left to right, front row) Jack Ham, Glen Edwards, Mike Wagner; (rear) L.C. Greenwood, Joe Greene, Jack Lambert, Mel Blount.

THE MOST FAMOUS PLAY IN FOOTBALL HISTORY

Today it's known as The Immaculate Reception. With twenty-two seconds on the clock, the Steelers were losing to the Raiders in the '72 playoffs. (Right) A desperate Terry Bradshaw fired one of his patented armor-piercing passes to Frenchy Fuqua, number 33, which hits Raider defender Jack Tatum. . . .

(Left) Meanwhile, a hustling Franco Harris, number 32 , is trailing the play. The ball falls and falls. . . .

Harris scoops it up. . . .

Three Rivers Stadium, 1972 AFC playoff game, twenty-two seconds left on the clock, Oakland-7, Pittsburgh-6. Fourth and ten on the Steelers' forty. If this is not desperation, nothing is. Terry Bradshaw, as was his wont, fires a pass to Frenchy Fuqua that could pierce an armored plate.

Raiders' strong safety Jack Tatum, in hot pursuit, gets in the way. The ball hits his shoulder pad and squirts back toward the line of scrimmage. Rookie-of-the-Year Franco Harris, having completed his assignment, is trailing the play. He sees the ball, falling, falling, falling, until Harris scoops it up and races for the end zone.

Final score: Pittsburgh-13, Oakland-7.

Pandemonium.

The Immaculate Reception is Chuck Noll's single all-time favorite Steelers moment. "Up until that point I was the one who was believing that this was a good football team," he smiles at the memory. "This was a sign that this was a team of destiny."

He races for the goal line. . . .

He scores! It's a mob in the end zone (left). The Steelers win their first championship—of any kind—in forty years.

Confident symbol of the super '70s: Terry Bradshaw prepares to pass against Denver's defense.

THE OFFENSE

In the early days, as L.C. Greenwood recalls it, the offense was not the most stellar. One day Joe Greene, coming off the field, grabbed Bradshaw and said, "Three downs and punt. Don't worry about scoring. We'll score. Just run the football. Make sure you don't throw an interception that they can run into the end zone."

Early in the Noll years, the Steelers developed their complex trap system. "Very few teams did that," Coach Dick Hoak says, "pull and run, sweeps. We used quicker, smaller, and brighter lineman—once play started their assignment changed, so they had to be smart enough to stay fluid in the game. Nobody used our system. 'You start trapping when you get off the bus,' one guy complained to me. He was right."

THE OFFENSIVE LINE

The offensive line is the most faceless group on a football team. They make no glory plays, have no statistics to flaunt—no one keeps stats on seconds protecting quarterback, holes opened for runners, or guys belted on the screen pass. Toiling in obscurity, they get no Blitzburgh banners. Their *raison d'etre* is to protect, to wallow in the ditch so Franco Harris can run for daylight.

"Our guys were a heck of an asset," L.C. Greenwood says. "Unknown and undersized, they ate up Minnesota's Purple People Eaters, Dallas's Doomsday Defense." They were good, too, because in practice they faced the Steel Curtain.

"The mixture is what made that team so great," says Larry Brown, a tight end and offensive tackle from 1971 to 1984. "I felt very fortunate just to be a part of it. There was plenty of publicity to go around. Besides, the recognition for linemen and nonstatistical guys comes from the players on your team who respect what you do and how you do it.

"We were taught the value of technique, not muscle," Brown adds. "We needed to protect the quarterback, to stay between him and the guy who's going after him. You don't need to do it for a long time—four, five, six seconds, long enough for him to get the ball away."

The literal and figurative center of the offensive line was Mike Webster, all-time Steeler with fifteen years of service, 1974-88, and 220 games, 177 of them consecutive. "Nobody could outwork Mike," Brown recalls. "Physically, there were others who were taller, bigger, and stronger than Mike. But he was a good student, a tough guy who wanted to play. He also played with a fear of not being good or not being successful at what he did. He had leg injuries where anybody else—*anybody else*—

Larry Brown offers protection.

Offensive wizard Jon Kolb in the snow.

would not have played. But he felt he was the guy to get it done. He was a motivator. He kept you pumped up."

"I was always insecure enough to make sure that I did everything right," Webster admits. "You have to be so demanding of yourself. Because those aren't the Boy Scouts out there. It's a dangerous place. Plus, from the moment they draft you, they're trying to replace you, looking for somebody better. Then there's film—you can't get away with things. Eventually, you're going to see it with your boss. That puts a lot of pressure on you.

"When I was playing," he continues, "I never felt comfortable. I never let myself feel that I had arrived. I couldn't afford that luxury. I always had to perform the next play. If I had a bad play, I had to let it go. Otherwise, I'd have five or six bad plays in a row."

Webster was famous for using everything to his advantage, even, or especially, the snap count to get off the ball. And Webster blew off the ball faster than anyone in the league. "There was a secret to that," he smiles. "I cheated. I was always a half count ahead of everyone else."

If you played on the Steelers' offensive line, you trapped, which Webster did to great advantage. "It took a while to understand the theory," he says, "and longer than normal to get everything in sync. But you could cut the defense any number of ways. It was fun. When it was working, it was really pretty."

"Webster was flat-out the best," says Tunch Ilkin. "He knew what everybody was doing. He made all the line calls. Sometimes we'd be in a play, and the quarterback would be in a cadence, and Webbie would look back and

Best off-the-ball center ever, Mike Webster was an asset to the Pittsburgh team 1974-88.

Ray "The Old Ranger" Mansfield played in 182 consecutive games, a Steeler record.

say, 'Get out of it,' and they respected Webster so much they would change."

"Webster was a tough guy who'd tape up his jersey sleeves to intimidate the other team," Dan Rooney recalls. "He gave you everything he had."

In one game, Ralph Berlin recalls, Webster tore the cartilage in his knee so badly that he couldn't run or straighten it—he could barely walk. Did he come out of the game? No. Webster taped it, finished the season, played the Pro Bowl, and then had surgery. Another time he dislocated three fingers but fixed them in the huddle. "His nickname Iron Mike is richly deserved," Berlin says.

"Webster lifted weights in his hospital bed," coach George Perles recalls. "If he had to miss one day, he'd lift twice to make up for it." He had a homemade weight machine in the boiler room with Jon Kolb, Larry Brown, and Steve Furness. "That was the beginning of big-time weight lifting in the NFL."

"Webster and Kolb were the hardest workers and the most prepared," Ilkin says. "I'd go early, walk in the weight room, and they'd have been there for a good hour. When I'd leave, they'd be watching film."

"Jon was serious about weight training," Larry Brown remembers, "and I knew I had to be serious about it as well. If he said, 'We're going to be here at seven o'clock in the morning,' I'm going to be there before seven. He was very much about teaching and passing information along, and people being better."

For his part, Kolb, who played from 1969 to 1981 and coached from 1982 to 1991, felt that there were two personalities on the offensive line. On the right side, the strong side, Larry Brown and Gerry Mullins lined up against Joe Greene and L.C. Greenwood. On the left, or weak side, Kolb and Sam Davis practiced against Ernie Holmes and Dwight White.

With traps, technique, and tenacity, Ted Petersen opens a hole for Franco Harris.

As Kolb remembers it, the right side was a little more laid-back. "L.C. would come to practice with a toothpick in his mouth—literally," Kolb says, "and Joe Greene never took practice too seriously. So Larry and Gerry had a cake walk. On the left side, however, with Fats and Mad Dog, I had crazy people. They didn't know what practice was. Every time they put on pads they thought they were in a game."

Perhaps the attitude of the offensive line is best summed up by center Ray Mansfield, who played from 1964 to 1976 and holds the club record with 182 consecutive games. "I always worked hard," the Old Ranger says. "I hustled. I ran downfield. I was strong and quick, and I won every blocking award they had.

"My attitude was always 'Never say die, never be defeated. Go down fighting on the beach.'"

Terry Bradshaw takes the snap from Ray Mansfield. It would be five years before Bradshaw was ready to play championship ball.

THE QUARTERBACK

The road to the Super Bowl begins in Butler, with Terry Hanratty.

By 1969, when the Steelers drafted Butler native Terry Hanratty in the second round, he had been on the cover of *Time* and *Sports Illustrated*. He was a Notre Dame All-American, and he was coming home to lead his team to glory.

Or so it seemed.

Although he picked up the offensive system rather quickly and seemed to be maturing, the 1-13 season ate at him. "It was the longest year I ever spent in football, or any sport," Hanratty recalls. "Going back to grade school, I never lost more than one or two games in any

season. In the huddle, I would say out of frustration, 'Please don't hold.' Back then, holding was fifteen yards. We had trouble with first and ten. Imagine us first and twenty-five."

The other shoe fell on draft day in 1970 when the club picked Terry Bradshaw. Chuck Noll called Hanratty, then pulling National Guard duty in Fort Bragg, and said the choice was not a reflection on him, that the club drafted the best athlete available. As Hanratty recalls, "You've got to be pretty stupid to think that the number-one pick in the whole draft is not going to play."

From that day through the end of the 1975 season, Hanratty was a backup—no more. Joe Gilliam, who came in '72 and also left in '75, was supposed to challenge Bradshaw, but it was not to be. "You just couldn't go in and say, 'I want to be traded,'" Hanratty shrugs. "It just didn't happen. You had to bite the bullet."

Hanratty was a good soldier, charting, dissecting film, and feeding the other Terry information. Hanratty helped,

America's top draft pick, Terry Bradshaw, signed with the Steelers in 1970. William Bradshaw (left) and Dan Rooney were as happy about the deal as he was.

When the Steelers drafted Terry Bradshaw (center) Terry Hanratty (left) knew his days at quarterback would be few and far between. The third man is coach Babe Parilli.

Terry Bradshaw already was a fan favorite early in his career. He delights young adoring fans (above) with autographs at the Steelers' training camp.

and he's proud of his job, but he never wears his two Super Bowl rings. "Life is timing," he says, "and I've had good timing for the better part of my life. If that small portion is all the bad timing I'll ever have, I can live with that."

Dick Hoak's last year as a player was Terry Bradshaw's first, and he remembers the rookie quarterback well—six-three, 215 pounds, rifle arm. "Terry Bradshaw had more talent at his position than anybody I'd ever seen," Hoak says.

"He was as good a football player as I've ever seen in my life," Dan Rooney agrees. "And he may have been Noll's best effort. Chuck handled Bradshaw perfectly. He'd give him sympathy, he'd be tough. He'd talk to him and tell him what to do. He let Bradshaw call the plays. Chuck really did the job."

"Terry was not a surprise," Noll recalls. "Everybody had him right up there at number one. Terry's ability was to throw long. But it takes more than the quarterback. You can have the greatest talent in the world, but if you don't have people around you, you are not going to function very well. So we had to get the supporting cast. In 1970 our receiving corps was questionable, and our running game was not anything special. We needed shoring up in the offensive line. We needed weapons."

Yes, everyone knew that Bradshaw had talent to spare, but his transition, roughly 1970-74, was long and painful. Finally, in December 1974, Noll told Bradshaw he would not be pulled. Bradshaw never looked back. Along the way, he set Steeler records for total yards passing (27,989), single season (3,724), most three-hundred-yard passing

Terry Bradshaw's dedication and drive played as big a role as his talent in winning him four Super Bowl rings.

WHAT WAS THAT PLAY AGAIN?

One day in training camp, rookie quarterback Mark Malone was confused by a particular coverage. The Steelers' aerial offense lived off double in-routes: play action, receivers to a post, run in-routes. But what of the coverage—man-to-man, zone, single free safety, extra defender as free safety, and so on? Where to throw when the traffic went haywire?

One night, he went to ask Terry Bradshaw, the master of the double in-route. Bradshaw nodded sympathetically at the rookie's dilemma. "If Lynn Swann says he can get open," Bradshaw says, "I don't care if it's single man, two deep, three deep, blitz. I'm coming back and I'm looking at Swann. And if he isn't open, I'm throwing it hard and high, because I know my guys are going to be able to go up and catch it."

Quarterbacks (left to right) Joe Gilliam, Terry Hanratty, and Terry Bradshaw competed for the soul of the Steelers in 1974. Bradshaw would emerge victorious, and the Steelers would win their first Super Bowl, 16-6, against the Minnesota Vikings.

games (four), attempts (3,901), completions (2,025), touchdown passes (212), and so on.

"I didn't learn any football in college," Bradshaw says. "I didn't learn anything about coverages. I never read coverages. So I had this whole big adjustment. Had I been a mature young man, I wouldn't have taken my rookie year as hard.

"I was different," Bradshaw allows. "Chuck recognized my strengths—strong arm, impatient, hated short passes, loved to challenge safeties and corners as opposed to linebackers—and put this offense in for me. It wasn't a West Coast offense. It was one pass, from East Coast to West Coast. It was fun.

"The thing that I learned early," he adds, "is that you put a defense together, you put a running game together, you control the clock, you let your defense keep you in the game, you put sustaining drives together, you do play action, and *then* you go deep when people come up to stop the run. That's how we played. That's it, nothing fancy.

"The game plan basically never changed the whole time I was there," Bradshaw nods, "other than the ap-

plication during the week. After my fifth year, I can't recall ever feeling any pressure of losing my job again. That's a great feeling."

Another great feeling came from Most Valuable Player awards in Super Bowls XIII and XIV. "That gives you a sense of belonging," Bradshaw says, "of self-worth. It gives you a feeling that you are successful, that you have accomplished the most important part of your job, which is winning championships. We accomplished that."

Bradshaw pauses. "I just wanted to win. We won. I did my job. Isn't that it?

"Very few people can go through life and say that at one time they were the very best at what they did," Bradshaw considers. "I am one of those people who can say, not that I was the very best, but that we were, and that's a privilege. We did something together that no one can take away from us, and that we can't personally say, 'It's mine.'

"You get nothing out of life unless you get it with the help of other people. How unique it is to go through this experience together, with all these people who were put together. It's amazing. I'm very proud."

BRADSHAW'S LAST GAME

After 1982 Terry Bradshaw's elbow was shot. Off-season surgery didn't help, and it was clear that '83 would be his last campaign.

Truth was, Bradshaw just couldn't throw. The Steelers were 9-2 and steaming for the postseason. Then they lost three in a row and desperately needed a win against the Jets' vaunted New York Sack Exchange to clinch a playoff berth.

Chuck Noll calls on Bradshaw one last time. Just run the ball, Bradshaw is told.

Bradshaw nods dutifully.

He steps into the huddle. Big grin. Bradshaw comes out smokin', makes two touchdown passes, hurts his elbow, and sits. But by then, they've clinched it.

The Steelers win big, 34-7.

After the game, tackle Tunch Ilkin has a question. "Hey, Brad," he smiles, "I thought we were going to run the ball."

"Tunch," Bradshaw shakes his head, "I ain't no mailman. I'm a gunslinger." Bradshaw pauses. "I just wanted to show everybody I could do it because nobody thought I could."

Coach Noll and quarterback Bradshaw have one of their typical sideline conferences.

"Close, but no cigar" never applied to Terry Bradshaw, who got the cigar (above) and four Super Bowl rings in his 14-year career.

In 1976, the Steelers became the second team in pro football history to host two one-thousand-yard runners: Rocky Bleier (left) and Franco Harris.

THE RUNNING BACKS

As the decade turned, the Steeler offense wasn't much different from that of the Jock Sutherland days—a diet of running the ball with an occasional pass thrown in as a palliative. The running game was mediocre at best until it acquired the heart of Rocky Bleier and the mind of Franco Harris.

When Bleier came to training camp in 1968, he was small, slow, and marginal. He made the squad and then went to Vietnam, where he took shrapnel in his leg.

"When he got back he looked like something that had come out of a concentration camp," trainer Ralph Berlin remembers. "But the kid wanted to play."

Did he ever. Although Noll wanted to cut Bleier—did cut him, in fact—Dan Rooney put him on the notable-to-perform list. Then the injured Bleier, whom some

thought would never walk again, much less play the punishing game of professional football, put himself through the most rigorous rehab program in the history of the sport. "You do what you have to do during a period of time, and you don't think about it," Bleier says. "I was willing to do the work, everything I possibly could to make the team."

Weights, special shoes, yoga, and running mechanics. By 1973 Bleier was a different human being, weighing 218, bench pressing 465, squatting more than 600, running a 4.5 forty—off 4.8 as rookie. "That made the team for me," Bleier says. The next year he was a starter. In 1976, he rushed for one thousand yards. "It was a glorious achievement," Bleier remembers, "because it wasn't expected."

If Bleier was the war hero, the journeyman made good, Franco Harris was the star, the Rookie of the Year who

In 1976, Rocky Bleier rushed for one thousand yards, but not always through holes big enough for an eighteen-wheeler.

FIGHTING BACK

Rocky Bleier remains the sole Steeler whose life has been translated into celluloid—the film, *Fighting Back*. "What can you not think?" the Rock shrugs today. "It's pretty good. It's a movie. It's clearly dated, but it gives me a little more credibility."

Perhaps some of the credibility comes from his unique synergy with actor Robert Urich, who portrays Bleier in the film. The star of such hits as *Vegas*, *Lonesome Dove*, *Spenser for Hire*, and *Lazarus Man* had more than a few points in common with Bleier: midwesterner, blue collar, college football, and injured. "There were a lot of parallels he could draw upon," Bleier nods. "Bob did a good job."

The consensus, though, is that Art Carney was less successful as the Chief—he had the Irish down, of course, and the warmth, but Carney missed the Chief's tough streak. One reason might be that Carney and the Chief never met. Since they were filming, Bleier says, the Chief wanted to stay out of Carney's way. Carney was working, after all, and the Chief didn't want to bother him. "Mr. Rooney," Bleier smiles, "was like that."

When Rocky Bleier returned wounded from Vietnam, some people didn't expect him to walk again, much less play professional football.

never looked back, what Dan Rooney calls "a winner, the guy who brought it to fruition. He came in 1972. We won our first division in 1972. Not only was he a great player in terms of ability, but he was the soul of the team. He's such a good person."

Joe Greene agrees. "The guy who made us real good was Franco Harris. There were a lot of good players on that team. But to me the single most important guy, the big money player, the guy who'd get you the tough first down, the guy who kept the ball when you needed to keep it, the guy the team rallied around, was Franco Harris."

Yet Greene and company weren't so sure at first. Yes, Harris played at Penn State, albeit behind Lydell Mitchell, and was drafted number one. Still, at that first camp Harris seemed slow and unsure of himself. Then in a preseason game in Atlanta, Harris was given the ball and a route off the left side. When the hole didn't open, some

backs might have completed the assignment anyway, punching into the pile and getting whatever they could. Not Harris. Turning at full speed, he dashed through the middle, cut to the sideline, and went seventy-five yards for a touchdown. The bench went nuts. "We got us one!" Greene yelled. "That was the happiest moment I ever had in Steeler football."

"The Steelers' offense was tailor-made for me," Harris recalls. "I was very lucky because I was able to have the success that I did. They just let me develop my talent to fit into that scheme. They didn't try to confine me. I had vision, anticipation. My strong suit was reading— I could read certain situations rather quickly, I could see

When Franco Harris, left, and Terry Bradshaw were on their game, the Steelers won and won.

Offense in the early '70s meant run, run, and run. Frenchy Fuqua motors up the middle.

a guy flinch and know what was going to develop. I was also good at reacting. If something didn't happen a certain way, I had the quickness to react.

"We had a good offensive line," Harris adds. "They weren't big, but with our scheme of traps and specials I was always able to adjust. I would have the read that I needed—a split-second for 1-2-3, and I would make the adjustment to what I had to do. Because no two plays are ever going to be alike. If you beat the defense one time, you can believe they're going to adjust to it. And if you think they're not going to adjust to it, you're crazy. They're professional football players. They don't want to be beat that second or third time. So I knew they were going to do something differently. Then I had to think differently. I had to adjust to that situation.

"The fun of running," Harris smiles, "was reading, vision, and doing what I had to do at that time—making something happen to make the team successful. I always looked for something big. Make the big play. Play the situation. Have fun with it. That's why I enjoyed it for so long. I had fun.

"I could run right into the pile and get what I could get. To me, that's not being a running back, that's not the essence, the art of running. If it's clogged up, we're not going to get anything anyway, so why not try to make something happen that helps the team? That was my style: Just make something happen.

"I learned early at Penn State to always be around the ball, be around the action. Maybe there'll be a fumble. Maybe I'll throw a block. Because of that attitude the Immaculate Reception happened. So it pays off."

Oh, it paid off all right. Harris is the all-time Steeler leader in touchdowns (100), yards rushing (11,950), one-hundred-yard games (47), attempts (2,881), yards from scrimmage (14,234), and so on. It all added up to a one-way ticket to Canton. "I never thought about the Hall of Fame along the way," he says. "It never crossed my mind. Once it was over, I started to think about it. But not while I was playing. When I got there and got into it, that was the best thing of all time. To be in that select group—it really hit me when I walked up on stage during breakfast and put on my Hall of Fame jacket. It was an unbelievable moment."

"**B**ig plays are not called to be a big play," Lynn Swann says. "They're just called."

THE WIDE RECEIVERS

Wide receivers. When he discusses the pre-1974 years, Chuck Noll shrugs and flutters a hand—there wasn't much for Terry Bradshaw to throw to. Superior arm needed superior talent; it's as simple as that.

It was Noll's pledge to bring the players. In 1974 it was Lynn Swann and John Stallworth, arguably the two greatest wide receivers the team has ever had, and certainly the best tandem. Of Swann alone, Jack Butler says, "His big thing was his great timing and his ability to jump. His timing was phenomenal. He knew when to go up. Great hands, great eye-hand coordination. He was a tough little guy and took a lot of big hits."

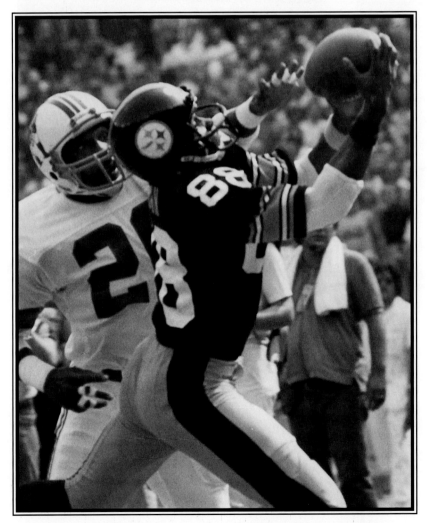

Lynn Swann led the team five times in receptions, 1974-82.

Dan Rooney agrees, "Swann was a tremendous player. He made phenomenal catches. He deserves to be in the Hall of Fame."

When Swann and Stallworth came, "We were looking for the opportunity to do the very best we could," Swann recalls.

"We were still known primarily as a strong defensive team," Swann continues, "very physical, with a conservative offensive team, a running attack. But when John and I arrived we became dangerous throwing the football—we could beat teams throwing the football. John and I established a reputation that if we put the ball in the air we could hurt you very badly with only three to five catches in the ballgame. But it wasn't something we lived off."

As Bradshaw matured as a quarterback, he threw more and more, most often to Swann, enough so that Swann led the team in receptions five times, amassing more than five thousand yards and fifty-one touchdowns. And all of them seemed to be the elevator variety. No, Swann shakes his head, "I can't say that Bradshaw intentionally threw passes high so I could outleap coverage. Because the go-to person isn't that guy who is open all the time. He's that person that you know, in the clutch situation, you can go to high, and if he can't make the catch, it won't get picked off."

Swann's other half was John Stallworth, who came the same year, 1974, but stayed another five years—'87 to Swann's '82. He finished as the team's all-time, all-everything receiver—receptions (537), yards-career (8,723), yards-season (1,395), one-hundred-yard games (25), touchdowns (63), passes caught in consecutive games (67), and so on—and never looked like he

Lynn Swann's Three Greatest Hits

As a wide receiver, Lynn Swann had unparalleled leaping ability—he could catch anything, anywhere, no matter how high.

But he could also take a hit. "I took a fair amount of punishment," Swann agrees. "I caught a lot of passes over the middle. If you're only going to get four to seven opportunities in the ball game, you're not going to argue about where the ball is or the coverage. If you get hit, you get hit; it's part of the game."

In a life of deadly blows, Lynn Swann's Three Baddest Belts:

Vikings. Swann comes across on a deep goal-line route. Double coverage. Swann beats 'em, is open. Bradshaw—surprise!—throws it high. Swann leaps to make the catch, high, very high, the ball is on the tips of his fingers. He is hit in midair, hard enough to break two ribs. Swann is on the ground. Bradshaw comes over, looks at Swann writhing on the ground, and mutters, "Damn, I threw it too high, didn't I?"

Broncos. Swann racing across the middle, catches the ball, Denver defender Tom Jackson crushes him—what Swann recalls as the hardest hit of his life. "My sinuses have never been that open in my entire life," Swann recalls. "I could smell the one-stick campfire in the Rocky Mountains." Jackson, angry, swears, "He still caught it. I've got to hit him harder."

Browns. The pass leads Swann to the outside, where he is nailed. "They thought they'd killed me," he says. "I'm in great pain. I get back to the huddle. I can barely breathe. Bradshaw asks if I'm okay. 'Yeah,' I say, 'but don't throw me another pass.'"

Lynn Swann makes another miracle catch during Super Bowl XIV.

broke a sweat. Swann got all the ink, Stallworth wound up with the numbers.

"Swann was from Southern California, Los Angeles," Stallworth says. "I was from Huntsville, Alabama. There is the difference in our styles. I was steady and consistent in getting open and catching the vast majority of passes that were thrown my way. Maybe I didn't do that with a lot of panache, but I was there and I got the job done. I was able to come up with the big catch when we needed the big catch.

After fourteen years, John Stallworth retired with many team records, including all-time pass receptions, yards receiving, and touchdowns on receptions.

and put it up deep." Stallworth smiles. "We did get around to throwing the ball. I enjoyed that, particularly after I got Bradshaw to look at my side. Early on, it was a chore."

If we remember Lynn Swann for the leaping catch in Super Bowl X, we are likely to remember John Stallworth for games like the one against Cincinnati his rookie year, when he caught an unremarkable pass for five yards and a touchdown. "It was an ugly catch," Stallworth says. After Stallworth fell down in the end zone, a Bengal defender drove his face into the turf. "It was not very pretty," Stallworth chuckles, "but I got the job done."

FINALE

"There is no question that the values, goodness, ethics, and character of the people associated with this football team had everything to do with its success," comments Dan Rooney. "They were good—but there are a lot of good players. A team has to be one—you have to take the various elements that you have—and they all have to come together. That group of people did that. They believed that the success of the team was more important than individual success. When that team walked on the field, they thought they were going to win—and everybody else thought so, too."

"It's a tribute to Mr. Rooney, Dan Rooney, Chuck Noll, and Joe Greene," former coach George Perles says, "that even though we won Super Bowls everybody didn't come unglued and think they were a star and start bickering for the money, prestige, and recognition."

But what did happen, what they did not reckon with at the time, was that the '70s were gone and that everyone on that golden Team of the Decade got old at once.

"It wasn't a flashy thing that sold a whole lot of newspapers," Stallworth adds, not bitterly, "or caused people to call me to endorse products. But when put in the context of what the team wanted to accomplish, it was very valuable."

Of course, he didn't want to come to Pittsburgh—the Steelers played grinding defensive and offensive football with little room for wide receivers. "If I had my choice," Stallworth recalls, "I would have gone to the Raiders or Miami, where they threw the ball, where they put it up,

Pittsburgh Steelers:

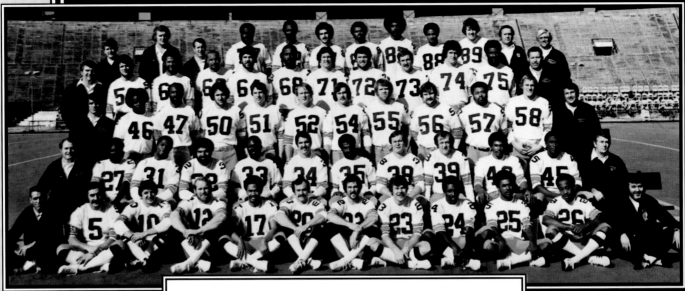

1974 NFL CHAMPIONS
Super Bowl IX: Steelers 16, Vikings 6
January 12, 1975, Tulane Stadium, New Orleans, La.

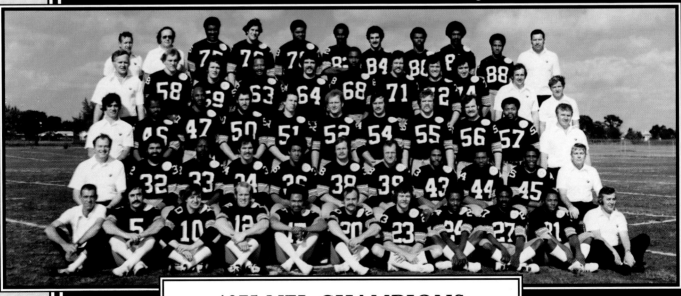

1975 NFL CHAMPIONS
Super Bowl X: Steelers 21, Cowboys 17
January 18, 1976, Orange Bowl, Miami, Fla.

THE TEAM OF THE '70S

1978 NFL CHAMPIONS
SUPER BOWL XIII: STEELERS 35, COWBOYS 31
January 21, 1979, Orange Bowl, Miami, Fla.

1979 NFL CHAMPIONS
SUPER BOWL XIV: STEELERS 31, RAMS 19
January 20, 1980, Rose Bowl, Pasadena, Calif.

Rod Woodson knocks the ball loose, displaying the moves that have made the perennial Steeler MVP one of the most successful cornerbacks in the NFL. The play ended with Carnell Lake running the fumble to the three, setting up the game-winning touchdown, 1992.

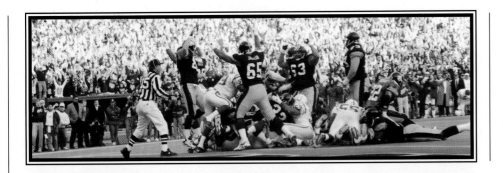

CHAPTER 6

ENTERING THE 1990s

Renaissance II

All good things must come to an end, and the Steeler Dynasty was no different. Hobbled by age and riddled with injuries, the club settled into a decade-long decline after the fourth Super Bowl victory in January 1980. After not making the playoffs in 1980-81, they came back to win two more division titles, but no more. There were flashes of glory and fine players, but it was not enough. In 1985 they suffered their first losing season in fourteen years, and in '88 bottomed out at 5-11. After 1991, Chuck Noll retired.

In 1992 head coach Bill Cowher, a believer in the Steelers' proud tradition, picked up essentially where the team had left off in the 1970s. That year, with players like Neil O'Donnell, Carnell Lake, Rod Woodson, Yancey Thigpen, Ernie Mills, and Greg Lloyd, the Steelers took their first division crown since 1984. The following year saw them in the playoffs again, in '94 another division title, and '95 an AFC championship and a trip to Super Bowl XXX. So near and yet so far.

Now Cowher and the club face the perils of free agency, setting the stage for 1996—and beyond.

> "So you have to ask yourself, 'Do I feel lucky?'"
>
> **Clint Eastwood**
> *Dirty Harry*

(Above) Culmination of a rebuilding effort: Byron "Bam" Morris scores the winning touchdown in the 1995 AFC Championship Game versus the Colts.

Running back Walter Abercrombie played for the
Steelers, 1982-87.

Strong, quick, but ultimately no Franco Harris,
Frankie Pollard led the team in rushing in 1984-85.

1980-1991: THE END OF AN ERA

"Football can be very cruel," shrugs Hall of Fame linebacker Jack Ham "Our defense in 1980-81 just wasn't good enough anymore. Plays we made before, we could no longer make. A bunch of players aged all at once, and we were a bunch of steps away. It's that way with life."

In January 1980, the Steelers won their fourth Super Bowl in six years. That December, they failed to make the playoffs for the first time since 1971. The 1970s were over.

Injuries had hurt, as well as age, and lack of replacement parts equal to the retirees. Although there were many good players, Mark Malone was no Terry Bradshaw, and neither was Bubby Brister; Weegie Thompson was no Lynn Swann; Frankie Pollard was no Franco Harris. And no man of woman born was Joe Greene.

In 1972 tight end Ben McGee came to trainer Ralph Berlin and shook his head. "Doc," he said, "I'm sore from

The changing of the guard: (left to right) quarterbacks Mark Quinn, Terry Bradshaw, Mark Malone,
and Cliff Stoudt.

one Sunday to the next." It was time to go. "I always wondered what happened to the great teams," Berlin muses. "The Green Bay Packers. The Baltimore Colts. The Dallas Cowboys. I found out what happened. They all got old.

"Our guys got old," Berlin adds. "And they got old all at one time. Time, heat, and rest will cure everything. But

In the '80s, talented Dwayne Woodruff had the unpleasant chore of replacing Mel Blount.

Mark Malone was drafted to replace Bradshaw in 1980, but the fans did not offer him a warm welcome.

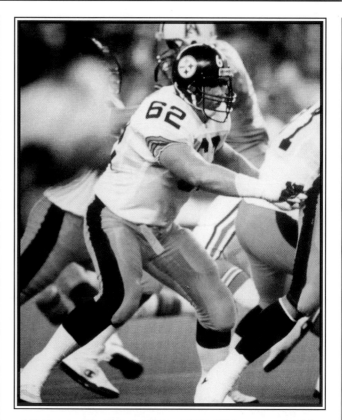

All-Pro tackle Tunch Ilkin, 1980. Ilkin was valuable on the offensive line for 13 seasons.

Centerpiece of a solid, if not great, defense, Bryan Hinkle signs autographs at training camp.

as you get older, you need a lot more time, heat, and rest." Berlin shakes his head. "It was somebody else's turn."

Indeed, as the Team of the Decade missed the postseason, Rocky Bleier, Mike Wagner, and Dwight White all retired. Over the decade, the rest would follow, one by

one. "We were fortunate to have good people," Chuck Noll recalls. "When the system is set up through the draft, and you draft last, you don't get the fertile minds you had before. We had a nucleus of some, but we didn't have the great All-Pros."

There were other problems as well. In some ways, the 1980s were symbolized by the bad luck of two number-one draft picks. Running back Tim Worley, class of '89, was lost to substance abuse, and defensive lineman Gabe Rivera, the ill-fated Señor Sack, class of '83, was crippled in an auto accident. "We had a lot of good luck before that," Noll says. "It has a way of balancing out."

Lupe Sanchez, Preston Gothard, Rich Erenberg—the list of mediocre players seems endless. The heart of the Super Bowl XXX team dates from the late '80s, when the Steelers were once again drafting higher. "But they were young," Noll says of names like Lloyd, Lake, Dawson, and Woodson. "They were just coming on. It takes a while to develop"

ONE FOR THE BOOKS

Quarterback-turned-receiver Mark Malone makes a catch against the Giants.

Guaranteed: You will win money on this bet. Who had the longest touchdown reception in Steeler history?

Lynn Swann?

John Stallworth?

Louis Lipps?

Wrong!

On November 8, 1981, in Seattle, it was a little-known receiver named . . . Mark Malone.

Drafted in 1980, versatile athlete Malone had been scouted by pro teams at a number of positions, including halfback and tight end by the Jets and Dolphins, but he thought of himself as quarterback. That's how he came to the Steelers.

In Pittsburgh, he not only clocked the club's fastest time in the forty, but as Terry Bradshaw's apprentice, he also knew all the receiver routes.

So it was natural that when receiver Calvin Sweeney pulled up lame, Chuck Noll pressed Malone into service.

Slot right, Steelers on their own ten-yard line. Bradshaw calls a hitch route, a six-yard hook. Malone goes out, beats the coverage, and is wide open. Bradshaw chucks it.

"All I could think of," Malone recalls, "is if I don't catch this I will never live it down."

But caught it he did, and with speed to spare and an open field, Malone dashed ninety yards for a touchdown. "Luckily," Malone says, "I made it into the end zone. As it stands," Malone grins, "I'm one-for-one, touchdown and ninety yards."

Defensive lineman, number one draft pick, the infamous Señor Sack, Gabe Rivera's career was cut short by a tragic auto accident.

Reggie Collier played in the United States Football League and with Dallas. Then in 1987 he became the Steeler quarterback during the strike season.

"It was disappointing," says Tunch Ilkin, an undersized offensive lineman who came after the fourth Super Bowl, got cut, got called back, and stayed for the next thirteen years. "When I came here I thought we'd get a Super Bowl. But my career coincided with the demise of the Steeler Dynasty. I had this fear that the year I retired the Steelers would win another Super Bowl. There'd be a certain symmetry to that."

Not that they weren't close. In '84, for example, the 9-7 Steelers beat Denver in the playoffs, then faced red-hot Danny Marino and the Dolphins—and got blown out, 45-28. In 1989, the 9-7 Steelers upset the Oilers in the 'Dome, and nearly took the Broncos in the next game, losing a heartbreaker 24-23 on a fumbled snap in Mile High. "We had a good football team," Ilkin says. "Just not quite good enough. We didn't have that many great players."

At first they limped along on Cliff Stoudt's guts and Terry Bradshaw's ailing arm. But no player felt the frus-

After the Dynasty, the Steelers boasted good teams, not great ones. Such was the 1987 offensive unit.

trations of the '80s more than Mark Malone, Bradshaw's supposed second coming.

Malone was a big, well scouted, truly gifted, a number-one pick like Bradshaw but ten years after.

So what went wrong?

Merril Hoge ran for the big plays, 1987-93.

Linebacker David Little, devastating hitter, 1981-92.

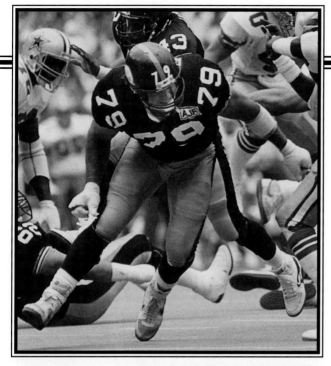

A quarterback depends on ten other guys all doing their jobs at once. The offensive line gives protection, with guard John Rienstra in the center, 1988.

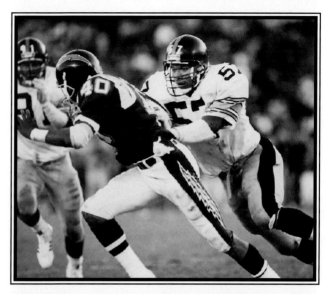

Linebacker Mike Merriweather's fifteen sacks in '84 remain a Steelers record. He was a three-time Pro Bowler in his six-year Steeler career.

Tunch Ilkin ponders another Steeler loss.

When Malone came to camp in 1980, his locker stood between Bradshaw's and Bleier's. Looking around the room, he saw Joe Greene, Mike Webster, Lynn Swann, and John Stallworth. "It was an overwhelming experience," Malone recalls. "The first thing you ask yourself, regardless of how highly people consider your talent, is 'Do I belong here? Can I play at this level with the people in this room?' I was excited to have that opportunity—but a little daunted, with a little trepidation."

On paper, at least, Malone was a perfect match for the Steelers. "My athletic abilities fit their style of offense," he recalls. "Run the football, have a strong arm, be a powerful guy who can stand in there and take a hit, and throw the football down the field. This was not an intricate passing game," Malone shakes his head.

"We had a very tenacious, strong, and extremely quick offensive line that allowed us to run the football against anybody. But when that talent started to retire, it was much more difficult to execute that same offensive game plan with the same success."

A lot of the pressure fell on Malone to make everything right. "The quarterback depends more on the people around him than any other one position in football," he says without bitterness. "Throwing the football, unaccosted, is your

Changes in the offensive system ultimately dictated that strong-armed Steeler quarterback Bubby Brister play elsewhere.

Wide receiver Weegie Thompson caught three touchdown passes in one game against the Green Bay Packers in 1986. He was a Steeler, 1984-89.

job. But there's a lot that has to happen before you can do your job. With a mass of humanity trying to pummel you into the ground, you depend on other guys doing their jobs to provide you time. As a quarterback, you have two and a half to three seconds to make the decisions, find the open person, and then throw the football."

Malone sighs. "We had players who gave everything they had and more. But we didn't have the talent to win games at a rate that would put us in the playoffs." He turns a hand. "This was not the wealth of talent the city enjoyed in the late '70s. We were just another football team."

After going 10-6 in '83 and 9-7 in '84, it seemed as if back-to-back playoff losses knocked the stuffing out of the Steelers. They were losers in '85, going 7-9, 6-10 in '86, 8-7 in '87, and a rock-bottom 5-11 in '88. "Being thirty minutes away from a Super Bowl hurt this team more than anything," Malone says. "The next four years were disastrous."

Having tried the Bradshaw body double, the club went back down south, to Louisiana, in fact, for the Bradshaw voice double. But the young Bubby Brister, like the young Bradshaw, was a long way from a championship. "Bubby has a great arm," Malone nods, "but his demeanor and knowledge of the game at this level were going to take some time."

They had the time, but not much else. "In the '80s," Dan Rooney says, "we really played well. We did some things that were pretty good." In '84, for example, with Mike Webster and John Stallworth still playing, Donnie Shell snagged seven interceptions. Dwayne Woodruff, Gary Dunn, David Little, Robin Cole, and Bryan Hinkle were a credible defensive unit. Linebacker Mike Merriweather alone accounted for fifteen sacks. Rookie of the Year wide receiver Louis Lipps pulled off a seventy-five-yard punt return against the New Orleans Saints.

Talented running back, number one draft pick, Tim Worley's career ended prematurely.

In 1991, as the Steelers tried once again to redefine themselves, quarterbacks Bubby Brister (left) and Neil O'Donnell both started eight games.

backers Jerrol Williams, Jerry Olsavsky, and Greg Lloyd as the team's hired assassins, the club didn't merely play, they punished. As Woodson said, "When you come to play the Pittsburgh Steelers, you're going to remember it."

Like the best Steeler teams, they never lost their poise. Losing to Miami 14-0 in what seemed like three feet of water, Carnell Lake intercepted a Marino pass to turn the game around. The final: Steelers, 34-14.

In the AFC Wild Card Playoff Game against Houston, the extra effort didn't fail them. Jerry Olsavsky busted through the line and blocked a punt. Rod Woodson got a big overtime hit and fumble recovery to set up a Gary Anderson field goal. The final: Steelers 26-23.

Finally, in Denver, the team began to feel as though it was '72 or '76: as if they were a team of destiny. Merril Hoge galloped for 120 yards, and Pittsburgh took a 23-17 lead into the fourth quarter. But a bad snap, and a Denver recovery, ruined the two-minute drill, and the Steelers lost 24-23. It was the '80s, and it was that close.

The '90s didn't open much better. Joe Greene returned in '87 as a coach with his perennial fire, but he couldn't get the ball over the goal line, and neither could anybody else. Tom Moore's offense was ungainly, and Joe Walton's ultimately unworkable. The old Steelers standbys—manage the field with defense, establish a running game, control the clock, and get the big play—had seemingly evaporated.

At first, bringing Joe Walton to design a new offense seemed like a great idea, until the squad tried to master the new terms, patterns, and systems. "We weren't very good," Walton says bluntly. "Chuck wanted to change the system, but as he said, change is always difficult."

By '86, the team played well, but it was largely too little, too late. Lipps had good hands and better moves. Malone could throw. Webster and Tunch Ilkin could block. Ernest Jackson and Walter Abercrombie could run. . . but ignominy of ignominies, for the first time Cleveland beat the Steelers in Three Rivers.

Observers agree that 1989 may have been Chuck Noll's best year. It was certainly his last hurrah: He orchestrated one of the greatest turn-arounds in club history. After the two most humiliating losses in Steeler history—a 51-0 drubbing by the Browns and a 41-10 disaster in Cincinnati—Noll never let the team panic. Rallying his troops and redirecting them, he piloted the club to a 9-7 finish, returning to the playoffs for the first time in five years.

With Bubby Brister taking that newfangled shotgun snap, Rookie of the Year Carnell Lake joining All-Everything Rod Woodson in the defensive secondary, and line-

Playing Well Is the Best Revenge

It is fair to say that quarterback Mark Malone was literally booed out of Pittsburgh. Traded to hometown San Diego in 1988, he faced his former team in a Jack Murphy Stadium shoot-out late in the season. Final score: 20-14 Chargers.

After the game, his former teammates came over, hugged him, and told him they were happy for him.

"To a certain extent," Malone says, "it was a good feeling. But there was some mixed emotion. There was some vindication, but there was some sadness, too."

When the season opened with four straight games without an offensive touchdown, it was time to tinker again. The one bright spot: rookie tight end Eric Green. At six-foot-five and 275 pounds, he was a simply huge target that was too good to be true—and too big to miss.

With Brister and sophomore quarterback Neil O'-Donnell sharing time in the pocket, 1991 was an another offensively scrambled season. Each had eight starts as Joe Walton's offense unraveled. After the Steelers gave up fifty-two points to Buffalo, Joe Greene publicly blasted the team, the talent, and the strategy, a display of double-barreled emotion that was just devastating. The club finished 7-9, and, after thirty-nine years in professional football, Chuck Noll retired.

The good news, director of football operations Tom Donahoe says, is that "this franchise never hit rock bottom. There was never a free fall when it came all the way down. That's a credit to Chuck and Mr. Rooney. They stayed competitive throughout the '80s. It still was good football. They just couldn't get going on a consistent basis."

"We always thought that we could win," recalls Louis Lipps, the top receiver of the '80s, two-time Steeler MVP, and all-time number-two receiver, with 358 receptions for more than six thousand yards. "We always felt that we had the talent to put it all together."

"Professional football is a struggle to win every week, regardless of how good a team is," adds former wide receiver Weegie Thompson, who played 1984-89 and scored a record three touchdowns against Green Bay in '86. "Personally, I had to work hard at the game. But I enjoyed the challenge. So it was an enjoyable six years."

The end of an era: Chuck Noll's last game as head coach, December 22, 1991.

THE PITTSBURGH STEELERS

1992-1995: COWHER POWER

When Bill Cowher introduced himself to Pittsburgh in January 1992, the assembled snickered when he said there was much talent on the team he was inheriting. But Cowher knew better, for Chuck Noll had built another champion team, one that would win three division titles in four years and revisit the Super Bowl. Yet Noll's creation was still an embryo. All it needed was to be born, smacked on the bottom, and taught how to walk. The players would do the rest.

"It wasn't like the cupboard was bare," Tom Donahoe says. "Maybe some of the guys weren't as focused as they could have been. Maybe they needed to hear a different voice. Maybe it needed a different direction, a firmer hand, more discipline, more communication between coach and players. It could have been a lot of factors. The players knew when they talked to Coach Cowher that he expected to win the first year. Usually, if you give players an excuse, they'll take it. But Bill's approach from the beginning was that there was a good nucleus here, and there's no reason why we can't put something together and start winning some football games."

(Left to right) Donald Evans, Gerald Williams, and Greg Lloyd combine to stuff the run, 1992-style.

Barry Foster (left) tied an NFL record in 1992 with twelve one-hundred-yard games, winning the AFC rushing title with 1,690 yards. He broke five Steeler rushing records and was named the team's MVP.

Fourth and goal, and all the chips are down. The Sixty-Minute Men stop a Drew Bledsoe quarterback sneak to secure a victory against the New England Patriots on December 5, 1993.

Bill Cowher's first game as head coach with Steelers President Dan Rooney (right).

To do that, they first needed to revamp the offense— one more time. Bubby Brister was in the Bradshaw mold, an air-it-out, end-to-end passer, and Tom Moore had designed an offense to best use Brister's talents. But Moore

had left after 1989, and the club not only drafted Neil O'Donnell, but within three years brought Ron Erhardt to design a system for him.

The new system consisted not of bombs and Hail Marys but of flares and screens—low-risk short routes for a high completion rate. "Neil's a great quarterback," Brister says. "They decided to go with him. Obviously, they made a pretty good choice. He's played well, and he's led the team.

"I came to make something happen," Brister adds. "If we needed a long gainer, we'd go for it. If we were third and fifteen, we'd run a sixteen-yard route. Now the game has changed." He does not speak with regret. "Now you play it safe and don't make mistakes. I'd been there and done my best. Things just didn't work out."

But they did for O'Donnell, whose performance in the new offensive system was exemplary. In '93, for example, he set a team record for attempts, 486, completions, 270, for a total of 3,208 yards (third all-time.) In '95 his four three-hundred-yard passing games were a

In 1993 in a game against the Rams, Rod Woodson punished future Steelers teammate Jerome Bettis by pushing his face in the dirt.

single-season record, as were his single-game attempts, fifty-five, and completions, thirty-four—while his completion rate skyrocketed to 63.9 percent.

O'Donnell could throw all those passes in part because of the new school of offensive linemen. Gone were the small, quick trappers—Jon Kolb, Mike Webster, and Tunch Ilkin. In came the new breed, the three-hundred-pounders set not to fool anybody, but simply to hold the line and give the quarterback time to throw. Bill Cowher's first draft pick told the tale: Leon Searcy, an offensive tackle who tipped the scales at 304. Complementing Dermontti Dawson (a mere 286), John Jackson (293), Todd Kalis (296), and Justin Strzelczyk (291), Searcy brought to mind Don Rickles's memorable line: "What do you eat for dinner? Furniture?"

And they got receivers. Although the Dynasty essentially had Swann and Stallworth, the Steelers' new aerial corps ran in and out the way teams once used messenger guards (like a young fellow named Noll in Cleveland). Ernie Mills (of the big play and easy smile), Yancey Thig-

To jump start the Steelers' moribund offense, Coach Cowher brought in offensive coordinator Ron Erhardt (right) to design a system that would fit quarterback Neil O'Donnell, 1992.

Defensive back Rod Woodson denies a Detroit Lion receiver this ball.

Kicker Gary Anderson is the all-time leading Steeler scorer with 1,343 points in 13 seasons.

Foul weather won't stop the Steelers' offensive tackle John Jackson.

pen (of the great hands and notable speed), Kordell Stewart (who by his own definition is a quarterback—although he can still snag 'em), Andre Hastings (of the very-tough, plays-hurt variety), and Charles Johnson (of high school hurdling and basketball fame) all saw duty in 1995; they gave the club what Dan Rooney flatly calls "the best group of receivers we've ever had—as a group."

They're not bad individually, either. When he talks, Andre Hastings exudes the quiet confidence of winners—but winners who know how hard it is to get there. Blossoming in '95, he had a personal high ten catches for eighty-six yards against Miami, specialized in the much-needed third-down reception, and in Kansas City, busted off a seventy-two-yard punt return for a touchdown. "I try," he smiles. "He's competitive," Ernie Mills says, "and very confident."

For his part, Mills "got better and better and better," Hastings says. Coming into his own in '95, the smart, fluid Mills led the team with eight touchdown catches, including a sixty-two-yard go-ahead touchdown reception against New England and one thirty-seven-yarder

Tight end Eric Green was 1993's leading receiver.

(Left to right, sitting) Deon Figures, Charles Johnson; (standing) Chad Brown, Ariel Solomon, and Joel Steed at the Steelers training camp in 1994.

The Colorado Connection, Sixty-Minute Man Chad Brown disguised as a civilian.

to the Colts' one-yard line to set up the game-winning touchdown. Not to mention his catch that won the AFC Championship.

"Each year has gotten better for me," Mills admits. "Last year, '95, was the most fun of all. Everything clicked and we won games as a team. I had a great time."

Maybe because he played his own game. "My style is laid-back but aggressive," he says "Running full speed, all out, not worrying about getting hit hard, but just making the play. I'm a tough guy, so no matter how many times they hit me, I'm going to get up and go right back at 'em. I'll make the catch every time.

"Hit me as hard as you want," Mills smiles, "as many times as you want, and I'll be there to make that big play at the end."

For his part, Yancey Thigpen doesn't have to worry about taking hits, because he can outrun just about anyone on the planet (except maybe Rod Woodson). Emerging as the Steelers' premier receiver in '95, the explosive speedster earned his first Pro Bowl spot while setting an all-time club record with eighty-five receptions and becoming the first Steeler receiver in more than a decade to log more than one thousand yards (1,307, the second all-time club mark).

Why pick this year to blossom? "We had so much adversity," Thigpen nods. "No would knew how it would turn out. A lot of guys took it upon themselves and said, 'Let's do whatever it takes to overcome and get to the level where we want to be.' So a lot of people came out of nowhere and really performed well for us at a lot of positions."

Like the receivers?

"We're a good group of guys who work well together," Thigpen nods. "We push each other to get better. We have a group of guys that is not selfish. I think the team uses all the receivers' talent well. If I can have my input for a big impact, then we can be productive—as a group. Right now, I'm still playing and I feel like I have a lot of football left. I don't feel like I've done a lot. But I never like taking a step backward. Hopefully I can get the opportunity next year and break the record again. Last year was just a taste. Next year, we'll realize what we can do and begin to do even more on offense.

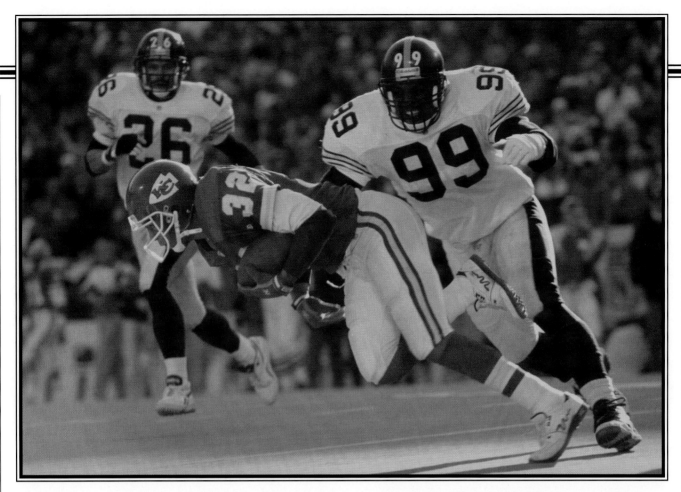

"This year," Thigpen continues, "we realized that when we put it all together, there wasn't a team in the National Football League that could beat us.

"It makes me proud to be compared with the best receivers Pittsburgh's ever had," Thigpen shakes his head. "But I can't agree that we're the best ever. Maybe the best season for a group of wide receivers. But until we go out and do it year after year, consecutively, we can't be compared to those guys."

The Steelers do have a running game, although it often gets lost in all the flying footballs and in the change of personnel during Cowher's four-year reign. The early standout was Barry Foster, who came in 1990 and left after '94. He left like Bill Dudley in '46, after a dust-up with the head coach.

But in his five seasons with the Steelers, Foster, a strong, Harris-style runner, had become the club's fourth all-time rusher (3,943 yards), set the single-season mark (1,690 yards, to lead the AFC, while his 390 attempts led the NFL), logged twenty hundred-yard games, and tied an NFL-record twelve one hundred-yarders in a single season.

When you say Blitzburgh, say veteran linebacker Levon Kirkland.

"We definitely had talent," Foster says, "but I felt that for the Steelers to get better we needed something new, a new direction. I'm glad Bill came. Bill did a great job putting it together.

"I was happy to be a part of that organization," Foster adds. "I'm proud to say that I was a part of that Steeler era. I thought I would end my career as a Steeler, and wanted to, but there was an incident where player and coach should never go. I was completely out of line—and it's one of the biggest regrets that I have. He felt he could never repair the relationship, so he traded me."

As in the Dynasty years, the defense starred before the offense. In '95, using a 3-4 system, Brentson Buckner, Joel Steed, and Ray Seals anchored the line, while linebackers Kevin Greene, Chad Brown, Levon Kirkland, Jerry Olsavsky, and Greg Lloyd were free to roam. Roam they did, wreaking much havoc. Lloyd alone is a one-man wrecking crew—Pro Bowl outside linebacker, devastating belter, and blitzer *par excellence*. At college, he

The Sixty-Minute Men drive 'em back during the 1994 AFC Championship Game.

majored in intensity, velocity, and un-apologetic violence.

"Greg brings mental toughness to the game," says safety Carnell Lake. "He's very strong and quick, a physical player who doesn't fear anything. He throws his body around like he's not worried about any injury or any consequence. Two linemen come at him, he doesn't think twice about blowing through them for the ball carrier." Lake pauses, "It's almost as if Greg has turned off the switch and is running on pure emotion. We feed off Greg."

Adds former teammate Barry Foster, "He's just ruthless—and about as tough as they come."

So is Carnell Lake.

"He's the ultimate warrior," Ernie Mills says. "He's big, strong, and fast. He's the best strong safety in the game."

"He's a tough dude," scout Jack Butler agrees. "He plays it one hundred percent."

The original franchise, the 1933 Pirates, was honored in '94 when the club wore these throwback uniforms, which were later auctioned off for charity.

"Bright guy, hard hitter," adds Tunch Ilkin. "Carnell will just tag you. Very physical, one of the best safeties in the game—and will be even better because of the year he spent at corner."

Yes, that year at corner. Lake, who had already switched from high school guard to running back, then to college linebacker, and on to professional safety, where he had garnered Pro-Bowl honors, moved to cornerback in '95 to cover for injured Rod Woodson. It was the Lake Effect—another stellar year, another Pro Bowl. "I wasn't

Blitzburgh linebacker Jerry Olsavsky brought guts, grit, and a good attitude to the Pittsburgh club.

Owner of the highest completion rate in Steelers history, quarterback Neil O'Donnell guns one.

prepared for all these moves," Lake says. "But this is a business," he shrugs. "And you better take care of business, or you'll be on your way out the door.

"The game moves so quickly," Lake considers. "You have coaches and opponents spending hours designing ways to outwit you. But all the time in the world can't beat a good game plan. You have to fight your battle first on the chalkboard and then apply it to a game.

"Because there's somebody on the other team that's just as fast as you," he adds. "If he gets that jump on you,

that inch, you can't really make it up. So the way to combat that is to try to get that jump on him. The only way to do that is to anticipate, to know what they are going to do before they do it. And the way to do that is to study."

Lake watches film, at home and at the office, to prepare his game. "If you don't force yourself too much," he says, "or put too much pressure on yourself, if you let things flow, it gets to be fun."

So was his move to cornerback. Oh, it was rocky at first, until Bill Cowher sat Lake down and told him that

"Nobody can beat us but ourselves. And we're not going to do that," insisted Steeler linebacker Greg Lloyd before Super Bowl XXX.

corners must have short memories. Put the play behind you and go on to the next one. "That calmed me down and took the pressure off me," Lake nods, "and I played better.

"I took that feeling into the Super Bowl," he adds. "Don't worry about it. Have fun and just play football and let whatever happens happen. I was comfortable and excited, but very calm. I thought I was a little too calm, and it worried me that I was too calm in a big game, but when you're calm you're ready."

The eye of the storm? Lake nods. "It takes a lot to get to that point," he allows. "But when you get there, you know it. Nothing seems to rattle you."

Except maybe Rod Woodson. "Rod and I didn't get along when I first got here," Lake recalls. "Rod was the veteran player who achieved success. Marquee name with the Steelers at the time. He was trying to teach a rookie who had never played defensive back something that would help me. I didn't want to hear it. I just wanted to

Big, quick, and deadly, All-Pro Dermontti Dawson readies the snap.

players in Steeler history to be part of that exclusive club.

"The true fans like defense," Woodson says, "the hard-hitting, the blue-collar mentality. And we are an attack defense—Pittsburgh and our defense is like a hand in a glove. I like the challenge of playing defense. 'You know where you're going, I don't. Let's play.' A good defense controls the tempo of a football game."

"He is a great, great athlete," scout Jack Butler says. "Supports well, kick-offs, extra teams—phenomenal. He's got everything you want."

What makes Rod Woodson a great football player?

"I don't know if Rod's a great football player," Woodson shrugs. "Rod enjoys the game. I've dedicated myself to the game. After my first Pro Bowl I learned how good someone could be in the NFL—if you use your mind. Studying film, understanding offenses, and getting a feel for the game. Then letting yourself go in the game.

"My goal," he says without irony, "is to be a decent player."

But September 3, 1995, a day that will live in infamy, almost ended it all—or so it seemed.

In the new season's first game, covering a standard swing pass to Detroit's Barry Sanders, Woodson planted his foot and moved to cover the receiver. "My foot stayed there," Woodson says, "but my knee kept going." The result: a torn ACL, surgery, and rehab. Woodson was lost for the year.

Or was he? Woodson set another record when he became the only player to suffer that kind of ligament injury and play again in the same season. It took medical miracles, of course, but also superhuman determination. "I had a coach that had the same crazy notion that I had," Woodson says. "There were days when I didn't think I

focus. The more I tuned him out, the more he felt it should be a part of my development."

Lake smiles. "We've become quite good friends. Rod is a tremendous athletic talent. He is a very good student of football, and is a hard worker. Attitude, motivation, and determination—all those things come when Rod gets on the football field. He doesn't settle for anything less than perfection. You can't help but admire and feed off that—and that's what I've been doing for seven years."

It's hard not to. Rod Woodson, six feet tall and two hundred pounds, runs a 4.3 forty, returns punts and kick-offs, intercepts like a wizard, tackles anything that moves, plays corner like a linebacker, blitzes, works man-to-man and zone, playing the run and the pass equally well. The three-time team MVP, he surprised no one in '93 when he was named NFL Defensive Player of the Year, joining Joe Greene, Mel Blount, and Jack Lambert as the only

The 1993 NFL Defensive Player of the Year struts his stuff. Jets receiver Rob Moore goes up for one, but so does his shadow, Rod Woodson.

ROD WOODSON, SO FAR...

Rod Woodson is now in his tenth season with the Steelers, and statistics cannot measure his impact on his team.

- One of five current players named to the NFL 75th Anniversary Team
- 1993 NFL Defensive Player of the Year
- Six-time Pro Bowler
- Three-time Steeler MVP
- Leads active Steelers in interceptions (thirty-two; tied with Jack Ham)
- All-time Steeler records for punt returns (256), punt return yards (2,362), kickoff returns (220), and kickoff return yards (4,894)
- All-time Steeler touchdowns on interceptions (four; tied with Jack Butler)
- Scored eight touchdowns, four on interceptions, two on punt returns, two on kickoff returns
- More than five-hundred tackles
- All-time best Steeler-owned restaurant

Moore has the ball, but Woodson has Moore . . .

. . . and foils the completion.

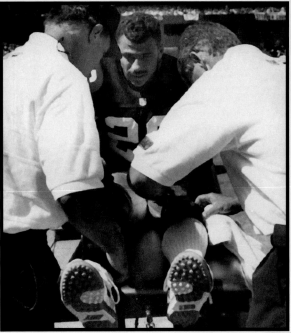

On September 3, 1995, Rod Woodson suffered a torn ACL (left). Four months later, he became the first player in National Football League history to return from so severe an injury in the same season.

(Above) Woodson shows off his reconstructed ACL to Cowboy Michael Irvin during Super Bowl XXX.

When teammate Rod Woodson was lost for the '95 season, All-Pro Carnell Lake moved from safety to cornerback—and never missed a step.

The Sixty-Minute Men in their natural habitat, the weight room. The Steelers' champion defense: (left to right, front row) Willie Williams, Brentson Buckner, Rod Woodson, Jason Gildon, Deon Figures; (back row) Chad Brown, Joel Steed, Ray Seals, Greg Lloyd, Kevin Henry, Levon Kirkland, Darren Perry, Carnell Lake.

A trio of All-Pros watch the action: (left to right) Greg Lloyd, Kevin Greene, Rod Woodson.

could come back. Then there were days when I said, 'This is great.'"

Woodson worked out, and Cowher encouraged him to visit, to stay in focus. "Leaving the window open made me more dedicated," Woodson says. "It gave me a reason to come back, to try."

If Cowher helped the tuned-up Woodson, think what he did for his entire team. Ernie Mills feels as if the four Cowher years leading up to Super Bowl XXX were on fast forward. The fleeting images appear something like this:

1992: Bill Cowher's on the sidelines, and he's shouting for a change. "You want emotion?" he bellows. "Watch this football team play football for sixty minutes. We'll show you emotion."

Performances like that, the "forty-guys-for-sixty-minutes" mantra, and an 11-5 record net him NFL Coach of the Year honors.

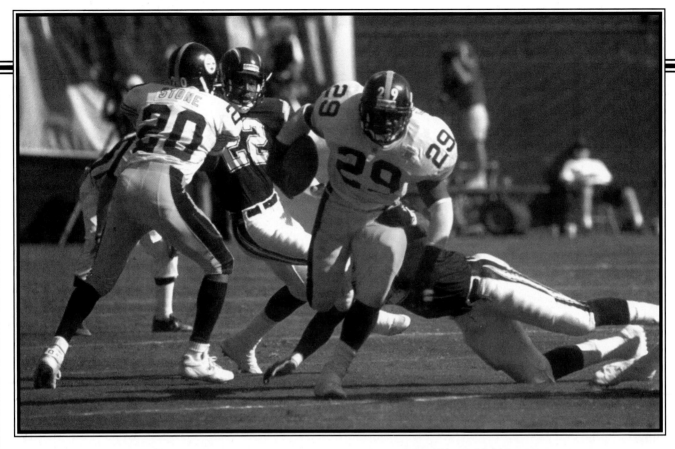

Record-setting running back Barry Foster was traded after the 1994 season.

"Let's have some fun," he says, "playing football our style."

Ernie Mills, tough guy with the sweet smile, shows great concentration in coverage, superb hands, and the strength to break tackles.

Greg Lloyd, heir to Jack Lambert as a quarterback's worst nightmare, creams a fellow. "That's a big play, big man," Cowher high-fives him, "that's a big play."

Steelers finish as AFC Central champs. The Oilers, heavily favored, go up 14-0 early. The Steelers respond with five interceptions.

1993: Cowher keeps the con going. "When you put your minds to it," he says, "there isn't anybody in this league who can beat you."

Even in a season of slow starts. Free agent Kevin Greene leads the team with the longest hair, best fan cheerleading, and 12.5 sacks.

Greg Lloyd punishes San Diego: eleven tackles, two forced fumbles, and one sack. "When we are playing emotional football for sixty minutes," he says to the players, "nobody in the National Football League can beat us." Wisely, no one argues.

Greg Lloyd belts quarterback Jim Kelly for a Buffalo loss—and yet another sack.

Rod Woodson, NFL Defensive Player of the Year, hauls down eight interceptions. He's got the smarts to snag 'em—and the moves to make 'em count.

1994: Yancey Thigpen *motors*. Greg Lloyd on the sidelines is in a frenzy. "They can't beat us," he foams. "And we ain't gonna beat ourselves. That's the name of the game."

A team-record fifty-five sacks. Five sacks against the Raiders.

Blitzburgh indeed.

Mike Tomczak passes for 343 yards against the Dolphins.

"Forget about the last play," Cowher exhorts. "Forget about the bad play. Focus on now."

"It isn't pretty," he adds. "Find a way and get it done."

At the AFC Championship game, the Steelers' first at home in fifteen years, Neil O'Donnell has thirty-two completions for 349 yards, but the team falls short. Fourth and goal, three yards away, O'Donnell's final toss is batted away. The Steelers lose, 17-13.

1995: It hardly began as a championship season. Trailing at the half, the Steelers nipped the Lions 23-20 to take the opener, then whacked always-tough Houston, 34-17. Then disaster struck: Three interceptions and two fumbles gave Danny Marino's Miami Dolphins a 23-10 win in game three, and five straight turnovers gave Minnesota a 44-24 victory in game four.

The Steelers came back strong for their third season victory, a 31-16 trouncing of the Chargers in game five. But a 20-16 loss to the upstart Jacksonville Jaguars in game six and a 27-9 loss to the Bengals in game seven left the club reeling with an anemic 3-4 record—with seemingly nowhere to go.

That's when Bill Cowher stepped up and turned some heads around. He announced that the new season would begin immediately—a season that was but nine games long, where the intensity would remain sky-high and they'd take on all comers one at a time.

The strategy worked. Barreling into the short season, the Steelers ran off eight straight victories before dropping the season finale to Green Bay, surprising an awful lot of people who neither knew nor appreciated the team's

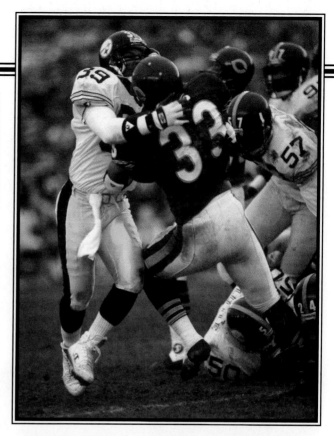

Free safety Darren Perry collars the runner during this game against the Bears in 1995. The Steelers came home victorious, 37-34.

grit and resolve. Taking a breather at last, they finished atop the AFC Central heap for the third time in four years.

Revenge was sweet: a 24-7 drubbing of Jacksonville in game eight; beating the Bears in Chicago for the first time in twelve tries in game nine, a squeaker of a 37-34 victory; a 20-3 pounding of Cleveland in game ten with Kordell Stewart at quarterback; a 49-31 thrashing of the Bengals in game eleven, coming from behind with twenty-one unanswered points in the fourth quarter. The Steelers first played the Browns in 1950; game twelve brought them together for the last time, a 20-17 marvel won in the fourth quarter on a twenty-seven-yard Norm Johnson field goal.

The Steelers shut down Houston 21-7 in game thirteen, and the Raiders 29-10 in game fourteen. They endured a nip-and-tuck battle with New England in game fifteen, storming ahead in the fourth quarter on a sixty-two-yard touchdown pass to the Miraculous Ernie Mills and a Greg Lloyd-induced fumble returned by Chris Oldham for the game-icing TD. Final: 41-27. By game six-

Kordell Stewart looks for a few more, 1995.

teen, the exhausted club came up short, losing 24-19 to Green Bay.

Ernie Mills hauled in one touchdown and five passes, Bam Morris ran like a demon, and Jerry Olsavsky and Levon Kirkland snagged one interception apiece as the Steelers shuffled all over Buffalo, 40-21, in the AFC divisional playoff. In the AFC Championship game, a game-ending busted pass in the end zone locked down a 20-16 Steeler win, with Mills and Morris again providing the offensive punch.

When the dust settled, Dermontti Dawson was named to another Pro Bowl, his fourth straight. Since Mike Webster's 1988 departure, Dawson had played in 120 straight games, with 115 starts. In fact, since Ray Mansfield arrived in '64 the Steelers have had only three—count 'em, three—centers over thirty years.

Greg Lloyd went to his fifth Pro Bowl. All-time he ranks fifth on the Steelers sack list with forty-nine. He has led the team in tackles five times and earned two team MVPs. Although Rod Woodson watched the season from

THE PLAYER DOTH PROTEST TOO MUCH

Shades of the Bluefield Bullet! Not since Bill Dudley has a Steeler been all things on offense—scrambling quarterback, glue-fingered wide receiver, resilient running back, and strong punter.

In 1995 multitalented rookie Kordell Stewart made thirty first downs (fourteen rushing, thirteen receiving, three passing), and scored on a seventy-one-yard touchdown reception. As a scrambling quarterback he threw to Ernie Mills for a touchdown against Cleveland. As a back, he rushed for a twenty-two-yard touchdown against New England. As a receiver, he caught six passes at Green Bay. Finally, as a punter, he booted one a respectable forty-one yards.

Even Bill Cowher calls him Slash, the nickname for the punctuation between quarterback/wide receiver/running back/punter.

Stewart may be uncommonly versatile, but he knows what comes first in his list of contributions:

"I'm capable of doing a lot of things," Stewart growls, "but I'm a quarterback. I've said that, and I always will say that. That Slash thing, that's fine and dandy. But I'm Kordell Stewart, and I'm a quarterback. Regardless of what anybody says, and regardless of what I can give the team, I'm capable of going out there and giving all the things a quarterback can give."

the sidelines, he was one of five active players named to the NFL's All-Time Seventy-fifth Anniversary team.

And Bill Cowher, with his third AFC Central Championship in four years, now had his first AFC title, the team's first since 1979—and Super Bowl XIV. He would soon be the youngest coach ever to play a Super Bowl. "If you stay at things," he says, "and don't ever stop believing, you make your own good fortune."

"Turning around a 3-4 record," offers Dermontti Dawson, "and going to a Super Bowl, we kind of rectified the situation. It was a dream season. We did it by paying attention to the small things. Spending more time at the

stadium instead of going home. Sitting back and taking a good look—what am I supposed to be doing? I studied game plans. I wanted to make sure I knew everything. I went back and reestablished how I went about learning every game."

On the field he learned from Mike Webster. "After fifteen years," Dawson says, "I don't care how tired he was, he ran up to the ball. He always gave one hundred percent, no matter what. I try to do the same.

"You have to give all the coaches credit," Dawson adds. "Instead of going in the tank, all those guys reassessed themselves. All the coaches, including Coach Cowher,

The ever-calm, always-temperate Coach Cowher gets doused, 1995.

were always positive. Always kept hope alive. Never dwelled on the negative. That was a big factor in the turnaround."

Nothing speaks more loudly about Bill Cowher and Renaissance II than the remarkable '95 recovery. Sputtering at 3-4, he could have made excuses, could have cited injuries (Woodson alone would have been sufficient), or free agency, or the ancient Steeler bugaboo, rebuilding. But he didn't. Cowher took the high road—all the way to Phoenix. "We had the talent," Dawson says, "and we knew if everybody did what they were capable of, we could do some things. That's what happened."

The night before Super Bowl XXX against the Dallas Cowboys, Jerry Olsavsky got on the team bus. "This is it, baby," he thought, and he knew all the guys were feeling it, too.

"Poise, sixty minutes, physical," Bill Cowher enjoined his players. They nearly pulled it off, but it was not to be. With the Steelers trailing 13-0 at the quarter and 20-7 at the half, the defense did what Steeler defenses have always done best—hunkered down and took the game back. Controlling the second half, the Steelers climbed back, 20-10, 20-17. Trailing by three points, the Steelers drove, and drove . . . until an errant pass, and a valiant 27-17 loss.

Not surprisingly, Carnell Lake puts it all into perspective. "Being part of winning and going to the Super Bowl was very special," he says. "Because when we started out we were supposed to be the hottest thing since the Internet. Then we disappointed a lot of people. But the team concept that Bill Cowher preached came through for us. We overcame a lot of shortcomings and disadvantages to wind up in the Super Bowl. I'd like to say I had something to do with that." He pauses. "It was really something."

"It was a great experience," Bill Cowher adds. "I don't like losing any games. But I was very proud of our football team, especially the way they responded after being down early. I think that was indicative of our 1995 season. We played sixty minutes of football, and we fought until the very end. They had every reason to walk out with their heads held high."

"This present team finally has its own identity," Dan Rooney says, knowing how terribly tough it is to succeed a legendary Dynasty. "These guys have finally overcome the situation."

RENAISSANCE II . . . AND BEYOND

It was a typically clear and cold Arizona morning, January 28, with the air as clean and crisp as an armadillo's scales. It had been sixteen years since the team had been to this party, a long and winding sixteen years. As Andy Russell says, in January 1980, if you had told that team, freshly victorious in their fourth Super Bowl in six years, that it would take that long to return, they'd have said you were crazy.

Same players, same desire, fresh blood every year.

But time and tide combine to erode skills; injuries ravage; rules change; people depart. Players are not replace-

After a characteristic big catch, we see the characteristic easy smile. Ernie Mills's clutch catch set up the winning touchdown during the AFC Championship Game in 1995.

able parts—no one is. NFL champions are made of precision thinking and pinpoint execution, astonishing effort and relentless intensity. "If you don't have a love for the game," Rod Woodson says, "and you don't appreciate the game, and you don't take the game seriously enough, it's not going to happen. No matter what you do."

The receiving corps has it, as does what Andy Russell calls "the rock 'em, sock 'em defense."

"I'm impressed with their superb athleticism and their great talent," he says. "They're stronger, bigger, and faster than we were. They would beat us."

They're Chuck Noll's lads, Lloyd, Woodson, and company. To Cowher's fire they brought Noll's predilection for great quickness, strength, and agility—classic Steeler traits, perfect for Blitzburgh: ride hell for leather and crush the quarterback. It's not only gorgeous, but it works, especially in this era of previously unimagined passing stats.

Still, Dynasties are hard to come by these days. Hard after their 1996 Super Bowl XXX appearance, Neil O'-Donnell, Kevin Greene, Leon Searcy—impact players on the AFC champions—all departed.

"You hate to lose guys," Dermontti Dawson says, "but you have to get used to it. That's just part of the game. You have to replace them." Dawson pauses. "But it takes a while for everybody to get on the same page."

A solid core of twenty players stood tall for Super Bowls IX-XIV, in the *ancien regime*, before free agency. Back then, players stayed on one team, identifying with it and the city. No longer. "You'll never have the loyalties you had then," Ralph Berlin says. "You'll never see that again. Because, with certain exceptions, these guys'll only be here for a cup of coffee."

"I don't know that there will ever be another period in the National Football League where there was assem-

Veteran center Dermontti Dawson, number 63, and 1995 rookie running back Erric "Peewee" Pegram, number 20, are two keys to the Steeler offense as the team continues to pursue a Super Bowl title in the 1990s.

Leadership means franchise stability. Insuring the future (left to right) Arthur Rooney II, Dan Rooney, Tom Donahoe.

bled a team like the Pittsburgh Steelers," Mark Malone says. "With the wealth of talent they had, with their ability to win four Super Bowls in six years. I don't know that we'll ever see that again."

"It's very difficult for coaches," Tunch Ilkin says. "It's like college—you only have a guy for a few years. In the process, you lose the dynasties and the opportunity to play with your buddies for fourteen years in one city."

Carnell Lake doesn't mince words. "Those losses are big losses, and when those guys left, they left voids. But one of the things about football is that things never stay the same, they are always changing. There are always new faces. I think that's what makes the game very special, and what keeps my interest, too, because I don't know what's going to happen from one day to the next. So it's a very exciting time for us. It will definitely test our char-

Kevin Greene pursued Bengal David Klingler (above), then pursued free agency after the 1995 season.

The Steelers and Browns met in 1994 (above) for a classic matchup in Cleveland Stadium. In '95, Pittsburgh slipped past the Browns to end the forty-six-year-old traditional rivalry with a 20-17 victory.

acter, test us as a team to see if we can overcome these losses and repeat—and maybe win."

Does free agency give Tom Donahoe fits? "It's frustrating," he allows. "No question about it. Personally, I don't like it. But it doesn't matter whether I like it or not. It's what we have. We have to deal with it and make the best of it.

"One thing that bothers me," Donahoe adds, "is that football is such a team game. You need so many people to be successful. I'm not sure that in the long term free agency is going to be good for this type of sport.

"When you go to a Super Bowl," Donahoe shakes his head, "and then you see guys who were a big part of it who aren't going to be here, it can frustrate you and get you down. But you can't let it. You have to go on. Whatever holes are created by free agency, we have to figure

out a way to plug them. The nice thing," he adds, "is that you can also sign some players. You still have a chance to be successful."

"Every year is a new challenge," Bill Cowher says. "There are going to be a lot of distractions, obstacles, and question marks. But we can deal with that. There's a good core of players on this team that will be able to keep us together. A lot of that has been built on the experience of the last couple of years. We've had success, and that builds confidence

"In today's system of free agency," he continues, "you have to be very cognizant of what you need now, and contractually, to be ready to fill the voids that may take place through free agency. We like to get players who have produced, but we also like to get players that we can feel comfortable with when adversity strikes, when you go through the bad times, so that these are the kind of guys who want to rally around you and respond to you. Rod Woodson, Greg Lloyd, Carnell Lake, Dermontti Dawson, and Yancey

Thigpen—these are the guys you're looking for. They understand the team commitment. They understand what teamwork is all about and are willing to make the sacrifices that go along with being successful.

"Still," Cowher smiles, "I like our prospects. It's going to be tough, but every year is tough. I don't know how it's going to unfold. But those are the challenges. And that's what creates the incentive to get back to where we were last year."

Another Super Bowl?

"You can't look for anything less," Kordell Stewart says.

"We're going to have to press on," Andre Hastings adds. "As players we can't be bothered by, or worried about, things we can't control."

There's a lot they can't control. Inside the club, they are grooming Dan's son, attorney Art II, to steer the ship. "I think you need succession," Dan Rooney says, "and I think he's capable."

Outside, the skies are dark. Houston, Baltimore, St. Louis, Los Angeles, Cleveland—*Cleveland*, for heaven's sake—have all pulled up stakes and moved. Rooney voted against all of them; bad for the game, he said, and rightfully so. Make no mistake about it: These are perilous times for the NFL, and nothing can be taken for granted. Not even the Steelers.

"Pittsburgh is a phenomenal community," Rooney says, "a great city. And the Steelers are one of our treasures. If someone were to ask me what I would view as the most successful thing I've done, I would say to keep the Steelers viable and in Pittsburgh. That's not been an easy task. It's been a balancing act, with all the different pressures and entities." Rooney shakes his head. "In the future, it's going to change. I think we will have more difficult problems." Rooney pauses. "It's not going to be easy."

In the old days, when the Chief ran the club out of his pocket notebook, sports teams were family businesses, like shoe stores or newsstands. Now corporations and the super-rich dump money in one day and sell out the next. There's not the same love there; too many fast-buck artists, too much turnover. There are not enough guys

He's Kordell Stewart and he's a quarterback—when he's not a running back, punter, or wide receiver.

like the Chief or his son, Dan—Pittsburgh guys who still live on North Lincoln Avenue on the North Side. Guys who still love the fans.

In the Steelers lobby in Three Rivers Stadium the proud tradition stands: four gleaming Lombardi trophies, symbols of the Dynasty, of the four Super Bowls, all in one Plexiglas box. Dan Rooney's plan is that when —not if, when—the Sixty-Minute Men, win Number Five, they will split 'em up, each trophy in its own separate case, a new Steel Curtain across the lobby, for Pittsburgh.

For the fans.

SUPER BOWL XXX

COWBOYS 27, STEELERS 17

January 28, 1996, Sun Devil Stadium, Tempe, Ariz.

The Steeler captains for Super Bowl XXX: (left to right) Fred McAfee, John L. Williams, Dermontti Dawson, Levon Kirkland, and Greg Lloyd.

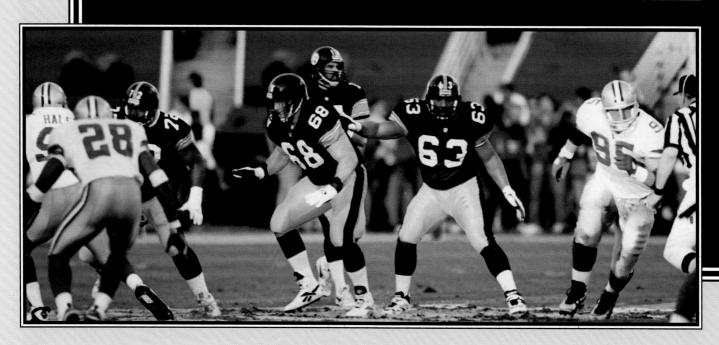

(Right) All-time single-season reception leader Yancey Thigpen celebrates his touchdown grab by spiking one.

———————

(Below) The three-hundred-pound offensive line gives quarterback Neil O'Donnell time to set up in the pocket, (left to right), Leon Searcy, Brenden Stai, Dermontti Dawson.

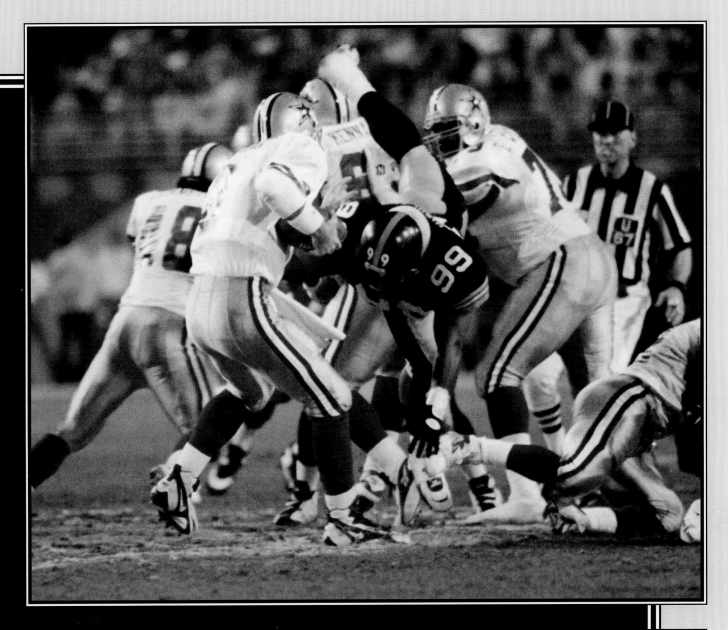

(Above) The Steelers won the battles but lost the war. Linebacker Levon Kirkland sacks Cowboy quarterback Troy Aikman.

(Left) Pittsburgh Steelers: 1995 American Football Conference champions.

The canonization of the faded kitchen dishrag: Terrible Towels aloft.

The Steelers are the official religion of Pittsburgh. Although all football fans seem rabid, Steelers fans are unique—indeed, it's hard to imagine the team playing for anyone else but the working class or their descendants. They embody the town traits of hard work, no glitz, and no self-aggrandizement. Their fans work hard in the mines and mills. They are self-made men and women in law offices and medical schools.

They're proud of their history, of Pittsburgh industry running the world. They will tell you with no little pride that Pittsburgh steel built the Brooklyn Bridge, the Panama Canal, the cannons of war, and the cars of Detroit.

That blue-collar ethic permeates Pittsburgh, a city of tradition, of ethnic neighborhoods and family loyalties. It's a hard place to live, Pittsburgh. It may be America's one-time most livable city, but it demands a lot from its people—tough jobs, tough weather, rugged landscape, and rugged history. Strikes, wars, and rebellions all passed through like winter's annual blizzards. The people who came from all over the globe had to be tough to move here, survive, and succeed. As Jack Lambert might say, this is not a place for sissies.

That may be why Pittsburghers are so proud. No one's lukewarm about the place. You either love it—or you get out. Nobody's mild about the 'Burgh.

Or football.

CHAPTER 7

FROM THE TERRIBLE TOWELS TO BLITZBURGH

The Fans

It's a hard game and you play it hard—nothing fancy. It is exquisitely fitting that Pittsburgh's football patriarch, arguably the single most beloved figure in city lore, is a former boxing champion who could—and did—wipe out one of his own coaches in an unbilled office bout, and flatten one of his own adult children with a hard right to the noggin.

The Steelers don't whine about the weather, they revel in it. They win in it.

Like all true religions, the Steelers have their home shrines (TVs with Terrible Towels), sacraments (kielbasa and Iron City), vestments (Steeler badges, pins, shirts, caps, scarves), and incantations (*DEE-fense!*). The fans celebrate Steeler tribal lore and legacy in hard hats, T-shirts, and face paint, reveling in the rituals of hard work and harder hits.

Black—coal, soot, darkness, dirt, unyielding. Pittsburgh.
Gold—bright, burnished, ingots, money, success. Steelers.

> "Louie, I think this is the beginning of a beautiful friendship."
>
> **Humphrey Bogart**
> *Casablanca*

195

"We won it for the fans." Steelers all-time iron man, center Mike Webster, played his heart out for fifteen years, 220 games, and four Super Bowls.

Never gold and black—black and gold. Black—crush them. Gold—reap success. Perfect.

The fans relish the totem colors. Black-and-gold fingernail painting. Black-and-gold face painting. Black-and-gold *teeth* painting, for heaven's sake.

Pass a firehouse or public house on game Sundays, and you'll hear the hoots and hollers. You know what the Steelers are doing.

The passion is passed from parent to child, generation to generation, from birth, it seems. There is no other way to account for the game in 1985 when a cherubic eight-year-old, upon seeing linebacker Mike Merriweather pick off a pass and run it back for a touchdown, shouted, "I've been waiting all my life to see that!"

So it's hard to imagine just what long-time ticket-meister Joe Carr would say these days. Just imagine, when two thousand souls rattling around old Forbes Field meant a big gate, what Carr would think of sixty thousand-plus in Three Rivers Stadium, on their feet, shouting *"Here we go, Steelers, here we go!"* He'd swear he was dreaming—or

swear off demon rum. That's reality these days.

So is the statement of Steelers broadcaster Myron Cope, who when the faithful were at a fever pitch during an Oilers game in the early '90s, screeched, "The football crowd is playing as big a factor in this game as the Steelers' defense."

High praise. Accurate reporting.

Indeed, the adulation has not gone unnoticed, either on the playing field or in the front office.

"The fans?" sophomore quarterback Kordell "Slash" Stewart asks. "They're awesome. You can't ask for better fans than we have. Football season, people are just rockin' it like crazy. It's perfect. We want to play football for this city—people *love* to come here and play."

"Three Rivers Stadium is a hard place for other people to win," adds Coach Bill Cowher. "Our people are a tremendous advantage here. Our people are very loud, very supportive. I wouldn't want to be on the other side.

"I think that's healthy," Cowher continues. "Steelers games—they're a happening, an event, and that's the way it should be. The best thing about it is that the people who lived through the '70s are now taking their kids and saying, 'When I was a kid this is the way it used to be.' The feeling that is generated throughout the city—that is what sports are all about. It can unite a city and create a sense of pride."

"The fans are a special part of Steeler history," adds Director of Football Operations Tom Donahoe. "They're passionate. They want to win, and they want to go to the Super Bowl every year. But they never give up on the team. I think their loyalty and consistency is remarkable.

"It never ceases to amaze me," Donahoe adds, "when we play a road game how many Steelers fans come to the hotel and to the game. When we play San Diego it almost seems like a home game. The Super Bowl in Phoenix, the whole week out there, it seemed like we were at home. When we came out to warm up, the Terrible Towels and the noise level were great, because our fans are passionate—they love football. As long as we give them a constant effort and play a physical brand of football, they can live with the results.

"Having said that," Donahoe adds, "the fans almost don't let us lose. Somebody has to do something so that we win each game—because of how much the fans are behind us.

"They're passionate, knowledgeable, and extremely loyal to this franchise," Donahoe sums up. "They have been a huge part of our success. So they're not something that we ever take lightly."

The equation is clear: The owners have a strong emotional commitment to Pittsburgh, the coaches have an unwavering commitment to the football product, and the players play hard—and play like they care. People respond to that—and the players respond to the people.

How important is all this? To hear Joe Greene tell it, the fans won 'em a Super Bowl. "They were great," he recalls. "They could boo us and talk about us, but they wouldn't let anybody else do it. There were times when they would make that stadium rock: *DEE-fense! DEE-fense! DEE-fense!*

"In Super Bowl XIV," Greene continues, "the Rams had us on the run. But late in the fourth quarter, when

Fan favorite Mike Merriweather's interceptions were a thing of beauty in the 1980s.

the sun started to go down, that field started to feel like Pittsburgh. This was a road game—there were 102,000 people in the Rose Bowl, but our fans were there and they were special. They stood up, wearing black and gold, yelling *DEE-fense! DEE-fense! DEE-fense!* Looking up at them, hearing them, feeling them, we knew we had to make a big play. That's when Lambert intercepted that pass. It turned the game around, and we won."

Broadcaster Myron Cope agrees. "Every Super Bowl has been like a home game. Of the 102,000 that day in the L.A. Coliseum, there must have been 40,000 in black and gold. This past Super Bowl in Phoenix, an NBC official told me privately that he always worries about dead Super Bowl crowds—they're played in neutral sites, and the games are often runaways. But when he came to Super Bowl XXX and saw the Steelers fans waving the Terrible Towels, he breathed a sigh of relief. "We're home free," he said.

"Because the Steelers fans are unlike any other football following," Cope continues. "Those teams of the

Suds 'n' sports have mixed at least since the Chief's dad ran a saloon next to Exposition Park. Blitzburgh fans at the 1995 AFC Championship Game.

'70s—they could have played a game in Zanzibar, and there'd be two hundred fans waiting for them at the hotel when they arrived. It's practically unheard of in my experience to find a fellow who's left the city, or been transferred, to adopt another city's football team. They're Steelers fans for life."

Who are these people and why are they saying all those nice things about them?

They are the secretaries wearing number 75 jerseys to work, because even though it's been fifteen years since Joe Greene retired he's still the best that ever was and ever will be. It's office workers slavering the salt mine in dolls, spreading signs across windows, and hanging banners, pennants, and pictures. It's the guys driving Steelermobiles, chock full of pompons, flags, and all matter of bric-a-brac. (The helmets alone are worth the price of

admission.) It's otherwise sane adults inventing radio handles, and identities, from the late pseudonymous Zivko Kovalchuk, the ersatz mayor of the Southside (actually, he lived in the East End and worked in the Strip, but he loved that make-believe gig), to Fanfare Frank, with his endless statistics, to innumerable others through the years. (Oh, to be a first-time caller!)

They have also been known to lift a few now and then. Indeed, the kinship between suds and sports has existed, well, at least since Art Rooney's dad ran a saloon near Exposition Park.

The progenitor of our modern era was Owney McManus's Fourth Avenue hangout. Owney and the Chief were great pals. Sometimes the backroom served as the unofficial team office, space being what it was in downtown hotels. Owney used to sponsor what he called Ham

The fabulous flying Steelheads, war-painted Steelers fans at Super Bowl XXX.

and Cabbage Specials, trains to take fans on road games to Philadelphia and New York. But the heart of the operation was the backroom, linoleum-decked, three steps above the sawdust floor, which became a gathering place for football players, fans, and pols. Never knew who you'd run into.

By 1960 the suits upstaged Owney, and high rollers could take a special train to see the Steelers meet the Browns in Cleveland. (Where the Steelers got clobbered, actually, 28-20.) A mere fifteen dollars included game ticket and lunch on the train.

Owney's joint wasn't so far from Froggy's, seventeen years and counting in FirstSide, the madeover Mon Wharf warehouse district. At one time, the Frog, who doubles in real life as Steve Morris, ran Bimbo's, near Forbes Field. Froggy's Saloon, while not specifically a sports bar, skews heavily male, heavily sports.

A season-ticket holder and veteran of all five Super Bowls, Froggy serves a Steelers Sunday brunch and ferries busloads of people to the game.

Terry Bradshaw could hear the boos as he went out hurt.

Sitting on a busy afternoon beneath a framed portrait of Joe Greene, Froggy shrugs. "Pittsburghers want a winner. We don't like losers. But we'll stay with a guy here—as long as he's a Steeler and as long as he's trying. Once he's not a Steeler anymore, he's the enemy."

So is everyone else, too, it seems. Froggy recalls the time that he and the troops were in a Florida hotel for Super Bowl XIII. The Steelers fans tried to buy some Dallas fans a drink. The Dallas fans were not receptive. As Froggy tells it, "The Steelers fans told 'em, 'Shut up, have a drink, or bet your money. Or if you want a fist fight, we'll be happy to accommodate you.'"

When an accommodation could not be reached, the Steelers mob threw the Dallas guys in the pool—fully dressed, mind you—and wouldn't let them out.

Up the river a bit, in Homestead, the legendary Joe Chiodo draws 'em all, mill hands to millionaires. He's been running his bridge-side saloon for nearly fifty years now, since he was a returning G.I., when there was still a Homestead works. (It is not known whether Chiodo has every single scrap of his memorabilia stuffed around the bar and office, but it seems that way.)

A nonstop talker, Chiodo has been a paying Steelers customer almost from the day the franchise opened—'34

Steelers fans will stop at nothing to show their commitment—or fanaticism.

or '35, things get a bit hazy these days. He was working for his father back then in the family shoe shop, and he took the streetcar to Forbes Field. "The place was ours," he recalls. "We sat anywhere we wanted."

When peace broke out, about the time Jock Sutherland was making the club respectable, Chiodo bought his first season tickets—and has had them ever since. They were the Steelers by then, and Chiodo remembers a bitter cold day at Forbes Field when a friend who worked the scoreboard—these were the days of hand-dropped numbers—let him and his friends stand by the fire to keep warm. They nearly set the scoreboard housing on fire, but they stayed warm. (It seems that Chiodo and Company weren't the only ones who were hot: The Steelers pummeled the Giants that day 63-7.) In '47 he started Chiodo's Football Group, and began to take trips, to New York, Philadelphia, Washington, Detroit, and Chicago. He chartered a bus to go to home games—Forbes Field, then Pitt Stadium, and finally Three Rivers. At its peak, the group boasted sixty-eight season ticket holders, now down to a mere three dozen. "From 1947 until today we have not missed a trip," he says proudly.

JOE CHIODO'S ALL-TIME FAN-FOOT-IN-THE-MOUTH STORY

You know Rege Phillips, right? Joe Chiodo's buddy, the one that holds the money for the bar tab? Well, here's how Rege puts his foot in his mouth all the way up to his kneecap.

Seems that when Joe and the boys fly down to Miami for Super Bowl XIII, Rege gets off the plane first and runs into a reporter. The reporter asks Rege if they brought their wives.

"What?" Rege says, "Bring our wives? Whoever heard of bringing a ham sandwich to a banquet?"

We-e-e-ll, Rege figures it's the end of it, but it's not. The reporter puts it in the paper, and it gets picked up by the Pittsburgh papers, and the next thing you know it's all over town.

Now Rege's wife is Marie —you probably knew that, too, 'cause if you know Rege you know Marie. Rege, well, he don't tell us what Marie says when he gets home, but Rege, he ain't too happy and he's got to say a lot of Hail Marys.

Later, Rege, he's coming on Joe's bus for Three Rivers, 'cept this time he brings the Little Woman. "Hey, Rege," Chiodo says, real friendly, "I see you brought the ham sandwich today."

Now the Missus turns about three shades of red, and most of what Rege says we can't print, but he does threaten Chiodo's life. "You ever mention that again," Rege makes a fist, "I'll kill you."

He's been more than loyal—he's even risked life and limb for the Steelers' honor. At Pitt Stadium one day, Chiodo got in the middle of a dust-up concerning the Rooneys' good name. Seems that some miscreant had insulted the Chief, and another fellow had a different opinion. Chiodo tried to break it up—only to get busted in the chops for his troubles.

Once, perhaps in a fit of madness, he even tried to hoist the colors in enemy territory. In the midst of hanging a Steelers banner off the Astrodome upper deck, Chiodo felt a long, tall Texan assure him that he would pitch him and his battle flag over the railing if the Yankee dared display enemy colors deep in the heart of Texas. Chiodo, a boisterous but ultimately sensible chap, allowed that he had seen the error of his ways.

Then there was the time in Chicago that Chiodo skipped the bus, but flew up for the game. Since he missed all the revelry, the lads all wanted him to have a libation before kickoff. "By 11 o'clock, I couldn't see," Chiodo recounts, "couldn't walk, couldn't talk." With no other recourse, they put Chiodo to bed. "I went to Chicago," he laments, "and I didn't see the game. I always wanted to see Soldier Field, and I still haven't seen Soldier Field."

Just over the hill in West Mifflin, there is the fabled Thompson Run Athletic Association, Bill Elwell, proprietor. (Rege Salley's his sidekick, and he counts, too.) The club has an annual stag sports banquet—where many a Steeler has appeared. But since this is a family publication, and the club's affairs are a mite, ah, risque, we will leave all other Thompson Run business in respectful silence.

Italian Armies, Polish Armies, Polish Hams, what-have-you: Gerela's Gorillas line up at Three Rivers.

It's these guys—the Chiodos, Elwells, Salleys, and thousands more like them—who backed the club, who coronated Big Daddy Lipscomb, Mean Joe, and Franco.

Franco Harris, as a running back, was something the Steelers had never seen before—a young, bright, and consistent power running back. He was a bull on the field—and a prince on the street. He lived on the North Side, attracting hordes of kids, blending together much of Pittsburgh with his mixed African-Italian heritage. A decent, soft-spoken man, he inspired the first—and arguably the greatest—of modern fan clubs: Franco's Italian Army. "The spirit of the town was incredible," the man himself recalls. "Franco's Italian Army was a big part of that. Bringing in the fans, and getting them behind us—I really enjoyed it."

The success of the club spawned a thousand imitators, some good, most bad to worse, a few just plain awful. The pick of the litter were Gerela's Gorillas, whom Myron Cope fed with information on the opposing squad's field-goal kicker, which they would gleefully paint on end-zone banners to try to rattle him. Not to be ethnically outdone, the Poles began Dobre Shunka, which translates roughly to "Sweet Ham," for Jack, but it never had Franco's panache. Then there were Joe Greene's Polish Armed Forces—the Green Babushka, Rocky's Flying Squirrels, Andy's Russellers, Mike Wagner's Wild Bunch, and perhaps the worst of all time, Cowher's Cowheads (*yeeesh!*).

A good reporter with a sense of the absurd, broadcaster Myron Cope (left) with the Voice of the Steelers, Jack Fleming.

You're in Steeler Country indeed: the redoubtable fans.

All this fanfare was accomplished to the dulcet tones of Jimmy Pol and his endless varieties of Greek-inflected polka-style Steeler fight songs. ("We're from the town with the great football team . . .") Only Pol, with his ear-bending accent, could rhyme "steel" and "thrill" and get away with it.

The simmering stewpot was mercilessly stirred by writer and radio commentator Myron Cope; indeed, no recounting of the Steelers phenomenon would be complete without mention of his insidious incitement of Pittsburgh's sleeping innocents.

Armed with a voice that rattles windows when he gets excited, Cope is a fellow who, despite his seemingly madcap manner, brings a keen journalist's eye—and integrity—to his broadcasts. People quote him, not because he's ludicrous (although he sometimes is), but because his information is good and his thinking is better. Although Cope sounds daffy, there is often more reason than rhyme in his seemingly mindless sayings and expressions.

A major voice on radio talk shows and Steelers broadcasts for nearly three decades, Cope is a great deal more thoughtful and reserved in person than his frenetic radio personality might suggest. Back in the early 1950s, when Pittsburgh broadcast legends Joe Tucker and Bob Prince called the action on WWSW, Cope was cutting his teeth writing sports, first at the *Erie Times* ("The older guys would go to dinner and I would get the bowling scores," he recalls), and later at the *Pittsburgh Post-Gazette*. By 1960 when the magazine world beckoned, Cope, a native Pittsburgher and lifelong resident, became a highly rated freelancer for such top-shelf outlets as *Sports Illustrated* and *The Saturday Evening Post*.

In 1968 WTAE asked Cope to do five-minute sports commentaries from his home every morning. "It was a lark and a few extra bucks," Cope recalls. The idea caught on, and Cope went to TV as well; when the Steelers moved to WTAE in '70 they asked Cope to be their radio color man. "I know nothing about doing that," he protested. The Steelers, a most persuasive lot, took him anyway.

By September 1973 Cope added his now-famous talk show. At first, he didn't want to do it. But the show caught on, running until the mid '90s, when Cope quasi-retired.

The famous Cope style? "A lot of the things I do just pop out of my mouth," he says. "'Yoi!' was one of them. So was 'that's a lot of garganzola.' I know that Gorgonzola is cheese. But garganzola is a good-sounding word to connote baloney.

"I've got to pinch myself," Cope continues. "I came along totally by accident, and then I was the color analyst for a team that had gone nowhere for years. All of a sudden you've got a dynasty being born. If this team had been the Tampa Bay Bucs all this would not have hap-pened. But the Steelers overwhelmed the town. I'm just a guy along for the ride.

"I've always tried to approach sports with a certain sense of fun," Cope adds. "And when you've got a perennial winner you can have a lot more fun. That, plus trying to bring some knowledge and being forthright, added up to the public's accepting me as an integral part of the team.

"With that in mind, over the years I think I was able to establish a great degree of credibility with the listeners. I shoot straight—and do my research. It was like a mania with me to be prepared for a talk show or a football game. The result was that I knew something about the game and I think that got across.

"A Steelers official once told me that in a very real way I was responsible for the success of this franchise—by

---

MYRON COPE'S FIVE FAVORITE NICKNAMES

Nothing warms a fans's heart as much as a good football nickname. Over the years, the faithful have roared for players from the Whites—Whizzer and Mad Dog—to Bags, Big Daddy, and the Bomber. Some players arrive with nicknames—Mean Joe trailed Joe Greene from Texas, Fats came from Ernie Holmes's grandpap.

Others acquire them along the way: His fellow players tagged Ray Mansfield the Old Ranger, Iron Mike was a natural for all-time games played leader Mike Webster.

But a lucky few have nicknames thrust upon them by Pittsburgh's grand monikermeister Myron Cope.

"Some guys," he says, "naturally suggest the need of a nickname, or a better nickname. When I decide a guy is ripe for one, I try to come up with something that has reason and originality. Then I'll take it to the player before I use it. After all, he should have the right to approve it."

Here are Cope's five favorites, in alphabetical order:

Eric "Big Bird" Green: "He looked like Big Bird."

Jack "Splat" Lambert: "Because the guy hit and splattered people. I played off the nursery rhyme, Jack Sprat —he's a tall, thin guy, too."

Chuck "The Emperor Chaz" Noll: This one was created on the spur of the moment at the Market Square rally after Super Bowl XIII. Cope had always called him Chaz, and when the Steelers won their third Super Bowl, he declared it a dynasty. "Every dynasty has to have an emperor. So I said, 'Everybody repeat after me: "All hail the Emperor Chaz."' (Predictably, Noll hated it.)

Erric "Peewee" Pegram: "He's small, he scoots around."

Ray "The Hotel Doorman" Seals: As in "the Hotel Doorman just busted through and picked up the quarterback like a piece of luggage." To make a living as a semipro player, Seals did indeed work as a doorman at the Hotel Syracuse.

Honorable Mention: Jack "The Hydroplane" Deloplaine: Well, of course. Anybody could have thought of that.

being honest and criticizing them when they deserved it, I gave them credibility."

Because of Cope's love for the absurd, he has become a receptacle for the fans' collective imagination—odd or catchy turns of phrase they've sent to him over the years. "I'm a magnet for that kind of stuff," Cope agrees. "I reject ninety-nine percent of it. But you get that nugget every once in a while."

He's had two world-class keepers from fans. One was Blitzburgh, which came from a radio caller. "You know when you have the right one," Cope says, "and I embraced it immediately. Blitzburgh is just perfect."

Then there's the Immaculate Reception, a fan call as well. Cope used it on the news at 11:00 the night of the Steelers' '72 miracle win—and the rest is history. "I was only the medium," he says. "It will go on forever."

Cope unleased the ultimate Steeler weapon—the Terrible Towel—in November 1975, just in time for Super Bowl X. It has endured, over the succeeding twenty years, elevating what for many is a used yellow dishrag into an *objet d'art*.

It was just Myron's luck that the gimmick caught on. WTAE wanted a Steeler promotion, and pressed into service, Cope responded. Like Cope himself, the Terrible Towel quickly became a talisman, good luck charm, and constant companion to the game. It was silly, out-of-step—and Pittsburgh all the way. (One corporate exec actually asked to be buried wearing his Steeler jersey—and clutching his Terrible Towel.)

Perhaps Cope's all-time coup was the time he convinced Frank Sinatra to show up and be inducted into Franco's Italian Army. It was back in '72, and the Steelers were training in Palm Springs before meeting San Diego in the deciding game of the season. While the Steelers were looking to win the division for the first time in franchise history, Cope's mission was to find Sinatra, who had been in retirement, and bring him to practice.

Easier said than done. Cope put the word out. Nothing doing.

Wednesday night the Steelers brass was sitting in a posh Palm Springs restaurant. Guess who walks in? Ol' Blue Eyes himself.

COACH STONE'S SIX ALL-TIME FAVORITE STEELERS

"This is not entertainment," Taylor Allderdice's offensive line coach Larry Stone growls. "This is football." At six feet and nearly three hundred pounds, Stone commands attention. An imposing, bearded figure, he likes his football neat—taking no prisoners, giving no quarter, asking none.

In real life, he calls the Dragons' plays from the booth. At home, he has his chair, his pins, and his Terrible Towel. "I've been a Steeler fan from the days when they were lucky to win the coin toss," he rumbles. "But I watch the game as a coach."

The players he admires, he says, "take deep pride in what they do. They approach football as work, and when demands are put on them, they stand up. Outlaws come to Pittsburgh to become heroes," he snarls approvingly.

Here is his all-time list:

John Stallworth. "Without question, as far as ability, he was outstanding. A money player—when you needed it, he was there."

Mel Blount. "I've never seen anyone play cornerback better. The corner should be the best athlete on the field, and he was."

Terry Bradshaw. "A winner. How many guys can say they went to the big show four times and walked away with four rings?"

Ray Mansfield. "This was a man who really was a field general. He knew defense, and he knew what to do, and he played."

Ernie Stautner. "He lifted play to a different level. When they couldn't win anything, he gave you 155 percent."

Rocky Bleier. "Bleier was the epitome of the game. He gave you everything he had—crippled, hurt, or sick, he came to play."

Cope writes him a message on a cocktail napkin, telling Sinatra the story of Franco's Italian Army, inviting him to practice, offering to induct him as a one-star general.

After a bit, Sinatra ambles over, pulls up a chair, and plops down next to Cope. He agrees.

Cope calls Army HQ and informs them the deal is set.

The next day, on the team bus, a seemingly irate Chuck Noll asks Cope about this distraction he's planning at practice.

Cope mumbles an excuse.

But the word leaks out; two hundred cameramen show up. No Sinatra. They start to rag Cope. Club official Jim Boston, telling a caller Sinatra's a no-show, feels a tap on his shoulder. Orange cardigan, white pork pie hat. "When Sinatra says he shows, he shows," the Voice says.

Sinatra, Cope and company all converge on the field. Franco, a humble rookie, demurs. "I'm practicing," he says. Noll, a monumental Sinatra fan, yells, "Franco, get over there."

Sinatra, bussed on both cheeks, is inducted.

The Steelers beat San Diego and win their first division title in forty years. A huge crowd showed up at the Greater Pitt Airport, including Franco's Italian Army,

You can't start 'em too young. The fans at Steelers training camp, circa 1972.

The Chief and the Chairman of the Board: Ol' Blue Eyes is inducted into Franco's Italian Army, Palm Springs, 1972.

with canine corps in tow—a Great Dane in a battle helmet. Just as the Army was about to promote Cope to two-star general—lights, camera—the Dane relieved himself on Cope's shoes. "That," Cope says, "was stardom."

There are other kinds of stardom, and the fans and players recognize both. Rocky Bleier was loved by the Pittsburgh fans, and he believes he knows why. "Because they could identify with me," he says, "with a guy who worked very hard, didn't have a whole lot of talent, made the team, and made a contribution. Pretty clean-cut, blue-collar guy. One of the boys. Father owned a bar. Went to Vietnam. Went to Notre Dame. How bad could he be?"

For his part, Tunch Ilkin credits the fans' intelligence. "Pittsburgh fans are the greatest," he says. "They are the most knowledgeable fans in sports. They listen to the talk shows, the pregame shows; they read everything, and they live and die with the Steelers. They appreciate good hard football. I was very blessed. This was a great place to play." Adds teammate Bubby Brister, "The people of Pittsburgh are great. I couldn't pick a better place to start my career."

"They always turned out, and they always backed the team," agrees former wide receiver Louis Lipps. "That was very important to us, to go out and perform for them. They were the greatest. They gave us that extra spark."

Number one draft choice, Rookie of the Year, receiver of the late eighties, infamous Loo-o-o-ou! Fan favorite Louis Lipps led the club in receptions, 1988, 1990-92.

He especially remembers the crowd yelling *Lo-o-o-o-o-u-u-u* whenever he took the field. "It was like a cold breeze going right through me, and I loved to respond when they were calling my name. I always wanted to do something positive."

"You have to get excited when you play here," Rod Woodson adds. "The fans scream so much we couldn't hear our audibles, so we had to get hand signals. I wouldn't go anywhere else."

"Yes," sums up Dan Rooney, "the fans have been phenomenal."

But they can be tough. As Jerry Olsavsky points out, they let you know what they're thinking—in a hurry. "When we play bad, we've got good fans, because they're

telling us, 'You guys stink out there, turn it around and start playing.' I appreciate that."

Some didn't. Yes, the fans are knowledgeable, and yes, they are loyal—perhaps to a fault. But they also have great expectations—and a lot to say if those expectations are not met. No one knows that more than former quarterback Mark Malone, the mere mortal who had to replace a legend.

"I had my ups and downs," he says. "But if I had it to do all over again, I'd come back. I don't know that I would want to play with any other city. There was a love affair with this team. They are the most rabid fans of any football franchise in America. That makes it an awfully difficult place to play. But it also makes it a very special place,

ALL-STAR, ALL-PRO, ALL THE TIME

With its pool tables, ubiquitous TVs, and merchandise, Rod Woodson's All-Star Grille, adjacent to Station Square on the South Side, is the model of a modern major sports restaurant. Although ritzier, Woodson's establishment joins a long but not necessarily distinguished line of Pittsburgh-area sports-related eateries and watering holes. Indeed, owning a joint has been the venerable pursuit of athletes since the first Olympians squeezed the grape.

Woodson—he's the slender fellow under the cap—follows such colleagues as Louis Lipps's Hot Licks, Willie Stargell and Brady Keys's All-Pro Chicken, Maury Wills's Stolen Base, the late Frank Gustine's gone-but-not-forgotten Oakland taproom, and a veritable cornucopia of other bars, beaneries, and hash houses—far too many to mention here.

The most telling artifact, in a large partition behind the cashier, is a wall of signed jerseys from the glory years, whose owners are all in the Hall of Fame, or should be: Swann, Stallworth, Bradshaw, Ham, Greene, Bleier, Harris, Lambert, Blount—and Woodson.

Outrageous Woodsonian ego?

No, they all say, he could have been one of them on the Dynasty teams of the '70s.

With its relentless pursuit of the sports theme—from helmets to oversized Steeler photos (many featuring Woodson) to the jerseyed wait staff (Donnie Shell will serve you drinks while Ray Seals brings the menu and Jerry Olsavsky buses your table)—upscale atmosphere, and up-to-the-minute menu, Woodson's three hundred-seat converted warehouse has rapidly become one of Pittsburgh's most popular places of the mid-90s.

For the Super Bowl special they sold tickets—and sold out the place—hosting the next best thing to a tailgate party: costumes, face painting, the whole bit. On a good night, for pre- and postgame nibbling, Woodson's does literally turnaway business, with nearly two hours considered not too long to wait for a table. One lure: Patrons never know which athletes will show up. They all eat free—any team, any time—as long as they mingle with the civilians.

Uh, Rod, isn't the mixture of three hundred-pound linemen and free food a bit dicey? "We're enjoying it right now," the perennial All-Pro chuckles. "We'll see if it gets out of hand."

"For Mr. Dan Rooney and the fans of Pittsburgh—this is for you." Bill Cowher holds aloft the AFC Championship trophy and dedicates it to the Steel City on January 14, 1996.

to play somewhere that demands that level of excellence and perfection.

"Because Steelers football, to a great many Steelers fans, is a religious experience. You put them in the privacy of their homes, or in a seat two hundred feet away, and the metamorphosis is startling.

"Do you take that personally?" Malone asks. "I've chosen not to. Yet when you hear that derision seeping in, it's difficult not to have it affect your ability to perform."

Especially when they turned on him. "It has to hurt," Malone recalls, "to have a percentage of fans express their disdain—although that was tempered to a great degree by the organization, the coaches, and the players. Those people had a belief and faith not in my abilities, but in the way I worked to try to succeed. It meant a lot more than what a few people said.

"Nevertheless, you do everything you can to insulate yourself," Malone adds. No talk shows, no newspapers. You try not to hear the boos. In the stadium, with bread on the line, brewskies under the belt, and remembering Bradshaw, "they're going to express a lament for you. And that's fine. But I've never met anybody on the street who has said an ill word to me," Malone adds. On the contrary, it was a smile, a slap on the back, a "hang in there. We'll get 'em next week." As such, Malone says, "I love these people, and I love the community."

How much? Mark Malone was a star athlete with good looks and high intelligence. He was born in San Diego, where he also finished his professional football career, and he went to school in Arizona. He now makes his living as a professional broadcaster, reporting on events all around the country. But he lives in Pittsburgh. "I look at my experience here as a complete positive. That's why I chose to live here."

Malone's not alone in such things. "One philosophy I've always had," Chuck Noll says, "is that you've got to

keep your feet on the ground. When they tell you you're great, you can't believe it, because you'll go off the deep end. When they tell you you're lousy, don't believe them, either." So when Emperor Chaz evoked the ire of the faithful, he ignored it. Like Malone, he neither read the papers nor tuned in the talk shows. "I never concerned myself with what anyone wrote," he says, "or whatever they did, because that was out of my control. We knew what we had to do. The free advice you get is probably worth just that."

Better is Noll's quote when he accepted his Hall of Fame ring on the field where he had so much success. "The thing that makes Three Rivers Stadium great," he said, "are the Hall of Fame fans." Indeed, they cheered themselves and their city as much as their football team.

"What I wasn't really aware of," comments Mike Wagner of the earlier Super Bowl years, "was how much fun the city was having. It gave them a good experience, something fun to share. Even though sports is not important to the world, it has given the city of Pittsburgh great pride. It helped contribute to a change here. So, it's more than just sports. Looking back on it as players, we have to remember that—and we have to recognize our contribution."

We end where we began: with a fan with a Steeler shrine in his house, Bill Cowher. "We're an extension of this city," he says, "and of the fan who watches us play."

Accepting the AFC Championship trophy, Bill Cowher held it aloft and said to sixty thousand screaming fans, "For Mr. Dan Rooney and the fans of Pittsburgh. This is for you."

He's a Pittsburgher, this Cowher—always was, always will be. Success won't alter that. His parents have season tickets and a Terrible Towel on the TV. He meant what he said.

So do the Rooneys.

With vision and an incredible ability to read a play and adjust, Hall of Famer Franco Harris gains his ten-thousandth yard.

HALL OF FAMERS

Arthur J. Rooney, 1933-88, founder, owner, president, chairman. Without his guidance, generosity, and spirit, the Pittsburgh franchise would not have survived or prospered.

Bert Bell, 1941-46, co-owner, 1941, head coach. Although Bell is enshrined because of his signal service to the league, he was the Chief's, and the club's, friend when they needed one.

Mel Blount, 1970-83, cornerback. Big, fast, devastating player who created a new standard for the position. Steeler record fifty-seven interceptions, led NFL with eleven in 1975.

Terry Bradshaw, 1970-83, quarterback. Incendiary passer, arguably greatest in NFL history. First man to pilot his club to four Super Bowl victories; Steeler record 27,989 yards in the air.

Bill Dudley, 1942, '45-46, back. Despite war-shortened career, Steelers' brightest star of the first two decades. Running, passing, receiving threat, led league in rushing his rookie season.

Joe Greene, 1969-81, defensive tackle, 1987-91, coach. Most dominant defensive player of his era, created a new winning attitude on hapless Steelers. His sixty-six sacks hold the second all-time club record.

Jack Ham, 1971-82, linebacker. Quiet, self-assured player, greatest coverage expert in the history of the game. His twenty-one fumble recoveries are a club record; he also had thirty-two interceptions and 25.5 sacks.

Franco Harris, 1972-83, running back. Power back *par excellence*, all-time Steeler rusher with 100 touchdowns, eight 1,000-yard seasons, 2,881 carries, and 11,950 yards.

John Henry Johnson, 1960-65, running back. Although he came to the club at the end of his career, he was a quintessential power back, good enough to notch the club's first two one-thousand-yard seasons.

Walt Kiesling, 1937-38, guard, head and assistant coach, 1939-61. Although a fine football man, his three turns as head coach resulted in but thirty wins and a .361 percentage.

Jack Lambert, 1974-84, linebacker. Intense, intimidating player, defensive captain and team leader, he registered twenty-eight interceptions and fifteen fumble recoveries.

Bobby Layne, 1958-62, quarterback. Provided the Steelers with their first great field general and passer, his 8,983 yards are the fourth all-time club best, and his 409 yards in a game are a Steelers high-water mark.

Johnny "Blood" McNally, 1934, '37-39, back, 1937-39, head coach. Quick, brainy halfback, he scatted for 168 yards receiving and four touchdowns to lead the club in 1937.

Chuck Noll, 1969-91, head coach. Orchestrated and conducted the most successful team makeover in NFL history. Member of exclusive two-hundred-win club, only NFL coach to win four Super Bowls.

Ernie Stautner, 1950-63, tackle. Playing in an era before many defensive statistics were kept, the Steelers defensive leader, master of the bone-jarring hit and coughed-up ball.

With the fans screaming DEE-fense! in the Rose Bowl, Hall of Fame linebacker Jack Lambert snags one to turn the tide against the Rams in Super Bowl XIV.

Eight Steelers Who Should Be in the Hall of Fame

Although Steeler history is rich with players, coaches, and executives who are enshrined in the Pro Football Hall of Fame, there are others who deserve the honor.

Many think that the voters feel that there are already enough Steelers represented. Others believe that the voters have not sufficiently reviewed these players' individual contributions.

Whatever the reason, in alphabetical order, here are eight Steelers who deserve to be in the Hall of Fame:

Jack Butler, defensive back, 1951-59. Heady, hard-hitting, franchise player of the '50s. Holds a host of Steeler interception records: fifty-two career (second), ten single-season (second), 827 yards (first), four touchdowns (tied first), four in a game (first).

L.C. Greenwood, defensive end, 1969-81. The most dominating defensive end on the most dominating defensive line in history. Used great height and speed to stuff run, sack quarterbacks, and deflect passes. His 73.5 sacks remain a Steeler record.

Dan Rooney, various positions, 1955-74, president, 1975-96. Great franchises are made, not born. In an era of greed and owner turnover, he had the vision, patience, and concern to create one of the sport's great franchises and help bring stability to the NFL

Donnie Shell, safety, 1974-87. One of the league's most feared players, he combined hard work with devastating hits to carve out a stellar fourteen-season career and rewrite the rules for strong safeties. His fifty-one interceptions are an all-time Steeler mark for safeties.

John Stallworth, wide receiver, 1974-87. Playing fourteen years, he tallied numerous all-time Steeler marks, including pass receptions (537), receiving yards (8,723 career, 1,395 single game), one-hundred-yard games (twenty career, seven single season), and career TDs receiving (sixty-three).

Lynn Swann, wide receiver, 1972-82. Master of the impossible catch and big play, Swann used his great leaping ability to garner Super Bowl X MVP honors with four game-breaking catches. He led team five years in receiving, and amassed 336 receptions for 5,462 yards.

Mike Webster, center, 1974-88. All-time Steeler Iron Man center holds club service record, fifteen years and 220 games (177 consecutive). A wily, strong work-ethic player, he anchored the offensive line, called plays, and blocked superbly, contributing to four Super Bowl champions.

Rod Woodson, cornerback, 1987-96. A quick, canny cornerback and punt and kick returner, he leads active Steelers in interceptions (thirty-two), and holds all-time club records for punt returns (256), yards (2,362), kickoff returns (220), yards (4,894), including 982 in a single season.

Plus two more to watch:

Carnell Lake, safety, 1989-96. Heady, hard-hitting Pro Bowl player, master of coverage and crushing hits, Lake has led the team in tackles, and tied the club record for consecutive games with sack (six). His five fumbles recovered in 1989 tie the second all-time single-season Steeler mark.

Greg Lloyd, linebacker, 1988-96. Lethal hits and devastating quickness netted this two-time team MVP and Blitzburgh leader forty-nine career sacks to lead current team and place fourth all-time. He also has tied all-time consecutive games with a sack (six).

Defensive back Jack Butler intercepted fifty-two career passes, including a record four in one game, but he never made it to the Hall of Fame.

For the Fiftieth Season Banquet in 1982, the Steelers picked an all-time team: (left to right, front row) John Stallworth, Terry Bradshaw, Jack Butler; (second row) Franco Harris, Lynn Swann, Rocky Bleier, Larry Brown, Gerry Mullins, Art Rooney, Mike Webster, Sam Davis, Jon Kolb; (third row) announcer Howard Cosell, Joe Greene, Mel Blount, Andy Russell, Dwight White, Jack Ham, Donnie Shell, Elbie Nickel, Pat Brady, Roy Gerela, L.C. Greenwood, Mike Wagner. Missing from photo: Jack Lambert, Ernie Stautner.

IT'S A *WHAT*?

In 1963 the Steelers adopted their team logo, three hypocycloids, the four-pointed starlike figures you see everywhere. Math majors no doubt recall that the hypocycloid is a curve traced by a point of the circumference of a circle rolling internally. In any event, it was originally developed in 1958 as a marketing tool for US Steel, representing the lightness, smartness, and versatility of steel. When the Steelers picked up the image in '62, the story goes, they weren't sure they liked it, so they placed the logo only on the right side of the helmet—where it remains today.

ALL-TIME TRIVIA QUESTION

Over the years, the Steelers have had players named Washington, Adams, Jefferson—even Nixon, Ford, and Carter. They've also had three Bradshaws, two Lamberts, and two Woodsons. Name them and their years.

FINALLY, THE GREATEST OF ALL TIME

It's a question that Chuck Noll always refused to answer when he was coaching: Winning four Super Bowls in six years, were the Steelers the best team in history?

Retired and away from the battlefield, Noll is more pensive and expansive. "I would like to think that," he says. "From that time, we played exceptionally well, we had good football players who were good people. We had a coaching staff that prepared them very well. We had a group of people who worked very well together. We had that spark. It was something to see, to experience—something you remember."

Franco Harris (left) and Joe Greene hoist Chuck Noll on their shoulders after their Super Bowl IX victory.

ALL-TIME TRIVIA ANSWER

Charley Bradshaw, 1961-66

Jim Bradshaw, 1963-67

Terry Bradshaw, 1970-83

Frank Lambert, 1965-66

Jack Lambert, 1974-84

Marv Woodson, 1964-69

Rod Woodson, 1987-96

FIVE WHO SURPRISED THE SUPERSCOUT

Jack Butler played—brilliantly—in the 1950s. Then he scouted, first for the Steelers, then for the Blesto talent combine. In a half-century, he has seen more football players than he can count. Known for having a good eye for the kinds of qualities that are actually visible in a player, Butler admits to sometimes missing those more intangible qualities that must be sensed on intuition. Here are five stars who surprised the superscout:

Andy Russell: "I could never figure out how he did what he did. When I scouted him, I said, 'You really want to draft this guy? As a linebacker?' He's not very big."

Jack Lambert: "Big, skinny guy—there's no way in the world he could play middle linebacker. I never thought he'd be as good as he was."

Rocky Bleier: "He broke all the rules. He shouldn't have been playing. He shouldn't have been on the team. What can you say? You can't measure the heart or the head."

Jack Ham: "He sits there, and they'd start a play, and he's hardly moving, and he gets by the blockers like nothing, all at once he makes a tackle. How he did it, I'll never know."

Mike Webster: "I thought, 'No way—too short, no speed, no quickness.' He's an ordinary guy. He turned out to be a great football player. So nobody knows everything."

Jack Lambert, intense on the bench.

YEAR-BY-YEAR RESULTS

1995
BILL COWHER, Head Coach

		Steelers	Opp.	
9/ 3	Detroit	23	20	[W]
9/10	at Houston	34	17	[W]
9/18	at Miami	10	23	[L]
9/24	Minnesota	24	44	[L]
10/ 1	San Diego	31	16	[W]
10/ 8	at Jacksonville	16	20	[L]
10/19	Cincinnati	9	27	[L]
10/29	Jacksonville	24	7	[W]
11/ 5	at Chicago (OT)	37	34	[W]
11/13	Cleveland	20	3	[W]
11/19	at Cincinnati	49	31	[W]
11/26	at Cleveland	20	17	[W]
12/ 3	Houston	21	7	[W]
12/10	at Oakland	29	10	[W]
12/16	New England	41	27	[W]
12/24	at Green Bay	19	24	[L]

W 11, L 5 (H 6-2, A 5-3)   407   327

AFC Playoff Game

1/ 6	Buffalo	40	21	[W]

AFC Championship Game

1/14	Indianapolis	20	16	[W]

Super Bowl XXX

1/28	Dallas	17	27	[L]

1994
BILL COWHER, Head Coach

		Steelers	Opp.	
9/ 4	Dallas	9	26	[L]
9/11	at Cleveland	17	10	[W]
9/18	Indianapolis	31	21	[W]
9/25	at Seattle	13	30	[L]
10/ 3	Houston	30	14	[W]
10/16	Cincinnati	14	10	[W]
10/23	at New York Giants	10	6	[W]
10/30	at Arizona (OT)	17	20	[L]
11/ 6	at Houston (OT)	12	9	[W]
11/14	Buffalo	23	10	[W]
11/20	Miami (OT)	16	13	[W]
11/27	at L.A. Raiders	21	3	[W]
12/ 4	at Cincinnati	38	15	[W]
12/11	Philadelphia	14	3	[W]
12/18	Cleveland	17	7	[W]
12/24	at San Diego	34	37	[L]

W 12, L 4 (H 7-1, A 5-3)   316   234

AFC Playoff Game

1/ 7	Cleveland	29	9	[W]

AFC Championship Game

1/15	San Diego	13	17	[L]

1993
BILL COWHER, Head Coach

		Steelers	Opp.	
9/ 5	San Francisco	13	24	[L]
9/12	at Los Angeles Rams	0	27	[L]
9/19	Cincinnati	34	7	[W]
9/27	at Atlanta	45	17	[W]
10/ 3	AFC Central idle			
10/10	San Diego	16	3	[W]
10/17	New Orleans	37	14	[W]
10/24	at Cleveland	23	28	[L]
10/31	AFC Central idle			
11/ 7	at Cincinnati	24	16	[W]
11/15	Buffalo	23	0	[W]
11/21	at Denver	13	37	[L]
11/28	at Houston	3	23	[L]
12/ 5	New England	17	14	[W]
12/13	at Miami	21	20	[W]
12/19	Houston	17	26	[L]
12/26	at Seattle	6	16	[L]
1/ 2	Cleveland	16	9	[W]

W 9, L 7 (H 6-2, A 3-5)   308   281

AFC Wild Card Playoff Game

1/ 8	at Kansas City (OT)	24	27	[L]

1992
BILL COWHER, Head Coach

		Steelers	Opp.	
9/ 6	at Houston	29	24	[W]
9/13	New York Jets	27	10	[W]
9/20	at San Diego	23	6	[W]
9/27	at Green Bay	3	17	[L]
10/ 4	AFC Central idle			
10/11	at Cleveland	9	17	[L]
10/19	Cincinnati	20	0	[W]
10/25	at Kansas City	27	3	[W]
11/ 1	Houston	21	20	[W]
11/ 8	at Buffalo	20	28	[L]
11/15	Detroit	17	14	[W]
11/22	Indianapolis	30	14	[W]
11/29	at Cincinnati	21	9	[W]
12/ 6	Seattle	20	14	[W]
12/13	at Chicago	6	30	[L]
12/20	Minnesota	3	6	[L]
12/27	Cleveland	23	13	[W]

W 11, L 5 (H 7-1, A 4-4)   299   225

AFC Playoff Game

1/ 9	Buffalo	3	24	[L]

1991
CHUCK NOLL, Head Coach

		Steelers	Opp.	
9/ 1	San Diego	26	20	[W]
9/ 8	at Buffalo	34	52	[L]
9/15	New England	20	6	[W]
9/22	at Philadelphia	14	23	[L]
9/29	AFC Central idle			
10/ 6	at Indianapolis	21	3	[W]
10/14	New York Giants	20	23	[L]
10/20	Seattle	7	27	[L]
10/27	at Cleveland	14	17	[L]
11/ 3	at Denver	13	20	[L]
11/10	at Cincinnati (OT)	33	27	[W]
11/17	Washington	14	41	[L]
11/24	Houston	26	14	[W]
11/28	at Dallas	10	20	[L]
12/ 8	at Houston	6	31	[L]
12/15	Cincinnati	17	10	[W]
12/22	Cleveland	17	10	[W]

W 7, L 9 (H 5-3, A 2-6)   292   344

1990
CHUCK NOLL, Head Coach

		Steelers	Opp.	
9/ 9	at Cleveland	3	13	[L]
9/16	Houston	20	9	[W]
9/23	at L.A. Raiders	3	20	[L]
9/30	Miami	6	28	[L]
10/ 7	San Diego	36	14	[W]
10/14	at Denver	34	17	[W]
10/21	at San Francisco	7	27	[L]
10/29	L.A. Rams	41	10	[W]
11/ 4	Atlanta	21	9	[W]
11/11	AFC Central idle			
11/18	at Cincinnati	3	27	[L]
11/25	at New York Jets	24	7	[W]
12/ 2	Cincinnati	12	16	[L]
12/ 9	** New England	24	3	[W]
12/16	at New Orleans	9	6	[W]
12/23	Cleveland	35	0	[W]
12/30	at Houston	14	34	[L]

W 9, L 7 (H 6-2, A 3-5)   292   240

★★Noll's 200th win

1989
CHUCK NOLL, Head Coach

		Steelers	Opp.	
9/10	Cleveland	0	51	[L]
9/17	at Cincinnati	10	41	[L]
9/24	Minnesota	27	14	[W]
10/ 1	at Detroit	23	3	[W]
10/ 8	Cincinnati	16	26	[L]
10/15	at Cleveland	17	7	[W]
10/22	at Houston	0	27	[L]
10/29	Kansas City	23	17	[W]
11/ 5	at Denver	7	34	[L]
11/12	Chicago	0	20	[L]
11/19	San Diego	20	17	[W]
11/26	at Miami	34	14	[W]
12/ 3	Houston	16	23	[L]
12/10	at New York Jets	13	0	[W]
12/17	New England	28	10	[W]
12/24	at Tampa Bay	31	22	[W]

W 9, L 7 (H 4-4, A 5-3)   265   326

AFC Wild Card Playoff Game

12/31	at Houston (OT)	26	23	[W]

AFC Playoff Game

1/ 7	at Denver	23	24	[L]

1988
CHUCK NOLL, Head Coach

		Steelers	Opp.	
9/ 4	Dallas	24	21	[W]
9/11	at Washington	29	30	[L]
9/18	Cincinnati	12	17	[L]
9/25	at Buffalo	28	36	[L]
10/ 2	Cleveland	9	23	[L]
10/ 9	at Phoenix	14	31	[L]
10/16	Houston	14	34	[L]
10/23	Denver	39	21	[W]
10/30	at New York Jets	20	24	[L]
11/ 6	at Cincinnati	7	42	[L]
11/13	Philadelphia	26	27	[L]
11/20	at Cleveland	7	27	[L]
11/27	Kansas City	16	10	[W]
12/ 4	at Houston	37	34	[W]
12/11	at San Diego	14	20	[L]
12/18	Miami	40	24	[W]

W 5, L 11 (H 4-4, A 1-7)   336   421

1987
CHUCK NOLL, Head Coach

		Steelers	Opp.	
9/13	San Francisco	30	17	[W]
9/20	at Cleveland	10	34	[L]
9/27	New York Jets		(Cancelled)	
10/ 4	at Atlanta	28	12	[W]
10/11	at Los Angeles Rams	21	31	[L]
10/18	Indianapolis	21	7	[W]
10/25	Cincinnati	23	20	[W]

		Steelers	Opp.	
11/ 1	at Miami	24	35	[L]
11/ 8	at Kansas City	17	16	[W]
11/15	Houston	3	23	[L]
11/22	at Cincinnati	30	16	[W]
11/29	New Orleans	16	20	[L]
12/ 6	Seattle	13	9	[W]
12/13	at San Diego	20	16	[W]
12/20	at Houston	16	24	[L]
12/26	Cleveland	13	19	[L]

W 8, L 7 (H 4-3, A 4-4) — 285 299

1986
CHUCK NOLL, Head Coach

		Steelers	Opp.	
9/ 7	at Seattle	0	30	[L]
9/15	Denver	10	21	[L]
9/21	at Minnesota	7	31	[L]
9/28	at Houston (OT)	22	16	[W]
10/ 5	Cleveland	24	27	[L]
10/13	at Cincinnati	22	24	[L]
10/19	New England	0	34	[L]
10/26	Cincinnati	30	9	[W]
11/ 2	Green Bay	27	3	[W]
11/ 9	at Buffalo	12	16	[L]
11/16	Houston	21	10	[W]
11/23	at Cleveland (OT)	31	37	[L]
11/30	at Chicago (OT)	10	13	[L]
12/ 7	Detroit	27	17	[W]
12/13	at New York Jets	45	24	[W]
12/21	Kansas City	19	24	[L]

W 6, L 10 (H 4-4, A 2-6) — 307 336

1985
CHUCK NOLL, Head Coach

		Steelers	Opp.	
9/ 8	Indianapolis	45	3	[W]
9/16	at Cleveland	7	17	[L]
9/22	Houston	20	0	[W]
9/30	Cincinnati	24	37	[L]
10/ 6	at Miami	20	24	[L]
10/13	at Dallas	13	27	[L]
10/20	St. Louis	23	10	[W]
10/27	at Cincinnati	21	26	[L]
11/ 3	Cleveland	10	9	[W]
11/10	at Kansas City	36	28	[W]
11/17	at Houston	30	7	[W]
11/24	Washington	23	30	[L]
12/ 1	Denver	23	31	[L]
12/ 8	at San Diego	44	54	[L]
12/15	Buffalo	30	24	[W]
12/21	at New York Giants	10	28	[L]

W 7, L 9 (H 5-3, A 2-6) — 379 355

1984
CHUCK NOLL, Head Coach

		Steelers	Opp.	
9/ 2	Kansas City	27	37	[L]
9/ 6	at New York Jets	23	17	[W]
9/16	Los Angeles Rams	24	14	[W]
9/23	at Cleveland	10	20	[L]
10/ 1	** Cincinnati	38	17	[W]
10/ 7	Miami	7	31	[L]
10/14	at San Francisco	20	17	[W]
10/21	at Indianapolis	16	17	[L]
10/28	Atlanta	35	10	[W]
11/ 4	Houston	35	7	[W]
11/11	at Cincinnati	20	22	[L]
11/19	at New Orleans	24	27	[L]
11/25	San Diego	52	24	[W]
12/ 2	at Houston (OT)	20	23	[L]
12/ 9	Cleveland	23	20	[W]
12/16	at L.A. Raiders	13	7	[W]

W 9, L 7 (H 6-2, A 3-5) — 387 310

**Noll's 150th win

AFC Playoff Game

12/30	at Denver	24	17	[W]

AFC Championship Game

1/ 6	at Miami	28	45	[L]

1983
CHUCK NOLL, Head Coach

		Steelers	Opp.	
9/ 4	Denver	10	14	[L]
9/11	at Green Bay	25	21	[W]
9/18	at Houston	40	28	[W]
9/25	New England	23	28	[L]
10/ 2	Houston	17	10	[W]
10/10	at Cincinnati	24	14	[W]
10/16	Cleveland	44	17	[W]
10/23	at Seattle	27	21	[W]
10/30	Tampa Bay	17	12	[W]
11/ 6	San Diego	26	3	[W]
11/13	at Baltimore	24	13	[W]
11/20	Minnesota	14	17	[L]
11/24	at Detroit	3	45	[L]
12/ 4	Cincinnati	10	23	[L]
12/10	at New York Jets	34	7	[W]
12/18	at Cleveland	17	30	[L]

W 10, L 6 (H 4-4, A 6-2) — 355 303

AFC Playoff Game

1/ 1	at L.A. Raiders	10	38	[L]

1982
CHUCK NOLL, Head Coach

		Steelers	Opp.	
9/13	at Dallas	36	28	[W]
9/19	Cincinnati (OT)	26	20	[W]
9/26	New York Giants			(Cancelled)
10/ 3	at Denver			(Cancelled)
10/11	Philadelphia			(Cancelled)
10/17	at Washington			(Cancelled)
10/24	Cleveland			(Postponed)
10/31	at Cincinnati			(Cancelled)
11/ 7	Houston			(Cancelled)
11/14	New York Jets			(Cancelled)
11/21	at Houston	24	10	[W]
11/28	at Seattle	0	16	[L]
12/ 5	Kansas City	35	14	[W]
12/12	at Buffalo	0	13	[L]
12/19	at Cleveland	9	10	[L]
12/26	New England	37	14	[W]
1/ 2	Cleveland	37	21	[W]

W 6, L 3 (H 4-0, A 2-3) — 204 146

AFC Tournament

1/ 9	San Diego	28	31	[L]

1981
CHUCK NOLL, Head Coach

		Steelers	Opp.	
9/ 6	Kansas City	33	37	[L]
9/10	at Miami	10	30	[L]
9/20	New York Jets	38	10	[W]
9/27	New England (OT)	27	21	[W]
10/ 4	at New Orleans	20	6	[W]
10/11	Cleveland	13	7	[W]
10/18	at Cincinnati	7	34	[L]
10/26	Houston	26	13	[W]
11/ 1	San Francisco	14	17	[L]
11/ 8	at Seattle	21	24	[L]
11/15	at Atlanta	34	20	[W]
11/22	at Cleveland	32	10	[W]
11/29	Los Angeles	24	0	[W]
12/ 7	at Oakland	27	30	[L]
12/13	Cincinnati	10	17	[L]
12/20	at Houston	20	21	[L]

W 8, L 8 (H 5-3, A 3-5) — 356 297

1980
CHUCK NOLL, Head Coach

		Steelers	Opp.	
9/ 7	Houston	31	17	[W]
9/14	at Baltimore	20	17	[W]
9/21	at Cincinnati	28	30	[L]
9/28	Chicago	38	3	[W]
10/ 5	at Minnesota	23	17	[W]
10/12	Cincinnati	16	17	[L]
10/20	Oakland	34	45	[L]
10/26	at Cleveland	26	27	[L]
11/ 2	Green Bay	22	20	[W]
11/ 9	at Tampa Bay	24	21	[W]
11/16	Cleveland	16	13	[W]
11/23	at Buffalo	13	28	[L]
11/30	Miami	23	10	[W]
12/ 4	at Houston	0	6	[L]
12/14	Kansas City	21	16	[W]
12/22	at San Diego	17	26	[L]

W 9, L 7 (H 6-2, A 3-5) — 352 313

1979
CHUCK NOLL, Head Coach

		Steelers	Opp.	
*9/ 3	at New England (OT)	16	13	[W]
9/ 9	Houston	38	7	[W]
9/16	at St. Louis	24	21	[W]
9/23	Baltimore	17	13	[W]
9/30	at Philadelphia	14	17	[L]
10/ 7	at Cleveland	51	35	[W]
10/14	at Cincinnati	10	34	[L]
10/22	Denver	42	7	[W]
10/28	Dallas	14	3	[W]
11/ 4	Washington	38	7	[W]
11/11	at Kansas City	30	3	[W]
11/18	at San Diego	7	35	[L]
11/25	Cleveland (OT)	33	30	[W]
12/ 2	Cincinnati	37	17	[W]
12/10	at Houston	17	20	[L]
12/16	Buffalo	28	0	[W]

W 12, L 4 (H 8-0, A 4-4) — 416 262

*Noll's 100th win

AFC Playoff Game

12/30	Miami	34	14	[W]

AFC Championship Game

1/ 6	Houston	27	13	[W]

SUPER BOWL XIV (Pasadena, Ca.)

1/20	Los Angeles	31	19	[W]

1978
CHUCK NOLL, Head Coach

		Steelers	Opp.	
9/ 3	at Buffalo	28	17	[W]
9/10	Seattle	21	10	[W]
9/17	at Cincinnati	28	3	[W]
9/24	Cleveland (OT)	15	9	[W]
10/ 1	at New York Jets	28	17	[W]
10/ 8	Atlanta	31	7	[W]
10/15	at Cleveland	34	14	[W]
10/23	Houston	17	24	[L]
10/29	Kansas City	27	24	[W]
11/ 5	New Orleans	20	14	[W]
11/12	at Los Angeles	7	10	[L]
11/19	Cincinnati	7	6	[W]
11/27	at San Francisco	24	7	[W]
12/ 3	at Houston	13	3	[W]
12/ 9	Baltimore	35	13	[W]
12/16	at Denver	21	17	[W]

W 14, L 2 (H 7-1, A 7-1) — 356 195

AFC Playoff Game

12/30	Denver	33	10	[W]

AFC Championship Game

1/ 7	Houston	34	5	[W]

SUPER BOWL XIII (Miami, Fla.)

1/21	Dallas	35	31	[W]

1977
CHUCK NOLL, Head Coach

		Steelers	Opp.	
9/19	San Francisco	27	0	[W]
9/25	Oakland	7	16	[L]
10/ 2	at Cleveland	28	14	[W]
10/ 9	at Houston	10	27	[L]
10/17	Cincinnati	20	14	[W]
10/23	Houston	27	10	[W]
10/30	at Baltimore	21	31	[L]
11/ 6	at Denver	7	21	[L]
11/13	Cleveland	35	31	[W]
11/20	Dallas	28	13	[W]
11/27	at New York Jets	23	20	[W]
12/ 4	Seattle	30	20	[W]
12/10	at Cincinnati	10	17	[L]
12/18	at San Diego	10	9	[W]

W 9, L 5 (H 6-1, A 3-4) 283 243

AFC Playoff Game

12/24	at Denver	21	34	[L]

1976
CHUCK NOLL, Head Coach

		Steelers	Opp.	
9/12	at Oakland	28	31	[L]
9/19	Cleveland	31	14	[W]
9/26	New England	27	30	[L]
10/ 4	at Minnesota	6	17	[L]
10/10	at Cleveland	16	18	[L]
10/17	Cincinnati	23	6	[W]
10/24	at New York Giants	27	0	[W]
10/31	San Diego	23	0	[W]
11/ 7	at Kansas City	45	0	[W]
11/14	Miami	14	3	[W]
11/21	Houston	32	16	[W]
11/28	at Cincinnati	7	3	[W]
12/ 5	Tampa Bay	42	0	[W]
12/11	at Houston	21	0	[W]

W 10, L 4 (H 6-1, A 4-3) 342 138

AFC Playoff Game

12/19	at Baltimore	40	14	[W]

AFC Championship Game

12/26	at Oakland	7	24	[L]

1975
CHUCK NOLL, Head Coach

		Steelers	Opp.	
9/21	at San Diego	37	0	[W]
9/28	Buffalo	21	30	[L]
10/ 5	at Cleveland	42	6	[W]
10/12	Denver	20	9	[W]
10/19	Chicago	34	3	[W]
10/26	at Green Bay	16	13	[W]
11/ 2	at Cincinnati	30	24	[W]
11/ 9	Houston	24	17	[W]
11/16	Kansas City	28	3	[W]
11/24	at Houston	32	9	[W]
11/30	at New York Jets	20	7	[W]
12/ 7	Cleveland	31	17	[W]
12/13	Cincinnati	35	14	[W]
12/20	at Los Angeles	3	10	[L]

W 12, L 2 (H 6-1, A 6-1) 373 162

AFC Playoff Game

12/27	Baltimore	28	10	[W]

AFC Championship Game

1/ 4	Oakland	16	10	[W]

SUPER BOWL X (Miami, Fla.)

1/18	Dallas	21	17	[W]

1974
CHUCK NOLL, Head Coach

		Steelers	Opp.	
9/15	Baltimore	30	0	[W]
9/22	at Denver (OT)	35	35	[T]

9/29	Oakland	0	17	[L]
10/ 6	at Houston	13	7	[W]
10/13	at Kansas City	34	24	[W]
10/20	Cleveland	20	16	[W]
10/28	Atlanta	24	17	[W]
11/ 3	Philadelphia	27	0	[W]
11/10	at Cincinnati	10	17	[L]
11/17	at Cleveland	26	16	[W]
11/25	at New Orleans	28	7	[W]
12/ 1	Houston	10	13	[L]
12/ 8	at New England	21	17	[W]
12/14	Cincinnati	27	3	[W]

W 10, L 3, T 1 (H 5-2, A 5-1-1) 305 189

AFC Playoff Game

12/22	Buffalo	32	14	[W]

AFC Championship Game

12/29	at Oakland	24	13	[W]

SUPER BOWL IX (New Orleans, La.)

1/12	Minnesota	16	6	[W]

1973
CHUCK NOLL, Head Coach

		Steelers	Opp.	
9/16	Detroit	24	10	[W]
9/23	Cleveland	33	6	[W]
9/30	at Houston	36	7	[W]
10/ 7	San Diego	38	21	[W]
10/14	at Cincinnati	7	19	[L]
10/21	New York Jets	26	14	[W]
10/28	Cincinnati	20	13	[W]
11/ 5	Washington	21	16	[W]
11/11	at Oakland	17	9	[W]
11/18	Denver	13	23	[L]
11/25	at Cleveland	16	21	[L]
12/ 3	at Miami	26	30	[L]
12/ 9	Houston	33	7	[W]
12/15	at San Francisco	37	14	[W]

W 10, L 4 (H 7-1, A 3-3) 347 210

AFC Wild Card Playoff Game

12/22	at Oakland	14	33	[L]

1972
CHUCK NOLL, Head Coach

		Steelers	Opp.	
9/17	Oakland	34	28	[W]
9/24	at Cincinnati	10	15	[L]
10/ 1	at St. Louis	25	19	[W]
10/ 8	at Dallas	13	17	[L]
10/15	Houston	24	7	[W]
10/22	New England	33	3	[W]
10/29	at Buffalo	38	21	[W]
11/ 5	Cincinnati	40	17	[W]
11/12	Kansas City	16	7	[W]
11/19	at Cleveland	24	26	[L]
11/26	Minnesota	23	10	[W]
12/ 3	Cleveland	30	0	[W]
12/10	at Houston	9	3	[W]
12/17	at San Diego	24	2	[W]

W 11, L 3 (H 7-0, A 4-3) 343 175

AFC Playoff Game

12/23	Oakland	13	7	[W]

AFC Championship Game

12/31	Miami	17	21	[L]

1971
CHUCK NOLL, Head Coach

		Steelers	Opp.	
9/19	at Chicago	15	17	[L]
9/26	Cincinnati	21	10	[W]
10/ 3	San Diego	21	17	[W]
10/10	at Cleveland	17	27	[L]
10/18	at Kansas City	16	38	[L]
10/24	Houston	23	16	[W]
10/31	at Baltimore	21	34	[L]

11/ 7	Cleveland	26	9	[W]
11/14	at Miami	21	24	[L]
11/21	New York Giants	17	13	[W]
11/28	Denver	10	22	[L]
12/ 5	at Houston	3	29	[L]
12/12	at Cincinnati	21	13	[W]
12/19	Los Angeles	14	23	[L]

W 6, L 8 (H 5-2, A 1-6) 246 292

1970
CHUCK NOLL, Head Coach

		Steelers	Opp.	
9/20	Houston	7	19	[L]
9/27	at Denver	13	16	[L]
10/ 3	at Cleveland	7	15	[L]
10/11	Buffalo	23	10	[W]
10/18	at Houston	7	3	[W]
10/25	at Oakland	14	31	[L]
11/ 2	Cincinnati	21	10	[W]
11/ 8	New York Jets	21	17	[W]
11/15	Kansas City	14	31	[L]
11/22	at Cincinnati	7	34	[L]
11/29	Cleveland	28	9	[W]
12/ 6	Green Bay	12	20	[L]
12/13	at Atlanta	16	27	[L]
12/20	at Philadelphia	20	30	[L]

W 5, L 9 (H 4-3, A 1-6) 210 272

1969
CHUCK NOLL, Head Coach

		Steelers	Opp.	
9/21	Detroit	16	13	[W]
9/28	at Philadelphia	27	41	[L]
10/ 5	St. Louis	14	27	[L]
10/12	at New York	7	10	[L]
10/18	at Cleveland	31	42	[L]
10/26	Washington	7	14	[L]
11/ 2	Green Bay	34	38	[L]
11/ 9	at Chicago	7	38	[L]
11/16	Cleveland	3	24	[L]
11/23	at Minnesota	14	52	[L]
11/30	at St. Louis	10	47	[L]
12/ 7	Dallas	7	10	[L]
12/14	New York	17	21	[L]
12/21	at New Orleans	24	27	[L]

W 1, L 13 (H 1-6, A 0-7) 218 404

1968
BILL AUSTIN, Head Coach

		Steelers	Opp.	
9/15	New York	20	34	[L]
9/22	at Los Angeles	10	45	[L]
9/29	Baltimore	7	41	[L]
10/ 5	at Cleveland	24	31	[L]
10/13	at Washington	13	16	[L]
10/20	New Orleans	12	16	[L]
10/27	Philadelphia	6	3	[W]
11/ 3	at Atlanta	41	21	[W]
11/10	at St. Louis	28	28	[T]
11/17	Cleveland	24	45	[L]
11/24	San Francisco	28	45	[L]
12/ 1	St. Louis	10	20	[L]
12/ 8	at Dallas	7	28	[L]
12/15	at New Orleans	14	24	[L]

W 2, L 11, T 1 (H 1-6, A 1-5-1) 244 397

1967
BILL AUSTIN, Head Coach

		Steelers	Opp.	
9/17	Chicago	41	13	[W]
9/24	St. Louis	14	28	[L]
10/ 1	at Philadelphia	24	34	[L]
10/ 7	at Cleveland	10	21	[L]
10/15	New York	24	27	[L]

		Steelers	Opp.	
10/22	Dallas	21	24	[L]
10/29	at New Orleans	14	10	[W]
11/ 5	Cleveland	14	34	[L]
11/12	at St. Louis	14	14	[T]
11/19	at New York	20	28	[L]
11/26	Minnesota	27	41	[L]
12/ 3	at Detroit	24	14	[W]
12/10	Washington	10	15	[L]
12/17	at Green Bay	24	17	[W]

W 4, L 9, T 1 (H 1-6, A 3-3-1) 281 320

1966
BILL AUSTIN, Head Coach

		Steelers	Opp.	
9/11	New York	34	34	[T]
9/18	Detroit	17	3	[W]
9/25	Washington	27	33	[L]
10/ 2	at Washington	10	24	[L]
10/ 8	at Cleveland	10	41	[L]
10/16	Philadelphia	14	31	[L]
10/30	at Dallas	21	52	[L]
11/ 6	Cleveland	16	6	[W]
11/13	St. Louis	30	9	[W]
11/20	Dallas	7	20	[L]
11/27	at St. Louis	3	6	[L]
12/ 4	at Philadelphia	23	27	[L]
12/11	at New York	47	28	[W]
12/18	at Atlanta	57	33	[W]

W 5, L 8, T 1 (H 3-3-1, A 2-5) 316 347

1965
MIKE NIXON, Head Coach

		Steelers	Opp.	
9/19	Green Bay	9	41	[L]
9/26	at San Francisco	17	27	[L]
10/ 3	New York	13	23	[L]
10/ 9	at Cleveland	19	24	[L]
10/17	St. Louis	7	20	[L]
10/24	at Philadelphia	20	14	[W]
10/31	Dallas	22	13	[W]
11/ 7	at St. Louis	17	21	[L]
11/ 4	at Dallas	17	24	[L]
11/21	Washington	3	31	[L]
11/28	Cleveland	21	42	[L]
12/ 5	at New York	10	35	[L]
12/12	Philadelphia	13	47	[L]
12/19	at Washington	14	35	[L]

W 2, L 12 (H 1-6, A 1-6) 202 397

1964
BUDDY PARKER, Head Coach

		Steelers	Opp.	
9/13	Los Angeles	14	26	[L]
9/20	New York	27	24	[W]
9/27	Dallas	23	17	[W]
10/ 4	at Philadelphia	7	21	[L]
10/10	at Cleveland	23	7	[W]
10/18	at Minnesota	10	30	[L]
10/25	Philadelphia	10	34	[L]
11/ 1	Cleveland	17	30	[L]
11/ 8	at St. Louis	30	34	[L]
11/15	Washington	0	30	[L]
11/22	at New York	44	17	[W]
11/29	St. Louis	20	21	[L]
12/ 6	at Washington	14	7	[W]
12/13	at Dallas	14	17	[L]

W 5, L 9 (H 2-5, A 3-4) 253 315

1963
BUDDY PARKER, Head Coach

		Steelers	Opp.	
9/15	at Philadelphia	21	21	[T]
9/22	New York	31	0	[W]
9/29	St. Louis	23	10	[W]
10/ 5	at Cleveland	23	35	[L]
10/13	at St. Louis	23	24	[L]
10/20	Washington	38	27	[W]
10/27	Dallas	27	21	[W]
11/ 3	at Green Bay	14	33	[L]
11/10	Cleveland	9	7	[W]
11/17	at Washington	34	28	[W]
11/24	Chicago	17	17	[T]
12/ 1	Philadelphia	20	20	[T]
12/ 8	at Dallas	24	19	[W]
12/15	at New York	17	33	[L]

W 7, L 4, T 3 (H 5-0-2, A 2-4-1) 321 295

1962
BUDDY PARKER, Head Coach

		Steelers	Opp.	
9/16	at Detroit	7	45	[L]
9/23	at Dallas	30	28	[W]
9/30	New York	27	31	[L]
10/ 6	Philadelphia	13	7	[W]
10/14	at New York	20	17	[W]
10/21	Dallas	27	42	[L]
10/28	Cleveland	14	41	[L]
11/ 4	Minnesota	39	31	[W]
11/11	at St. Louis	26	17	[W]
11/18	Washington	23	21	[W]
11/25	at Cleveland	14	35	[L]
12/ 2	St. Louis	19	7	[W]
12/ 9	at Philadelphia	26	17	[W]
12/16	at Washington	27	24	[W]

W 9, L 5 (H 4-3, A 5-2) 312 363

Playoff Bowl (Miami, Fla.)

1/ 6	Detroit	10	17	[L]

1961
BUDDY PARKER, Head Coach

		Steelers	Opp.	
9/17	at Dallas	24	27	[L]
9/24	New York	14	17	[L]
10/ 1	at Los Angeles	14	24	[L]
10/ 8	at Philadelphia	16	21	[L]
10/15	Washington	20	0	[W]
10/22	Cleveland	28	30	[L]
10/29	San Francisco	20	10	[W]
11/ 5	at Cleveland	17	13	[W]
11/12	Dallas	37	7	[W]
11/19	at New York	21	42	[L]
11/26	St. Louis	30	27	[W]
12/ 3	Philadelphia	24	35	[L]
12/10	at Washington	30	14	[W]
12/17	at St. Louis	0	20	[L]

W 6, L 8 (H 4-3, A 2-5) 295 287

1960
BUDDY PARKER, Head Coach

		Steelers	Opp.	
9/24	at Dallas	35	28	[W]
10/ 2	at Cleveland	20	28	[L]
10/ 9	New York	17	19	[L]
10/16	St. Louis	27	14	[W]
10/23	at Washington	27	27	[T]
10/30	Green Bay	13	19	[L]
11/ 6	at Philadelphia	7	34	[L]
11/13	at New York	24	27	[L]
11/20	Cleveland	14	10	[W]
11/27	Washington	22	10	[W]
12/11	Philadelphia	27	21	[W]
12/18	at St. Louis	7	38	[L]

W 5, L 6, T 1 (H 4-2, A 1-4-1) 240 275

1959
BUDDY PARKER, Head Coach

		Steelers	Opp.	
9/26	Cleveland	17	7	[W]
10/ 4	Washington	17	23	[L]
10/11	at Philadelphia	24	28	[L]
10/18	at Washington	27	6	[W]
10/25	New York	16	21	[L]
11/ 1	at Chicago Cards	24	45	[L]
11/ 8	Detroit	10	10	[T]
11/15	at New York	14	9	[W]
11/22	at Cleveland	21	20	[W]
11/29	Philadelphia	31	0	[W]
12/ 6	at Chicago Bears	21	27	[L]
12/13	Chicago Cards	35	20	[W]

W 6, L 5, T 1 (H 3-2-1, A 3-3) 257 216

1958
BUDDY PARKER, Head Coach

		Steelers	Opp.	
9/28	at San Francisco	20	23	[L]
10/ 5	Cleveland	12	45	[L]
10/12	Philadelphia	24	3	[W]
10/19	at Cleveland	10	27	[L]
10/26	at New York	6	17	[L]
11/ 2	Washington	24	16	[W]
11/ 9	at Philadelphia	31	24	[W]
11/16	New York	31	10	[W]
11/23	at Chicago Cards	27	20	[W]
11/30	Chicago Bears	24	10	[W]
12/ 7	at Washington	14	14	[T]
12/13	Chicago Cards	38	21	[W]

W 7, L 4, T 1 (H 5-1, A 2-3-1) 261 230

1957
BUDDY PARKER, Head Coach

		Steelers	Opp.	
9/29	Washington	28	7	[W]
10/ 5	Cleveland	12	23	[L]
10/13	Chicago Cards	29	20	[W]
10/20	at New York	0	35	[L]
10/27	Philadelphia	6	0	[W]
11/ 3	at Baltimore	19	13	[L]
11/10	at Cleveland	0	24	[L]
11/24	Green Bay	10	27	[L]
12/ 1	at Philadelphia	6	7	[L]
12/ 7	New York	21	10	[W]
12/15	at Washington	3	10	[L]
12/22	at Chicago Cards	27	2	[W]

W 6, L 6 (H 4-2, A 2-4) 161 178

1956
WALT KIESLING, Head Coach

		Steelers	Opp.	
9/30	Washington	30	13	[W]
10/ 6	Cleveland	10	14	[L]
10/14	Philadelphia	21	35	[L]
10/21	at New York	10	38	[L]
10/28	at Cleveland	24	16	[W]
11/ 4	New York	14	17	[L]
11/11	at Philadelphia	7	14	[L]
11/18	Chicago Cards	14	7	[W]
11/25	at Chicago Cards	27	38	[L]
12/ 2	Los Angeles	30	13	[W]
12/ 9	at Detroit	7	45	[L]
12/16	at Washington	23	0	[W]

W 5, L 7 (H 3-3, A 2-4) 217 250

1955
WALT KIESLING, Head Coach

		Steelers	Opp.	
9/26	Chicago Cards	14	7	[W]
10/ 2	at Los Angeles	26	27	[L]
10/ 9	New York	30	23	[W]
10/15	Philadelphia	13	7	[W]
10/23	at New York	19	17	[W]
10/30	at Philadelphia	0	24	[L]
11/ 5	at Chicago Cards	13	27	[L]
11/13	Detroit	28	31	[L]
11/20	at Cleveland	14	41	[L]

		Steelers	Opp.	
11/27	Washington	14	23	[L]
12/ 4	Cleveland	7	30	[L]
12/11	at Washington	17	28	[L]
W 4, L 8 (H 3-3, A 1-5)		**195**	**285**	

1954
WALT KIESLING, Head Coach

		Steelers	Opp.	
9/26	at Green Bay	21	20	[W]
10/ 2	Washington	37	7	[W]
10/ 9	at Philadelphia	22	24	[L]
10/17	Cleveland	55	27	[W]
10/23	Philadelphia	17	7	[W]
10/31	at Chicago Cards	14	17	[L]
11/ 7	New York	6	30	[L]
11/14	at Washington	14	17	[L]
11/20	San Francisco	3	31	[L]
11/28	Chicago Cards	20	17	[W]
12/ 5	at New York	3	24	[L]
12/12	at Cleveland	7	42	[L]
W 5, L 7 (H 4-2, A 1-5)		**219**	**263**	

1953
JOE BACH, Head Coach

		Steelers	Opp.	
9/27	at Detroit	21	38	[L]
10/ 3	New York	24	14	[W]
10/11	Chicago Cards	31	28	[W]
10/17	at Philadelphia	7	23	[L]
10/24	Green Bay	31	14	[W]
11/ 1	Philadelphia	7	35	[L]
11/ 8	at Cleveland	16	34	[L]
11/15	at New York	14	10	[W]
11/22	Cleveland	16	20	[L]
11/29	Washington	9	17	[L]
12/ 6	at Chicago Cards	21	17	[W]
12/13	at Washington	14	13	[W]
W 6, L 6 (H 3-3, A 3-3)		**211**	**263**	

1952
JOE BACH, Head Coach

		Steelers	Opp.	
9/28	Philadelphia	25	31	[L]
10/ 4	Cleveland	20	21	[L]
10/12	at Philadelphia	21	26	[L]
10/19	Washington	24	28	[L]
10/26	at Chicago Cards	34	28	[W]
11/ 2	at Washington	24	23	[W]
11/ 9	Detroit	6	31	[L]
11/16	at Cleveland	28	29	[L]
11/23	Chicago Cards	17	14	[W]
11/30	New York	63	7	[W]
12/ 7	at San Francisco	24	7	[W]
12/14	at Los Angeles	14	28	[L]
W 5, L 7 (H 2-4, A 3-3)		**300**	**273**	

1951
JOHN MICHELOSEN, Head Coach

		Steelers	Opp.	
10/ 1	New York	13	13	[T]
10/ 7	at Green Bay	33	35	[L]
10/14	San Francisco	24	28	[L]
10/21	at Cleveland	0	17	[L]
10/28	at Chicago Cards	28	14	[W]
11/ 4	Philadelphia	13	34	[L]
11/11	Green Bay	28	7	[W]
11/18	Washington	7	22	[L]
11/25	at Philadelphia	17	13	[W]
12/ 2	at New York	0	14	[L]
12/ 9	Cleveland	0	28	[L]
12/16	at Washington	20	10	[W]
W 4, L 7, T 1 (H 1-4-1, A 3-3)		**183**	**235**	

1950
JOHN MICHELOSEN, Head Coach

		Steelers	Opp.	
9/17	New York	7	18	[L]
9/24	at Detroit	7	10	[L]
10/ 1	at Washington	26	7	[W]
10/ 7	Cleveland	17	30	[L]
10/15	at New York	17	6	[W]
10/22	Philadelphia	10	17	[L]
10/29	at Cleveland	7	45	[L]
11/ 5	at Philadelphia	9	7	[W]
11/12	Baltimore	17	7	[W]
11/23	at Chicago Cards	28	17	[W]
12/ 3	Washington	7	24	[L]
12/10	Chicago Cards	28	7	[W]
W 6, L 6 (H 2-4, A 4-2)		**180**	**195**	

1949
JOHN MICHELOSEN, Head Coach

		Steelers	Opp.	
9/25	New York Giants	28	7	[W]
10/ 3	Washington	14	27	[L]
10/ 8	Detroit	14	7	[W]
10/16	at New York Giants	21	17	[W]
10/23	New York Bulldogs	24	13	[W]
10/30	Philadelphia	7	38	[L]
11/ 6	at Washington	14	27	[L]
11/13	Los Angeles	7	7	[T]
11/20	at Green Bay	30	7	[W]
11/27	at Philadelphia	17	34	[L]
12/ 4	at Chicago Bears	21	30	[L]
12/11	at New York Bulldogs	27	0	[W]
W 6, L 5, T 1 (H 3-2-1, A 3-3)		**224**	**214**	

1948
JOHN MICHELOSEN, Head Coach

		Steelers	Opp.	
9/26	at Washington	14	17	[L]
10/ 3	Boston	24	14	[W]
10/10	Washington	10	7	[W]
10/17	at Boston	7	13	[L]
10/24	at New York	27	34	[L]
10/31	Philadelphia	7	34	[L]
11/ 7	Green Bay	38	7	[W]
11/14	Chicago Cards	7	24	[L]
11/21	at Detroit	14	17	[L]
11/28	at Philadelphia	0	17	[L]
12/ 5	New York	38	28	[W]
12/12	at Los Angeles	14	31	[L]
W 4, L 8 (H 4-2, A 0-6)		**200**	**243**	

1947
JOCK SUTHERLAND, Head Coach

		Steelers	Opp.	
9/21	Detroit	17	10	[W]
9/29	Los Angeles	7	48	[L]
10/ 5	at Washington	26	27	[L]
10/12	at Boston	30	14	[W]
10/19	Philadelphia	35	24	[W]
10/26	at New York	38	21	[W]
11/ 2	at Green Bay	18	17	[W]
11/ 9	Washington	21	14	[W]
11/16	New York	24	7	[W]
11/23	at Chicago Bears	7	49	[L]
11/30	at Philadelphia	0	21	[L]
12/ 7	Boston	17	7	[W]
W 8, L 4 (H 5-1, A 3-3)		**240**	**259**	
Eastern Division Playoff				
12/21	Philadelphia	0	21	[L]

1946
JOCK SUTHERLAND, Head Coach

		Steelers	Opp.	
9/20	Chicago Cards	14	7	[W]
9/29	at Washington	14	14	[T]
10/ 6	New York	14	17	[L]
10/13	Boston	16	7	[W]
10/20	at Green Bay	7	17	[L]
10/27	at Boston	33	7	[W]
11/ 3	Washington	14	7	[W]
11/10	at Detroit	7	17	[L]
11/17	Philadelphia	10	7	[W]
11/24	at New York	0	7	[L]
12/ 1	at Philadelphia	7	10	[L]
W 5, L 5 T 1 (H 4-1, A 1-4-1)		**136**	**117**	

1945
JIM LEONARD, Head Coach

		Steelers	Opp.	
9/25	at Boston	7	28	[L]
10/ 7	New York	6	34	[L]
10/14	Washington	0	14	[L]
10/21	at New York	21	7	[W]
10/28	Boston	6	10	[L]
11/ 4	Philadelphia	3	45	[L]
11/11	Chicago Cards	23	0	[W]
11/18	at Philadelphia	6	30	[L]
11/25	at Chicago Bears	7	28	[L]
12/ 2	at Washington	0	24	[L]
W 2, L 8 (H 1-4, A 1-4)		**79**	**220**	

1944★
WALT KIESLING and
PHIL HANDLER, Head Coaches

		Steelers	Opp.	
9/24	Cleveland	28	30	[L]
10/ 8	Green Bay	7	34	[L]
10/15	at Chicago Bears	7	34	[L]
10/22	at New York	0	23	[L]
10/29	at Washington	20	42	[L]
11/ 5	Detroit	6	27	[L]
11/12	at Detroit	7	21	[L]
11/19	** Cleveland	6	33	[L]
11/26	** Green Bay	20	35	[L]
12/ 3	Chicago Bears	7	49	[L]
W 0, L 10 (H 0-6, A 0-4)		**108**	**328**	

*Combined with Chicago Cards
**Home game played in Chicago

1943★
WALT KIESLING and
GREASY NEALE, Head Coaches

		Steelers	Opp.	
10/ 2	** Brooklyn	17	0	[W]
10/ 9	** New York	28	14	[W]
10/17	at Chicago Bears	21	48	[L]
10/24	at New York	14	42	[L]
10/31	Chicago Cards	34	13	[W]
11/ 7	** Washington	14	14	[T]
11/14	at Brooklyn	7	13	[L]
11/21	Detroit	35	34	[W]
11/28	at Washington	27	14	[W]
12/ 5	** Green Bay	28	38	[L]
W 5, L 4, T 1 (H 4-1-1, A 1-3)		**225**	**220**	

*Combined with Philadelphia Eagles
**Home game played in Philadelphia

1942
WALT KIESLING, Head Coach

		Steelers	Opp.	
9/13	Philadelphia	14	24	[L]
9/20	at Washington	14	24	[L]
10/ 4	New York	13	10	[W]
10/11	at Brooklyn	7	0	[W]
10/18	at Philadelphia	14	0	[W]
10/25	Washington	0	14	[L]
11/ 1	at New York	17	9	[W]
11/ 8	at Detroit	35	7	[W]
11/22	Chicago Cards	19	3	[W]
12/ 6	at Green Bay	21	24	[L]
W 7, L 4 (H 3-2, A 4-2)		**167**	**119**	

1941
BERT BELL, ALDO DONELLI and WALT KIESLING, Head Coaches

		Steelers	Opp.	
9/ 7	at Cleveland	14	17	[L]
9/21	Philadelphia	7	10	[L]
10/ 5	New York	10	37	[L]
10/12	Washington	20	24	[L]
10/19	at New York	7	28	[L]
10/26	at Chicago Bears	7	34	[L]
11/ 2	at Washington	3	23	[L]
11/ 9	at Philadelphia	7	7	[T]
11/16	Brooklyn	14	7	[W]
11/23	Green Bay	7	54	[L]
11/30	at Brooklyn	7	35	[L]

W 1, L 9, T 1 (H 1-4, A 0-5-1) 103 276

1940
WALT KIESLING, Head Coach

		Steelers	Opp.	
9/ 8	Chicago Cards	7	7	[T]
9/15	New York	10	10	[T]
9/22	at Detroit	10	7	[W]
9/29	Brooklyn	3	10	[L]
10/ 6	Washington	10	40	[L]
10/13	at Brooklyn	0	21	[L]
10/20	at New York	0	12	[L]
10/27	at Green Bay	3	24	[L]
11/ 3	at Washington	10	37	[L]
11/10	Philadelphia	7	3	[W]
11/28	at Philadelphia	0	7	[L]

W 2, L 7, T 2 (H 1-2-2, A 1-5) 60 178

1939
WALT KIESLING and JOHN BLOOD, Head Coaches

		Steelers	Opp.	
9/14	at Brooklyn	7	12	[L]
9/24	Chicago Cards	0	10	[L]
10/ 2	Chicago Bears	0	32	[L]
10/ 8	New York	7	14	[L]
10/15	at Washington	14	44	[L]
10/22	Washington	14	21	[L]
10/29	at Cleveland	14	14	[T]
11/ 5	at Brooklyn	13	17	[L]
11/19	at New York	7	23	[L]
11/23	at Philadelphia	14	17	[L]
11/26	Philadelphia	24	12	[W]

W 1, L 9, T 1 (H 1-4, A 0-5-1) 114 216

1938
JOHN BLOOD, Head Coach

		Steelers	Opp.	
9/ 9	at Detroit	7	16	[L]
9/11	New York	14	27	[L]
9/16	at Philadelphia	7	27	[L]
9/23	at Brooklyn	17	3	[W]
10/ 3	at New York	13	10	[W]
10/ 9	Brooklyn	7	17	[L]
10/23	at Green Bay	0	20	[L]
11/ 6	Washington	0	7	[L]
11/20	at Philadelphia	7	14	[L]
11/27	at Washington	0	15	[L]
12/ 4	at Cleveland	7	13	[L]

W 2, L 9 (H 0-3, A 2-6) 79 169

1937
JOHN BLOOD, Head Coach

		Steelers	Opp.	
9/ 5	Philadelphia	27	14	[W]
9/19	at Brooklyn	21	0	[W]
9/26	New York	7	10	[L]
10/ 4	Chicago Bears	0	7	[L]
10/10	at Detroit	3	7	[L]
10/17	at Washington	20	34	[L]
10/24	Chicago Cards	7	13	[L]
10/31	Philadelphia	16	7	[W]
11/ 7	at New York	0	17	[L]
11/14	Washington	21	13	[W]
11/21	Brooklyn	0	23	[L]

W 4, L 7, (H 3-4, A 1-3) 122 145

1936
JOE BACH, Head Coach

		Steelers	Opp.	
9/13	Boston	10	0	[W]
9/23	at Brooklyn	10	6	[W]
9/27	New York	10	7	[W]
10/ 4	Chicago Bears	9	27	[L]
10/14	Philadelphia	17	0	[W]
10/18	at Chicago Bears	6	26	[L]
10/25	at Green Bay	10	42	[L]
11/ 1	Brooklyn	10	7	[W]
11/ 5	at Philadelphia	6	0	[W]
11/ 8	at Detroit	3	28	[L]
11/15	at Chicago Cards	6	14	[L]
11/29	at Boston	0	30	[L]

W 6, L 6 (H 4-1, A 2-5) 97 187

1935
JOE BACH, Head Coach

		Steelers	Opp.	
9/13	at Philadelphia	17	7	[W]
9/22	New York	7	42	[L]
9/29	Chicago Bears	7	23	[L]
10/ 6	at Green Bay	0	27	[L]
10/ 9	Philadelphia	6	17	[L]
10/20	Chicago Cards	17	13	[W]
10/27	Boston	6	0	[W]
11/ 3	Brooklyn	7	13	[L]

1934
LUBY DiMELIO, Head Coach

		Steelers	Opp.	
11/10	at Brooklyn	16	7	[W]
11/24	Green Bay	14	34	[L]
12/ 1	at Boston	3	13	[L]
12/ 8	at New York	0	13	[L]

W 4, L 8 (H 2-5, A 2-3) 100 209

(1934 continued)

		Steelers	Opp.	
9/ 9	Cincinnati	13	0	[W]
9/16	Boston	0	7	[L]
9/26	Philadelphia	0	17	[L]
10/ 3	New York	12	14	[L]
10/ 7	at Philadelphia	9	7	[W]
10/10	Chicago Bears	0	28	[L]
10/14	at Boston	0	39	[L]
10/21	at New York	7	17	[L]
10/28	at Brooklyn	3	21	[L]
11/ 4	at Detroit	7	40	[L]
11/11	at St. Louis	0	6	[L]
11/18	Brooklyn	0	10	[L]

W 2, L 10 (H 1-5, A 1-5) 51 206

1933
JAP DOUDS, Head Coach

		Steelers	Opp.	
9/20	New York	2	23	[L]
9/27	Chicago Cards	14	13	[W]
10/ 4	Boston	6	21	[L]
10/11	Cincinnati	17	0	[W]
10/15	at Green Bay	0	47	[L]
10/22	at Cincinnati	0	0	[T]
10/29	at Boston	16	14	[W]
11/ 5	at Brooklyn	3	3	[T]
11/12	Brooklyn	0	32	[L]
11/19	at Philadelphia	6	25	[L]
12/ 3	at New York	3	27	[L]

W 3, L 6, T 2 (H 2-3, A 1-3-2) 67 205

The Steelers own a trio of Super Bowl MVPs: running back Franco Harris (left), Super Bowl IX; wide receiver Lynn Swann (center), Super Bowl X; quarterback Terry Bradshaw (right), Super Bowls XIII–XIV.

TEAM RECORDS

GAMES WON

Season   14 (1978)
Most Consecutive 12 (1978–79)
Most Consecutive (One Season) 11 (1975)

SCORING

Most Points
Season   416 (1979)
Game   63 (11–30–52 vs. N.Y. Giants)

Most Points Against
Season   421 (1988)
Game   54 (11–23–41 vs. Green Bay,
12–8–85 vs. San Diego)

Fewest Points
Season   51 (1934—12 games)
202 (1965—14 games)

Fewest Points Allowed
Season   138 (1976—14 games)
117 (1946—11 games)

Most Points, Both Teams
Game   98 (12–8–85, San Diego 54 vs.
Pittsburgh 44)
90 (12–18–66, Pittsburgh 57
vs. Atlanta 33)
86 (10–7–79, Pittsburgh 51
vs. Cleveland 35)

Fewest Points, Both Teams
Game   0 (1933, Pittsburgh 0 vs.
Cincinnati 0)

Most Touchdowns
Season   52 (1979)
Game   9 (11–30–52 vs. N.Y. Giants)

Most Touchdowns Against
Season   50 (1968, 1969)
Game   8 (11–23–41 vs. Green Bay,
12–8–85 vs. San Diego)

Fewest Touchdowns Against
Season   14 (1976)

Most Touchdowns Rushing
Season   33 (1976)
Game   5 (11–7–76 vs. K.C., 9–20–81
vs. New York Jets)

Most Touchdowns Rushing Against
Season   20 (1947, 1988)
Game   6 (10–24–53 vs. G.B.,
10–14–34 vs. Boston)

Fewest Touchdowns Rushing Against
Season   5 (1976)

Most Touchdowns Passing
Season   28 (1978)
Game   5 (11–30–52 vs. N.Y. Giants;
10–7–79 vs. Wash.;
11–15–81 vs. Atlanta;
9–8–85 vs. Indianapolis)

Most Touchdowns Passing Against
Season   34 (1962)
Game   6 (9–8–91 vs. Buffalo)

Fewest Touchdowns Passing Against
Season   9 (1990, 1976, 1975, 1972)

Most Touchdowns (Defensive)
Season   7 (1983, 1987)
Game   3 (10–10–83 vs. Cincinnati)

Most Points After Touchdown
Season   50 (1979)
Game   9 (11–30–52 vs. N.Y. Giants)

Most Points After Touchdown Against
Season   49 (1968, 1969)

Most Field Goals
Season   34 (1995)
Game   6 (10–23–88 vs. Denver)

Most Field Goals Against
Season   26 (1988, 1991)
Game   7 (9–24–67 vs. St. Louis)

FIRST DOWNS

Most First Downs
Season   344 (1995)
Game   36 (11–25–79 vs. Cleveland)

Most First Downs By Opponents
Season   323 (1981, 1989)
Game   35 (11–23–86 vs. Cleveland)

Most First Downs, Both Teams
Game   58 (11–25–79 Pittsburgh 36
vs. Cleveland 22)

Most First Downs Rushing
Season   163 (1976)
Game   21 (11–7–76 vs. K.C.)

**Most First Downs Rushing
by Opponents**
Season   122 (1965)
Game   18 (11–9–69 vs. Chicago)

Most First Downs Passing
Season   193 (1995)
Game   21 (12–13–58 vs. Chi. Cards)

**Most First Downs Passing
by Opponents**
Season   194 (1991)
Game   22 (12–5–48 vs. N.Y. Giants)

Most First Downs Penalties
Season   34 (1978, 1995)

**Most First Downs Penalties
by Opponents**
Season   40 (1978)

NET YARDS

Most Net Yards Gained
Season   6,258 (1979)
Game   683 (12–13–58 vs. Chi. Cards)

Fewest Net Yards Gained
Season   3,354 (1965)
Game   53 (9–10–89 vs. Cleveland)

Most Net Yards Gained by Opponents
Season   5,805 (1988)
Game   559 (11–6–88 vs. Cincinnati)

**Fewest Net Yards Gained
by Opponents**
Season   3,074 (1974)
Game   70 (10–27–57 vs. Phila.)

RUSHING

Most Yards Gained Rushing
Season   2,971 (1976)
Game   361 (10–7–79 vs. Cleveland)

Fewest Yards Gained Rushing
Season   1,092 (1966)
Game   7 (10–30–66 vs. Dallas)

**Most Yards Gained Rushing
by Opponents**
Season   2,193 (1954)
Game   426 (11–4–34 vs. Detroit)

**Fewest Yards Gained Rushing
by Opponents**
Season   1,125 (1953—12 games)
1,321 (1995—16 games)
1,368 (1993—16 games)
1,377 (1967—14 games)
Game   –33 (10–2–43 vs. Brooklyn)

**Fewest Yards Rushing Allowed
by Opponents (per game)**
Season   84.7 (1982)

Most Rushing Attempts
Season   653 (1976)
Game   60 (10–3–50 vs. Boston)

Fewest Rushing Attempts
Season   368 (1954—12 games)
375 (1966—14 games)
Game   14 (9–30–90 vs. Miami,
11–17–91 vs. Washington)

Most Rushing Attempts by Opponents
Season   516 (1988)

**Fewest Rushing Attempts
by Opponents**
Season   363 (1962)
Game   10 (10–1–89 vs. Detroit)

PASSING

Most Yards Gained Passing
Season   3,917 (1995)
Game   472 (12–13–58 vs. Chi. Cards)

Fewest Yards Gained Passing
Season   652 (1945—11 games)
1,711 (1972—14 games)
Game   –16 (9–17–65 vs. St. Louis)

**Most Yards Gained Passing
by Opponents**
Season   3,941 (1988)
Game   422 (9–11–88 vs. Wash.)

**Fewest Yards Gained Passing
by Opponents**
Season   1,466 (1974)
Game   #28 (12–7–58 vs. Wash.)

Most Passes Attempted
Season   592 (1995)
Game   57 (12–19–93 vs. Houston)
55 (12–24–95 at Green Bay)
54 (1–15–95 vs. San Diego

Fewest Passes Attempted
Season   161 (1946, 1942—11 games)
277 (1976)
Game   0 (11–16–41 vs. Brooklyn,
11–13–49 vs. L.A.)

Most Passes Attempted by Opponents
Season   548 (1989)
Game   60 (12–16–95 vs. N.E.)

Fewest Passes Attempted
by Opponents
Season   162 (1946—11 games)
         339 (1974—14 games)
Game   8 (12–14–74 vs. Cin.,
              12–1–57 vs. Phil.)

Most Passes Attempted, Both Teams
Game   95 (12–19–93 Pittsburgh 57
            vs. Houston 38)

Most Passes Completed
Season 348 (1995)
Game   34 (11–5–95 at Chicago)

Fewest Passes Completed
Season   42 (1941—11 games)
       140 (1973—14 games)
Game   0 (11–16–41 vs. Brooklyn,
            11–13–49 vs. L.A.)

Most Passes Completed by Opponents
Season 334 (1991)
Game   39 (12–16–95 vs. N.E.)

Fewest Passes Completed
by Opponents
Season   64 (1946—11 games)
       147 (1974—14 games)
Game   3 (Several times)

SACKS

Most Sacks
Season   55 (1994)
Game   10 (11–29–92 vs. Cincinnati)

Most Sacks Allowed
Season   52 (1969, 1983)
Game   12 (11–20–66 vs. Dallas)

INTERCEPTIONS

Most Interceptions
Season   37 (1973)
Game   7 (11–30–52 vs. N.Y. Giants,
          (10–13–74 vs. K.C.)

Fewest Interceptions
Season   12 (1965 and 1964—14 games)

Most Interceptions by Opponents
Season   35 (1965)
Game   9 (12–12–65 vs. Phil.)

Fewest Interceptions by Opponents
Season   9 (1994)

Most Yards Interceptions Returned
Season 673 (1973)
Game 147 (10–17–54 vs. Cleveland)

Fewest Yards Interceptions Returned
Season   96 (1964—14 games)

Most Yards Interceptions Returned
by Opponents
Season 535 (1969)
Game 172 (12–12–65 vs. Phil.)

Fewest Yards Interceptions
Returned by Opponents
Season   47 (1975—14 games)

Most Touchdowns by Interceptions
Season   5 (1987)
Game   2 (10–1–95 vs. San Diego,
         (12–18–88 vs. Miami,
         10–1–84 vs. Cincinnati,
         10–10–83 vs. Cincinnati,
         9–30–73 vs. Houston,
         10–17–54 vs. Cleveland)

Most Touchdowns by Interceptions
by Opponents
Season   6 (1965 and 1964)
Game   3 (12–12–65 vs. Phil.,
         9–29–68 vs. Balt.)

Most Touchdowns by Interceptions,
Both Teams
Game   4 (12–12–65 Philadelphia 3
         vs. Pittsburgh 1)

PUNTING

Most Punts
Season   97 (1994)

Most Punts By Opponents
Season 100 (1979)

Fewest Punts
Season   51 (1958)
Game   1 (12–9–73 vs. Houston,
         10–26–86 vs. Cincinnati,
         12–2–90 vs. Cincinnati,
         10–27–91 vs. Cleveland,
         12–15–91 vs. Cincinnati)

Fewest Punts By Opponents
Season   54 (1960)
Game   0 (9–17–89 vs. Cincinnati)

Highest Punting Average
Season 47.0 (1961)

Highest Punting Average
by Opponents
Season 46.4 (1959)

PUNT RETURNS

Most Punt Returns
Season   71 (1976)

Most Punt Returns By Opponents
Season   51 (1970)

Most Yardage By Punt Returns
Season 774 (1974)

Most Yardage By Punt Returns
by Opponents
Season 678 (1993)

Most Touchdowns By Punt Returns
Season   3 (1952)
Game   1 (many times)

Most Touchdowns By Punt Returns
by Opponents
Season   3 (1959, 1993)
Game   2 (11–1–59 vs. St. Louis,
         10–24–93 vs. Cleveland)

KICKOFF RETURNS

Most Kickoff Returns
Season   74 (1988)

Most Kickoff Returns By Opponents
Season   88 (1995)

Most Kickoff Return Yardage
Season 1,575 (1988)

Most Kickoff Return Yardage
by Opponents
Season 1,668 (1979)

Most Touchdowns By Kickoff Returns
Season   2 (1952, 1988)
Game   1 (many times)

Most Touchdowns By Kickoff Returns
by Opponents
Season   3 (1986)
Game   1 (many times)

PENALTIES

Most Penalties
Season 122 (1977)

Most Penalties By Opponents
Season 112 (1981)

Most Penalty Yards
Season 986 (1989)

Most Penalty Yards By Opponents
Season 960 (1981)

FUMBLES

Most Fumbles
Season   47 (1979)
Game   10 (10–9–43 vs. N.Y. Giants)

Most Fumbles By Opponents
Season   42 (1976)
Game   9 (12–23–90 vs. Cleveland)

Most Fumbles Lost
Season   28 (1977—14 games)
        26 (1979—16 games)

Most Fumbles Lost By Opponents
Season   24 (1976)
Game   8 (12–23–90 vs. Cleveland)

SHUTOUTS

Most Shutouts
Season   5 (1976)

Most Shutouts Against
Season   6 (1934)

**Lethal linebacker Greg Lloyd demonstrates the Steelers' attack defense as
he stops the run behind the line of scrimmage.**

ALL-TIME LEADERS

Franco Harris

Terry Bradshaw

John Stallworth

RUSHING

Player	Years	Atts.	Yds.	Avg.	LG	TDs
Franco Harris	1972–83	2,881	11,950	4.1	75t	91
John Henry Johnson	1960–65	1,025	4,383	4.3	87	26
Frank Pollard	1980–88	953	3,989	4.2	52	20
Dick Hoak	1961–70	1,132	3,965	3.5	77	25
Barry Foster	1990–94	915	3,943	4.3	69	26
Rocky Bleier	1968, 1970–80	928	3,865	4.2	70t	23
Walter Abercrombie	1982–87	842	3,343	4.0	50t	22
Fran Rogel	1950–57	900	3,271	3.6	51	17
Merril Hoge	1987–93	819	3,115	3.8	41t	21
John Fuqua	1970–76	699	2,942	4.2	85	21
Tom Tracy	1958–63	727	2,712	3.7	64	15
Terry Bradshaw	1970–83	444	2,255	5.1	39	32
Preston Pearson	1970–74	573	2,243	3.9	47	8
Lynn Chandnois	1950–56	593	1,934	3.2	38	16
Earnest Jackson	1986–88	470	1,921	4.1	39	9
Sidney Thornton	1977–82	356	1,512	4.2	75	18
Bill Dudley	1942, 1945–46	343	1,505	4.4	42	14
Joe Geri	1949–51	411	1,500	3.6	45	10
Byron "Bam" Morris	1994–95	346	1,395	4.0	30t	16
Tim Worley	1989–91, 1993	336	1,338	4.0	38	5

PASSING
(Based on total yardage)

Player	Years	Atts.	Comps.	Yds.	Pct.	LG	TD	Ints.	Rtg.
Terry Bradshaw	1970–83	3,901	2,025	27,989	51.9	90t	212	210	71.1
Bubby Brister	1986–92	1,477	776	10,104	52.5	90	51	57	69.8
Neil O'Donnell	1990–95	1,871	1,069	12,867	57.1	89t	68	39	81.6
Bobby Layne	1958–62	1,156	569	8,983	49.2	78	67	81	70.7
Jim Finks	1949–55	1,382	661	8,854	47.8	78t	55	88	48.5
Mark Malone	1980–87	1,374	690	8,582	50.2	61t	54	68	62.1
Ed Brown	1962–65	736	339	5,821	44.7	85	30	50	57.7
Bill Nelsen	1964–67	589	274	4,440	46.5	87t	28	30	67.0
Dick Shiner	1968–69	513	245	3,278	47.8	63	25	27	54.7
Cliff Stoudt	1977–83	479	244	3,217	50.9	72	14	28	57.9
David Woodley	1984–85	339	179	2,630	52.8	80t	14	21	66.2
Kent Nix	1967–69	451	217	2,597	48.1	66	14	33	46.1
Terry Hanratty	1969–75	417	159	2,428	38.1	72t	24	34	42.6
Earl Morrall	1957–58	335	145	2,175	43.3	66	12	19	53.9
Joe Gilliam	1972–75	331	147	2,103	44.4	61t	9	17	53.3

PASS RECEIVING

Player	Years	No.	Yds.	Avg.	LG	TDs
John Stallworth	1974–87	537	8,723	16.2	74t	63
Louis Lipps	1984–91	358	6,018	16.8	89t	39
Lynn Swann	1974–82	336	5,462	16.3	68t	51
Elbie Nickel	1947–57	329	5,133	15.6	77t	37
Franco Harris	1972–83	306	2,284	7.5	44t	9
Merril Hoge	1987–93	241	2,054	8.5	40	13
Ray Mathews	1951–59	230	3,919	16.1	78t	34
Buddy Dial	1959–63	229	4,723	20.6	88t	42
Bennie Cunningham	1976–85	202	2,879	14.3	48	20
Roy Jefferson	1965–69	199	3,671	18.4	84t	29

THE PITTSBURGH STEELERS

Eric Green	1990–94	198	2,681	13.5	71t	24
Ron Shanklin	1970–74	166	3,047	18.4	81t	24
Lynn Chandnois	1950–56	163	2,062	12.6	55	8
Gary Ballman	1962–66	154	2,949	19.2	87t	22
Dwight Stone	1987–94	152	2,460	16.2	90	12
Fran Rogel	1950–57	150	1,087	7.2	64	2
Dick Hoak	1961–70	146	1,452	9.9	48	8
Val Jansante	1946–51	144	2,214	15.4	66	13
Walter Abercrombie	1982–87	138	1,353	9.8	59	7
John Fuqua	1970–76	135	1,247	9.2	57t	3

SCORING

Player	Years	Tot. TD	TDR	TDP	PAT	FG	TP
Gary Anderson	1982–94	0	0	0	416	309	1,343
Roy Gerela	1971–78	0	0	0	293	146	731
Franco Harris	1972–83	100	91	9	0	0	600
John Stallworth	1974–87	64	1	63	0	0	384
Lynn Swann	1974–82	53	1	51	0	0	**318
Mike Clark	1964–67	0	0	0	116	57	287
Lou Michaels	1961–63	0	0	0	91	62	277
Louis Lipps	1984–91	46	4	39	0	0	***276
Ray Mathews	1951–59	43	13	30	1	0	*261
Buddy Dial	1959–63	42	0	42	0	0	252
Elbie Nickel	1947–57	37	0	37	0	0	222
Merril Hoge	1987–93	34	21	13	0	0	204
Matt Bahr	1979–80	0	0	0	89	37	200
Dick Hoak	1961–70	33	25	8	0	0	198

INTERCEPTIONS

Player	Years	No.	Yds.	Avg.	LG	TDs
Mel Blount	1970–83	57	736	12.9	52t	2
Jack Butler	1951–59	52	827	15.9	52	4
Donnie Shell	1974–87	51	450	8.8	67	2
Dwayne Woodruff	1979–85, 87–90	37	689	18.6	78t	3
Mike Wagner	1971–80	36	491	13.6	65	0
Jack Ham	1971–82	32	218	6.8	32t	1
Rod Woodson	1990–94	32	658	20.6	63t	4
Jack Lambert	1974–84	28	243	8.7	31	0
Glen Edwards	1971–77	25	652	26.1	86t	1
Howard Hartley	1949–52	25	267	10.7	38	0
Clendon Thomas	1962–68	23	233	10.1	33	0

QUARTERBACK SACKS

Player	Years	No.
L.C. Greenwood	1969–81	73.5
Joe Greene	1969–81	66.0
Keith Willis	1982–87, 89–91	59.0
Greg Lloyd	1988–95	49.0
Dwight White	1971–80	46.0
Ernie Holmes	1972–77	40.0
Kevin Greene	1993–95	35.5
Gary Dunn	1977–87	35.0
Steve Furness	1972–80	32.0
Mike Merriweather	1982–87	31.0
Robin Cole	1977–87	27.0
Jack Ham	1971–82	25.5

OPPONENT FUMBLE RECOVERIES

Player	Years	No.
Jack Ham	1971–82	21
Donnie Shell	1974–87	19
Joe Greene	1969–81	16
Jack Lambert	1974–84	15
Robin Cole	1977–87	14
L.C. Greenwood	1969–81	14
Carnell Lake	1989–95	12
Mel Blount	1970–83	11
Mike Wagner	1971–80	11
Bryan Hinkle	1982–93	10
Greg Lloyd	1988–95	11

*   Includes one safety
**   Includes one touchdown on punt return (1974)
***   Includes three touchdowns on punt returns (1984, '85)

Gary Anderson

Mel Blount

Jack Ham

INDIVIDUAL RECORDS

SERVICE

Most Seasons

Career	15	Mike Webster (1974–88)
	14	Donnie Shell (1974–87)
	14	John Stallworth (1974–87)
	14	Larry Brown (1971–84)
	14	Mel Blount (1970–83)
	14	Terry Bradshaw (1970–83)
	14	Ernie Stautner (1950–63)
	13	Tunch Ilkin (1980–92)
	13	Joe Greene (1969–81)
	13	L.C. Greenwood (1969–81)
	13	Jon Kolb (1969–81)
	13	Sam Davis (1967–79)
	13	Ray Mansfield (1964–76)
	13	Gary Anderson (1982–94)

Most Games

Career	220	Mike Webster (1974–88)
	201	Donnie Shell (1974–87)
	200	Mel Blount (1970–83)
	197	Gary Anderson (1982–94)
	182	Ray Mansfield (1964–76)
	181	Joe Greene (1969–81)
	179	David Little (1981–92)
	177	Jon Kolb (1969–81)
	176	Tunch Ilkin (1980–92)
	174	L.C. Greenwood (1969–81)
	173	Ernie Stautner (1950–63)

Most Consecutive Games Played

	182	Ray Mansfield (1964–76)
	177	Mike Webster (1974–85)

SCORING

Most Total Points

Career	1,343	Gary Anderson (1982–94) 416 PATs, 309 FGs.
	731	Roy Gerela (1971–78), 293 PATs, 146 FGs.
	600	Franco Harris (1972–83), 100 TDs.
	384	John Stallworth (1974–87), 64 TDs.
	318	Lynn Swann (1974–81), 53 TDs.
Season	141	Norm Johnson (1995), 39 PATs, 34 FGs.
	139	Gary Anderson (1985) 40 PATs, 33 FGs.
	123	Roy Gerela (1973), 36 PATs, 29 FGs.
	119	Gary Anderson (1983), 38 PATs, 27 FGs.
	119	Roy Gerela (1972), 35 PATs, 28 FGs.
	118	Gary Anderson (1988), 34 PATs, 28 FGs.
	117	Gary Anderson (1984), 45 PATs, 24 FGs.
	116	Gary Anderson (1993), 32 PATs, 28 FGs.
	113	Gary Anderson (1992), 29 PATs, 28 FGs.
	110	Lou Michaels (1962), 32 PATs, 26 FGs.
	104	Matt Bahr (1979), 50 PATs, 18 FGs.
	104	Gary Anderson (1994), 32 PATs, 24 FGs.
	100	Gary Anderson (1991), 31 PATs, 23 FGs.
Game	24	Roy Jefferson (11–3–68 vs. Atlanta), 4 TDs.
	24	Ray Mathews (10–17–54 vs. Cleve.), 4 TDs.

Most Touchdowns

Career	100	Franco Harris (1972–83)
	64	John Stallworth (1974–87)
	53	Lynn Swann (1974–82)
	46	Louis Lipps (1984–91)
	43	Ray Mathews (1951–59)
	42	Buddy Dial (1959–63)
	37	Elbie Nickel (1947–57)
	34	Merril Hoge (1987–93)
	33	Dick Hoak (1961–70)
	32	Terry Bradshaw (1970–83)
	32	John Henry Johnson (1960–65)
Season	15	Louis Lipps (1985)
	14	Franco Harris (1976)
	12	Franco Harris (1979)
	12	Roy Jefferson (1968)
	12	Buddy Dial (1961)
Game	4	Roy Jefferson (11–3–68 vs. Atlanta)
	4	Ray Mathews (10–17–54 vs. Cleveland)
	3	Bam Morris (11–19–95 at Cincinnati)
	3	Erric Pegram (11–5–95 at Chicago)
	3	Barry Foster (9–27–93 vs. Atlanta)
	3	Merril Hoge (10–29–90 vs. L.A. Rams)
	3	Eric Green (10–14–90 vs. Denver)
	3	Merril Hoge (11–26–89 vs. Miami)
	3	Walter Abercrombie (12–13–86 vs. N.Y. Jets)
	3	Weegie Thompson (11–2–86 vs. Green Bay)
	3	Louis Lipps (9–8–85 vs. Indianapolis)
	3	John Stallworth (11–25–84 vs. San Diego)
	3	John Stallworth (11–4–84 vs. Houston)
	3	Jim Smith (9–28–80 vs. Chicago)
	3	Rocky Bleier (12–5–76 vs. Tampa Bay)
	3	Steve Davis (9–22–74 vs. Denver)
	3	Franco Harris (10–29–72 vs. Buffalo)
	3	Earl Gros (12–21–69 vs. New Orleans)
	3	John Henry Johnson (10–10–64 vs. Cleve.)

Center Ray Mansfield anchored the offensive line for 13 seasons and a team-record 182 consecutive games.

Most Field Goals

Career	309	Gary Anderson (1982–94)
	146	Roy Gerela (1971–78)
	62	Lou Michaels (1961–63)
	57	Mike Clark (1964–67)
Season	34	Norm Johnson (1995)
	33	Gary Anderson (1985)
	29	Roy Gerela (1973)
	8	Gary Anderson (1993)
	28	Gary Anderson (1992)
	28	Gary Anderson (1988)
	28	Roy Gerela (1972)
	27	Gary Anderson (1983)
	26	Lou Michaels (1961)
Game	6	Gary Anderson (10–23–88 vs. Denver)

Longest Field Goal

	55	Gary Anderson (11–25–84 vs. San Diego)
	54	Gary Anderson (12–8–91 vs. Houston)
	53	Gary Anderson (10–21–84 vs. Indianapolis)
	52	Gary Anderson (11–13–88 vs. Philadelphia)
	52	Gary Anderson (11–22–87 vs. Cincinnati)
	52	Gary Anderson (11–17–85 vs. Houston)
	50	Norm Johnson (11–19–95 at Cincinnati)
	50	Gary Anderson (9–13–87 vs. San Francisco)
	50	Gary Anderson (11–6–94 vs. Houston)
	50	Lou Michaels (9–15–63 vs. Philadelphia)

Most Field Goal Attempts

Career	395	Gary Anderson (1982–94)
	227	Roy Gerela (1971–78)
	109	Lou Michaels (1961–63)
Season	43	Roy Gerela (1973)
	42	Gary Anderson (1985)
	41	Norm Johnson (1995)
	41	Roy Gerela (1972)
	41	Lou Michaels (1963)
Game	8	Lou Michaels (12–2–62 vs. St. Louis)

Highest Field Goal Percentage

Career	82.9	Norm Johnson (1995) (41–34)
	78.2	Gary Anderson (1982–94) (395–309)
	64.3	Roy Gerela (1971–78) (227–146)
	56.9	Lou Michaels (1961–63) (109–62)
Season	93.3	Gary Anderson (1993) (30–28)
	87.0	Gary Anderson (1983) (31–27)
	83.3	Gary Anderson (1982) (12–10)
	82.9	Norm Johnson (1995) (41–34)
	82.8	Gary Anderson (1994) (29–24)
	81.5	Gary Anderson (1987) (27–22)
	81.0	Roy Gerela (1975) (21–17)
	80.0	Gary Anderson (1990) (25–20)
	78.6	Gary Anderson (1985) (42–33)
	77.8	Gary Anderson (1992) (36–28)
	77.8	Gary Anderson (1988) (36–28)
	75.0	Gary Anderson (1984) (32–24)

Most Consecutive Field Goals Made

	19	Gary Anderson (1994)

Most Extra Points

Career	416	Gary Anderson (1982–94)
	293	Roy Gerela (1971–78)
	116	Mike Clark (1964–67)
Season	50	Matt Bahr (1979)
	45	Gary Anderson (1984)
	44	Roy Gerela (1978 & 1975)
	40	Gary Anderson (1985)
	40	Roy Gerela (1976)
	39	Norm Johnson (1995)
Game	8	Gary Kerkorian (11–30–52 vs. N.Y. Giants)

Most Extra Point Attempts

Career	420	Gary Anderson (1982–94)
	306	Roy Gerela (1971–78)
Season	52	Matt Bahr (1979)
Game	8	Gary Kerkorian (11–30–52 vs. N.Y. Giants)

Most Consecutive Extra Points Made

	202	Gary Anderson (began 9–11–83 vs. Green Bay and ended 12–4–88 vs. Houston)

RUSHING

Most Yards Rushing

Career	11,950	Franco Harris (1972–83)
	4,383	John Henry Johnson (1960–65)
	3,989	Frank Pollard (1980–88)
	3,965	Dick Hoak (1961–70)
	3,943	Barry Foster (1990–94)
	3,865	Rocky Bleier (1968, 1970–80)
Season	1,690	Barry Foster (1992)
	1,246	Franco Harris (1975)
	1,186	Franco Harris (1979)
	1,162	Franco Harris (1977)
	1,141	John Henry Johnson (1962)
	1,128	Franco Harris (1976)
	1,082	Franco Harris (1978)
	1,055	Franco Harris (1972)
	1,048	John Henry Johnson (1964)
	1,036	Rocky Bleier (1976)
	1,006	Franco Harris (1974)
Game	218	John Fuqua (12–20–70 vs. Philadelphia)
	200	John Henry Johnson (10–10–64 vs. Cleve.)
	190	Barry Foster (9–13–92 vs. New York Jets)
	182	John Henry Johnson (12–11–60 vs. Phila.)
	179	Franco Harris (11–20–77 vs. Dallas)
	79	Barry Foster (9–18–94 vs. Indianapolis)

Most 100–Yard Rushing Games

Career	47	Franco Harris (1972–83)
	20	Barry Foster (1990–94)
	7	Earnest Jackson (1986–88)
	7	John Fuqua (1970–76)
	5	Rocky Bleier (1968, 1970–80)
Season	*12	Barry Foster (1992)
	7	Franco Harris (1972)
	6	Franco Harris (1976)

6 Franco Harris (1975)
6 Franco Harris (1974)
5 Franco Harris (1983)
5 Franco Harris (1979)
*T NFL Record

Most Rushing Attempts

Career	2,881	Franco Harris (1972–83)
	1,132	Dick Hoak (1961–70)
	1,025	John Henry Johnson (1960–65)
	953	Frank Pollard (1980–88)
Season	390	Barry Foster (1992)
	310	Franco Harris (1978)
	300	Franco Harris (1977)
	289	Franco Harris (1976)
Game	41	Franco Harris (10–17–76 vs. Cincinnati)
	35	Rocky Bleier (10–26–75 vs. Green Bay)
	33	Barry Foster (12–6–92 vs. Seattle)
	33	Barry Foster (9–13–92 vs. New York Jets)
	32	Franco Harris (12–2–79 vs. Cincinnati)
	32	Barry Foster (12–18–94 vs. Cleveland)
	31	Barry Foster (11–1–92 vs. Houston)
	31	Barry Foster (9–11–94 vs. Cleveland)
	31	Barry Foster (9–18–94 vs. Indianapolis)
	31	Barry Foster (11–20–94 vs. Miami)
	31	Franco Harris (10–23–83 vs. Seattle)
	30	Leroy Thompson (11–15–93 vs. Buffalo)
	30	John Fuqua (11–7–71 vs. Cleveland)
	30	John Henry Johnson (10–10–64 vs. Cleve.)

Most Touchdowns Rushing

Career	91	Franco Harris (1972–83)
	32	Terry Bradshaw (1970–83)
	26	John Henry Johnson (1960–65)
	26	Barry Foster (1990–94)
	25	Dick Hoak (1961–70)
Season	14	Franco Harris (1976)
	11	Barry Foster (1992)
	11	Franco Harris (1977 and 1979)
	10	Franco Harris (1975 and 1972)
Game	3	Bam Morris (11–19–95 at Cincinnati)
	3	Barry Foster (9–27–93 vs. Atlanta)
	3	Merril Hoge (11–26–89 vs. Miami)
	3	Rocky Bleier (12–5–76 vs. Tampa Bay)
	3	Earl Gros (12–21–69 vs. New Orleans)
	3	John Henry Johnson (10–10–64 vs. Cleve.)

Highest Rushing Average *(minimum 1500 yds.)*

Career	5.08	Terry Bradshaw (1970–83)
	4.39	Bill Dudley (1942, 1945–46)
	4.31	Barry Foster (1990–94)
	4.28	John Henry Johnson (1960–65)
	4.25	Sidney Thornton (1977–82)
	4.21	John Fuqua (1970–76)
Season	5.6	Franco Harris (1972)
	5.0	Sidney Thornton (1979)
	5.0	John Fuqua (1970)
	4.9	Dick Hoak (1968)

Longest Rushing Plays

97t	Bobby Gage (12–4–49 vs. Chicago Bears)
87t	John Henry Johnson (12–11–60 vs. Phil.)
85t	John Fuqua (12–20–70 vs. Philadelphia)
77t	Dick Hoak (10–20–68 vs. New Orleans)
75t	Franco Harris (11–19–72 vs. Cleveland)
75	Sidney Thornton (9–23–79 vs. Baltimore)
75	Busit Warren (11–11–45 vs. Chicago Cards)

TOTAL YARDS FROM SCRIMMAGE

Most Total Yards From Scrimmage

Career	14,234	Franco Harris (1972–83)
	8,834	John Stallworth (1974–87)
	6,406	Louis Lipps (1984–91)
	5,534	Lynn Swann (1974–82)
	5,417	Dick Hoak (1961–70)
	5,197	John Henry Johnson (1960–65)
	5,169	Merril Hoge (1987–93)
	5,159	Rocky Bleier (1968, 1970–80)
Season	2,034	Barry Foster (1992)
	1,477	Franco Harris (1979)
	1,460	Franco Harris (1975)
	1,395	John Stallworth (1984)
	1,367	John Henry Johnson (1962)
	1,330	Rocky Bleier (1976)
	1,308	Yancey Thigpen (1995)
	1,295	Buddy Dial (1963)

PASSING

Most Yards Passing

Career	27,989	Terry Bradshaw (1970–83)
	12,867	Neil O'Donnell (1990–95)
	10,104	Bubby Brister (1986–92)
	8,983	Bobby Layne (1958–62)
	8,854	Jim Finks (1949–55)
	8,582	Mark Malone (1980–87)
Season	3,724	Terry Bradshaw (1979)
	3,339	Terry Bradshaw (1980)
	3,208	Neil O'Donnell (1993)
	2,982	Ed Brown (1963)
	2,970	Neil O'Donnell (1995)
	2,915	Terry Bradshaw (1978)
	2,887	Terry Bradshaw (1981)
Game	409	Bobby Layne (12–13–58 vs. Chic. Cardinals)
	377	Neil O'Donnell (11–13–95 at Cincinnati)
	374	Mark Malone (9–30–85 vs. Cincinnati)
	364	Terry Bradshaw (11–25–79 vs. Cleveland)
	359	Neil O'Donnell (10–19–95 vs. Cincinnati)
	355	Neil O'Donnell (10–24–93 vs. Cleveland)
	353	Bubby Brister (10–14–90 vs. Denver)
	351	Mark Malone (12–21–86 vs. Kansas City)
	348	Joe Gilliam (9–22–74 vs. Denver)
	343	Mike Tomczak (11–20–94 vs. Miami)
	341	Neil O'Donnell (10–29–95 vs. Jacksonville)
	339	Terry Bradshaw (12–2–79 vs. Cleveland)
	337	Jim Finks (11–5–55 vs. Chicago Cardinals)
	334	Bill Nelsen (12–18–66 vs. Atlanta)

Most 300–Yard Passing Games

Career	5	Neil O'Donnell (1990–95)
	4	Terry Bradshaw (1970–83)
	3	Bubby Brister (1986–92)
	3	Jim Finks (1949–55)
Season	4	Neil O'Donnell (1995)
	3	Terry Bradshaw (1979)
	2	Bubby Brister (1988)

Most Passing Attempts

Career	3,901	Terry Bradshaw (1970–83)
	1,871	Neil O'Donnell (1990–95)
	1,477	Bubby Brister (1986–92)
	1,382	Jim Finks (1949–55)
	1,374	Mark Malone (1980–87)
	1,156	Bobby Layne (1958–62)
Season	486	Neil O'Donnell (1993)
	472	Terry Bradshaw (1979)
	425	Mark Malone (1986)
	424	Terry Bradshaw (1980)
	416	Neil O'Donnell (1995)
	387	Bubby Brister (1990)
	381	Cliff Stoudt (1983)
	373	Terry Bradshaw (1971)
	370	Neil O'Donnell (1994)
	370	Bubby Brister (1988)
	370	Terry Bradshaw (1981)
	368	Terry Bradshaw (1978)
	362	Ed Brown (1963)
	344	Jim Finks (1955)
Game	55	Neil O'Donnell (12–24–95 at Green Bay)
	52	Neil O'Donnell (10–19–95 vs. Cinc., 11–5–95 at Chicago)
	50	Joe Gilliam (9–22–74 vs. Denver)
	49	Bobby Layne (12–13–58 vs. Chic. Cardinals)
	49	Jim Finks (11–5–55 vs. Chicago Cardinals)
	48	Mark Malone (9–15–86 vs. Denver)
	46	Kent Nix (10–22–67 vs. Dallas)
	45	Mark Malone (9–16–85 vs. Cleveland)

Most Passes Completed

Career	2,025	Terry Bradshaw (1970–83)
	1,069	Neil O'Donnell (1990–95)
	776	Bubby Brister (1986–92)
	690	Mark Malone (1980–87)
	661	Jim Finks (1949–55)
	569	Bobby Layne (1958–62)
Season	270	Neil O'Donnell (1993)
	259	Terry Bradshaw (1979)
	246	Neil O'Donnell (1995)
	223	Bubby Brister (1990)
	218	Terry Bradshaw (1980)
	216	Mark Malone (1986)
	212	Neil O'Donnell (1994)
	207	Terry Bradshaw (1978)
	203	Terry Bradshaw (1971)
	201	Terry Bradshaw (1981)
Game	34	Neil O'Donnell (11–5–95 at Chicago)
	33	Neil O'Donnell (12–24–95 at Green Bay)
	31	Joe Gilliam (9–22–74 vs. Denver)

30	Terry Bradshaw (11–25–79 vs. Cleveland)
30	Neil O'Donnell (10–19–95 vs. Cincinnati)
29	Terry Bradshaw (9–19–82 vs. Cincinnati)
28	Kent Nix (10–22–67 vs. Dallas)
27	Jim Finks (9–26–54 vs. Green Bay)
26	Mike Tomczak (11–20–94 vs. Miami)
26	Mark Malone (9–30–85 vs. Cincinnati)
25	Neil O'Donnell (10–24–93 vs. Cleveland)

Most Consecutive Passes Completed

15	Bubby Brister (10–1–89 vs. Detroit)
13	Bill Nelsen (12–18–66 vs. Atl.[11], 9–17–67 vs. Chi. [2])
11	Bubby Brister (12–27–92 vs. Cleveland)
11	Neil O'Donnell (10–11–92 vs. Cleveland)
11	Mark Malone (11–25–84 vs. San Diego)

Highest Completion Percentage

Career (Minimum 500 Attempts)

57.1%	Neil O'Donnell (1,069/1,871, 1990–95)
52.5%	Bubby Brister (776/1,477, 1986–92)
51.9%	Terry Bradshaw (2,025/3,901, 1970–83)
50.2%	Mark Malone (690/1,374, 1980–87)
49.2%	Bobby Layne (569/1,156, 1958–62)
47.8%	Jim Finks (661/1,382, 1949–55)
47.8%	Dick Shiner (245/513, 1968–69)

Season (Minimum 250 Attempts)

59.1%	Neil O'Donnell (185/313, 1992, 246/416, 1995)
57.7%	Terry Bradshaw (165/286, 1975)
57.6%	Bubby Brister (223/387, 1990)
57.3%	Neil O'Donnell (212/370, 1994)
56.3%	Terry Bradshaw (207/368,1978)
55.6%	Neil O'Donnell (270/486, 1993)
54.9%	Terry Bradshaw (259/472, 1979)
54.7%	Bubby Brister (187/342, 1989)
54.5%	Neil O'Donnell (156/286, 1991)
54.4%	Terry Bradshaw (203/373, 1971)
54.3%	Terry Bradshaw (201/370, 1981)
54.0%	Mark Malone (147/272, 1984)

Game (Minimum 20 Attempts)

84.0%	Neil O'Donnell (21/25, 9–19–93 vs. Cinc.)
81.8%	Mark Malone (18/22, 11–25–84 vs. S.D.)
78.1%	Neil O'Donnell (25/32, 10–11–92 vs. Clev.)
77.4%	Neil O'Donnell (33/55, 12–24–95 at G.B.)
77.8%	Bubby Brister (21/27, 10–1–89 vs. Det.)
76.0%	Neil O'Donnell (19/25, 9–27–93 vs. Atlanta)
75.9%	Bubby Brister (22/29, 9–15–91 vs. N.E.)
75.0%	Bubby Brister (18/24, 11–25–90 vs. N.Y.J.)
75.0%	Bubby Brister (21/28, 10–14–90 vs. Den.)
75.0%	Terry Bradshaw (15/20, 12–5–82 vs. K.C.)
75.0%	Terry Bradshaw (18/24, 10–22–79 vs. Den.)
75.0%	Terry Bradshaw (21/28, 9–21–75 vs. S.D.)

Most Touchdown Passes

Career	212	Terry Bradshaw (1970–83)
	68	Neil O'Donnell (1990–95)
	67	Bobby Layne (1958–62)
	55	Jim Finks (1949–55)
	54	Mark Malone (1980–87)
	51	Bubby Brister (1986–92)

Season	28	Terry Bradshaw (1978)
	26	Terry Bradshaw (1979)
	24	Terry Bradshaw (1980)
	22	Terry Bradshaw (1981)
	21	Ed Brown (1963)
	20	Bubby Brister (1990)
	20	Bobby Layne (1959)
	20	Jim Finks (1952)
Game	5	Mark Malone (9–8–85 vs. Indianapolis)
	5	Terry Bradshaw (11–15–81 vs. Atlanta)
	4	Bubby Brister (12–23–90 vs. Cleveland)
	4	Bubby Brister (10–29–90 vs. L.A. Rams)
	4	Bubby Brister (10–14–90 vs. Denver)
	4	Mark Malone (11–25–84 vs. San Diego)
	4	Terry Bradshaw (9–28–80 vs. Chicago)
	4	Terry Bradshaw (11–4–79 vs. Washington)
	4	Dick Shiner (11–24–68 vs. San Francisco)
	4	Ed Brown (10–27–63 vs. Dallas)
	4	Jim Finks (10–17–54 vs. Cleveland)
	4	Jim Finks (11–16–52 vs. Cleveland)
	4	Jim Finks (11–30–52 vs. N.Y. Giants)

Most Passes Had Intercepted

Career	210	Terry Bradshaw (1970–83)
	88	Jim Finks (1949–55)
	81	Bobby Layne (1958–62)
Season	26	Jim Finks (1955)
	25	Terry Bradshaw (1979)
	24	Terry Bradshaw (1970)
	22	Terry Bradshaw (1971 and 1980)
Game	7	Tommy Wade (12–12–65 vs. Philadelphia)
	5	Mark Malone (9–20–87 vs. Cleveland)
	5	Terry Bradshaw (11–18–79 vs. San Diego)
	5	Terry Bradshaw (10–30–77 vs. Baltimore)
	5	John Gildea (12–1–35 vs. Boston)

Highest Passer Rating (among qualifiers)

Career	81.6	Neil O'Donnell (1990–95)
	71.1	Terry Bradshaw (1970–83)
	70.7	Bobby Layne (1958–62)
	69.8	Bubby Brister (1986–92)
	67.0	Bill Nelsen (1963–67)
Season	87.8	Terry Bradshaw (1975)
	87.7	Neil O'Donnell (1995)
	84.8	Terry Bradshaw (1978)
	84.0	Terry Bradshaw (1981)
	83.6	Neil O'Donnell (1992)
	81.6	Bubby Brister (1990)
	81.4	Terry Bradshaw (1982)

PASS RECEIVING

Most Receptions

Career	537	John Stallworth (1974–87)
	358	Louis Lipps (1984–91)
	336	Lynn Swann (1974–82)
	329	Elbie Nickel (1947–57)
	306	Franco Harris (1972–83)
	241	Merril Hoge (1987–93)
	230	Ray Mathews (1951–59)
	229	Buddy Dial (1959–63)

Season	85	Yancey Thigpen (1995)
	80	John Stallworth (1984)
	75	John Stallworth (1985)
	70	John Stallworth (1979)
	67	Roy Jefferson (1969)
	63	Eric Green (1993)
	63	John Stallworth (1981)
	62	Elbie Nickel (1953)
	61	Lynn Swann (1978)
	60	Buddy Dial (1963)
Game	12	J.R. Wilburn (10–22–67 vs. Dallas)
	11	John Stallworth (9–30–85 vs. Cincinnati)
	11	Roy Jefferson (11–3–68 vs. Atlanta)
	10	Yancey Thigpen (9–24–95 vs. Minn., 11–5–95 at Jacksonville)
	10	Andre Hastings (9–18–95 at Miami)
	10	Dick Compton (10–7–67 vs. Cleveland)
	10	Elbie Nickel (12–14–52 vs. Los Angeles)
	10	Val Jansante (11–30–49 vs. Philadelphia)

Most Yards Receiving

Career	8,723	John Stallworth (1974–87)
	6,018	Louis Lipps (1984–91)
	5,462	Lynn Swann (1974–82)
	5,133	Elbie Nickel (1947–57)
	4,723	Buddy Dial (1959–63)
	3,919	Ray Mathews (1951–59)
Season	1,395	John Stallworth (1984)
	1,307	Yancey Thigpen (1995)
	1,295	Buddy Dial (1963)
	1,183	John Stallworth (1979)
	1,134	Louis Lipps (1985)
	1,098	John Stallworth (1981)
	1,079	Roy Jefferson (1969)
	1,074	Roy Jefferson (1968)
Game	235	Buddy Dial (10–22–61 vs. Cleveland)
	205	Jimmy Orr (12–13–58 vs. Chic. Cardinals)
	202	Elbie Nickel (12–14–52 vs. Los Angeles)
	199	Roy Jefferson (11–3–68 vs. Atlanta)
	192	Jeff Graham (12–19–93 vs. Houston)
	192	Lynn Swann (12–2–79 vs. Cincinnati)

Most 100–Yard Receiving Games

Career	25	John Stallworth (1974–87)
	16	Louis Lipps (1984–91)
	10	Lynn Swann (1974–82)
Season	7	John Stallworth (1984)
	5	Louis Lipps (1989)
	4	Yancey Thigpen (1995)
	4	Louis Lipps (1985)
	4	John Stallworth (1981)
	4	Theo Bell (1980)

Most Touchdowns Receiving

Career	63	John Stallworth (1974–87)
	51	Lynn Swann (1974–82)
	42	Buddy Dial (1959–63)
	39	Louis Lipps (1984–91)
	37	Elbie Nickel (1947–57)
	34	Ray Mathews (1951–59)
	29	Roy Jefferson (1965–69)

Season	12	Louis Lipps (1985)
	12	Buddy Dial (1961)
	11	John Stallworth (1984)
	11	Lynn Swann (1978 & 1975)
	11	Roy Jefferson (1968)
Game	4	Roy Jefferson (11–3–68 vs. Atlanta)
	3	Eric Green (10–14–90 vs. Denver)
	3	Weegie Thompson (11–2–86 vs. Green Bay)
	3	Louis Lipps (9–8–85 vs. Indianapolis)
	3	John Stallworth (11–4–84 vs. Hou., 11–24–84 vs. San Diego)
	3	Jim Smith (9–28–80 vs. Chicago)
	3	Ray Mathews (10–17–54 vs. Cleveland)

Most Consecutive Games Caught Pass

	67	John Stallworth (began 10–9–77 vs. Houston and ended 12–12–82 vs. Buffalo)

PUNTING

Most Punts

Career	716	Bobby Walden (1968–77)
	429	Craig Colquitt (1978–81, 1983–84)
	375	Harry Newsome (1985–89)
	259	Mark Royals (1992–94)
	223	Pat Brady (1952–54)
	171	Joe Geri (1949–51)
Season	97	Mark Royals (1994)
	89	Mark Royals (1993)
	86	Harry Newsome (1986)
	84	Craig Colquitt (1981)
	82	Harry Newsome (1989)
	80	Craig Colquitt (1983)
	80	Pat Brady (1953)
	79	Bobby Walden (1971)
	78	Harry Newsome (1985)
Game	11	Mark Royals (12–5–93 vs. New England, 11–6–94 vs. Houston)
	10	Harry Newsome (11–9–86 vs. Buffalo)
	10	Harry Newsome (9–16–85 vs. Cleveland)
	10	Bobby Walden (12–7–69 vs. Dallas)

Highest Average Punting

Career	45.7	Bobby Joe Green (1960–61)
	44.5	Pat Brady (1952–54)
	41.5	Mark Royals (1992–94)
	41.4	Harry Newsome (1985–89)
	41.3	Craig Colquitt (1978–81, 1983–84)
	41.1	Bobby Walden (1968–77)
Season	47.0	Bobby Joe Green (1961)
	46.9	Pat Brady (1953)
	45.4	Harry Newsome (1988)
	45.2	Bobby Walden (1970)

Longest Punts

	82	Joe Geri (11–20–49 vs. Green Bay)
	75	Bobby Joe Greene (1960)
	74	Craig Colquitt (12–7–81 vs. Oakland), Bob Cifers (1947)

PUNT RETURNS

Most Punt Returns

Career	256	Rod Woodson (1987–95)
	139	Theo Bell (1976, 78–80)
	107	Louis Lipps (1984–91)
	99	Glen Edwards (1971–77)
	98	Jim Smith (1977–82)
	70	Rick Woods (1982–86)
	66	Lynn Chandnois (1950–56)
Season	53	Louis Lipps (1984)
	48	Andre Hastings (1995)
	45	Theo Bell (1979)
	43	Paul Skansi (1983)
	41	Rod Woodson (1993)
	41	Lynn Swann (1974)
	39	Rod Woodson (1994)
	39	Theo Bell (1976)
	38	Rod Woodson (1990)

Most Yards Punt Returns

Career	2,362	Rod Woodson (1987–95)
	1,259	Theo Bell (1976, 78–80)
	1,212	Louis Lipps (1984–91)
	941	Glen Edwards (1971–76)
	838	Bill Dudley (1942, 45–46)
Season	*656	Louis Lipps (1984)
	577	Lynn Swann (1974)
	474	Andre Hastings (1995)
	437	Louis Lipps (1985)
	435	Walt Slater (1947)

*NFL Rookie Record

Most Touchdowns Punt Returns

Career	3	Ray Mathews (1951–59), Louis Lipps (1984–89)
Season	2	Ray Mathews (1952), Louis Lipps (1985)
Game	1	Held by many, last time by Andre Hastings (72 yards, 9–10–95 at Houston)

Highest Average Punt Returns

Career	14.9	Bobby Gage (1949–50)
	14.4	Bill Dudley (1942, 45–46)
	12.8	Ray Mathews (1951–59)
	12.3	Lynn Swann (1974–78)
Season	16.0	Bobby Gage (1949)
	15.5	Walt Slater (1947)
	15.4	Ray Mathews (1951)
	14.1	Lynn Swann (1974)

Longest Punt Returns

	90	Brady Keys (9–20–64 vs. N.Y. Giants)
	82	Brady Keys (9–22–63 vs. N.Y. Giants)
	80t	Rod Woodson (10–25–92 vs. Kansas City)
	80t	Roy Jefferson (11–10–68 vs. St. Louis)

KICKOFF RETURNS

Most Kickoff Returns

Career	220	Rod Woodson (1987–95)
	122	Larry Anderson (1978–81)
	98	Dwight Stone (1987–94)
	92	Lynn Chandnois (1950–56)
	68	Ernie Mills (1991–95)
	64	Gary Ballman (1963–66)
	52	Preston Pearson (1970–74)
	49	Rich Erenberg (1984–86)
Season	54	Ernie Mills (1995)
	44	Rod Woodson (1991)
	39	Henry Odom (1983)
	37	Rod Woodson (1988)
	37	Larry Anderson (1978, 1981)
	36	Rod Woodson (1989)
	35	Rod Woodson (1990)
	34	Larry Anderson (1979)
	29	Dwight Stone (1988)
	28	Brady Keys (1962)
	28	Rich Erenberg (1984)
Game	7	Jack Deloplaine (9–26–76 vs. New England); Rich Erenberg (9–2–84 vs. Kansas City)

Most Yards Kickoff Returns

Career	4,894	Rod Woodson (1987–95)
	2,866	Larry Anderson (1978–81)
	2,720	Lynn Chandnois (1950–56)
	2,086	Dwight Stone (1987–94)
	1,711	Gary Ballman (1963–66)
Season	1,306	Ernie Mills (1995)
	982	Rod Woodson (1989)
	930	Larry Anderson (1978)
	880	Rod Woodson (1991)
	850	Rod Woodson (1988)
	825	Larry Anderson (1981)
	764	Rod Woodson (1990)
	758	Henry Odom (1983)
	732	Larry Anderson (1979)

Most Touchdowns Kickoff Returns

Career	3	Lynn Chandnois (1950–56)
Season	2	Lynn Chandnois (1952)
Game	1	Held by many, last time by Dwight Stone (92 yards, 2–4–88 vs. Houston)

Highest Average Kickoff Returns

Career	29.6	Lynn Chandnois (1950–56)
	26.7	Gary Ballman (1963–66)
	25.8	Mel Blount (1970–78)
	23.8	Brady Keys (1961–67)
	23.6	Ernie Mills (1991–95)
	23.5	Larry Anderson (1978–80)
Season	35.2	Lynn Chandnois (1952)
	32.5	Lynn Chandnois (1951)
	29.7	Mel Blount (1970)

Longest Kickoff Returns

101t	Don McCall (11–23–69 vs. Minnesota)
96t	Billy Wells (10–13–57 vs. Chicago Cards)
95t	Larry Anderson (10–2–78 vs. Clev.)
94t	Mike Collier (10–26–75 vs. Green Bay)

INTERCEPTIONS

Most Interceptions

Career	57	Mel Blount (1970–83)
	52	Jack Butler (1951–59)
	51	Donnie Shell (1974–87)
	37	Dwayne Woodruff (1979–85, 87–90)
	36	Mike Wagner (1971–80)
	32	Jack Ham (1971–82)
	32	Rod Woodson (1987–95)
	28	Jack Lambert (1974–84)
	25	Glen Edwards (1971–77)
	25	Howard Hartley (1949–52)
	23	Clendon Thomas (1962–68)
Season	11	Mel Blount (1975)
	10	Jack Butler (1957)
	10	Howard Hartley (1951)
	10	Bill Dudley (1946)
Game	4	Jack Butler (12–13–53 vs. Washington)

Most Yards Interceptions Returned

Career	827	Jack Butler (1951–59)
	736	Mel Blount (1970–83)
	689	Dwayne Woodruff (1979–85, 87–90)
	658	Rod Woodson (1987–95)
	652	Glen Edwards (1971–77)
	491	Mike Wagner (1971–80)
	450	Donnie Shell (1974–87)
Season	242	Bill Dudley (1946)
	186	Glen Edwards (1973)
	179	Tony Compagno (1948)
	168	Jack Butler (1952)
	153	Glen Edwards (1974)

Most Touchdowns on Interceptions

Career	4	Rod Woodson (1987–95)
	4	Jack Butler (1951–59)
	3	Dwayne Woodruff (1979–85, 87–90)
	3	Tony Compagno (1946–48)
Season	2	Rod Woodson (1994)
	2	Jack Butler (1954)
	2	Tony Compagno (1947)
	2	Sam Washington (1984)
Game	1	Held by many, most recently by Willie Williams and Alvoid Mays (10–1–95 vs. S.D.)

Longest Interception Returns

99t	Martin Kottler (9–27–33 vs. Chicago Cards)
86t	Glen Edwards (9–30–73 vs. Houston)
82t	Tony Compagno (11–7–48 vs. Green Bay)

Most Consecutive Games Intercepting a Pass

      6   Mel Blount (1975)

QUARTERBACK SACKS

Most Quarterback Sacks

Career	73.5	L.C. Greenwood (1969–81)
	66.0	Joe Greene (1969–81)
	59.0	Keith Willis (1982–87, 89–91)
	49.0	Greg Lloyd (1988–95)
	46.0	Dwight White (1971–80)
	40.0	Ernie Holmes (1972–77)
Season	15.0	Mike Merriweather (1984)
	14.0	Keith Willis (1983)
	14.0	Kevin Greene (1994) #
	12.5	Kevin Greene (1993)
	12.0	Keith Willis (1986)
	11.5	Ernie Holmes (1974)
	11.0	Joe Greene (1972)
Game	5.0	Joe Greene (12–10–72 vs. Houston)
	4.5	L.C. Greenwood (11–25–79 vs. Cleveland)
	4.0	Jerrol Williams (12–22–91 vs. Cleveland)
	4.0	Edmund Nelson (9–16–84 vs. Los Angeles Rams)

Most Consecutive Games With a Sack

      6   Joe Greene (1974)
      6   Ernie Holmes (1974)
      6   Greg Lloyd (1994)
      5   Dwight White (1972)

OPPONENT FUMBLE RECOVERIES

Most Opponent Fumbles Recovered

Career	21	Jack Ham (1971–82)
	19	Donnie Shell (1974–87)
	16	Joe Greene (1969–81)
	15	Jack Lambert (1974–84)
Season	6	Jack Lambert (1976)
	5	Carnell Lake (1989)
	5	Donnie Shell (1978)
	5	Joe Greene (1978)
	5	L.C. Greenwood (1971)
	5	John Reger (1955, 1957)
	5	Gary Glick (1957)

– NFL Leader

Ernie Holmes puts the head of Cleveland quarterback Brian Sipe in a vise grip. Holmes is tied with Joe Greene and Greg Lloyd for the most consecutive games with a sack (six).

ALL-TIME HEAD COACHES

Coach (Years)	Overall	Record
Austin, Bill (1966–68)	11–28–3	(.298)
Bach, Joe (1935–36, 52–53)	21–27–0	(.438)
Bell, Bert (1941)	0–2–0	(.000)
Cowher, Bill (1992–95)	44–24	(.647)
DiMelio, Luby (1934)	2–10–0	(.167)
Donelli, Aldo (1941)	0–5–0	(.000)
Douds, Forrest (1933)	3–6–2	(.364)
Kiesling, Walter (1939–40, 41–44★, 54–56)	30–55–5	(.361)
Leonard, Jim (1945)	2–8–0	(.200)
McNally, Johnny "Blood" (1937–39)	6–19–0	(.240)
Michelosen, Johnny (1948–51)	20–26–2	(.438)
Nixon, Mike (1965)	2–12–0	(.143)
Noll, Chuck (1969–1991)	209–156–1	(.572)
Parker, Raymond (1957–64)	51–48–6	(.514)
Sutherland, Jock (1946–47)	13–10–1	★(.563)

★Kiesling was co–head coach with Greasy Neale in 1943 (Phil.–Pitt.) and with Phil Handler in 1944 (Card.–Pitt.).

ALL-TIME ASSISTANT COACHES

April, Bobby 1994–95	Heinrich, Don 1966–68	Ramsey, Buster 1962–64
Bach, Joe 1935–36	Henry, Jack 1990–91	Reese, Cad 1934 36
Ball, Herman 1955	Hoak, Dick 1972–95	Riecke, Lou 1970–79
Blackledge, Ron 1982–91	Hodgson, Pat 1992–95	Ronzani, Gene 1954
Brazil, Dave 1989–91	Hughes, Jed 1984–88	Rooker, Harvey 1948
Bridgers, John 1969	Hunter, Hal 1985–88	Rooney, JP 1934–35
Butler, Jack 1961–63	Jones, Edgar 1953	Rust, Rod 1989
Capers, Dom 1992–94	Keane, Tom 1965	Skladany, Joseph 1947
Carson, Bud 1972–77	Kiesling, Walt ★1938–39, 41, 49–54, 57–61	Skorich, Nick 1955–57
Cherundolo, Charles 1948–57, 61	Kolb, Jon 1982–91	Snyder, Bob 1955
Coley, Max 1969–71	Kuharich, Joe 1946	Sortet, Wilbur 1940
Craft, Russ 1956	Layne, Bobby 1964–65	Souchak, Frank 1946
Davis, Robert 1951	LeBeau, Dick 1992–95	Spezzaferro, John 1976
DePasqua, Carl 1968	Leonard, Jim 1942	Stautner, Ernie 1963–64
DiMancheff, Boris 1958–59	Lewis, Art 1960–61	Stephenson, Kent 1992–95
Dorais, Gus 1952	Lewis, Marvin 1992–95	Stewart, George 1989–91
Doran, Jim 1964–65	Lewis, Tim 1995	Stilley, Ken 1959–63
Dotsch, Rollie 1978–81	McGraw, Thurman 1958–61	Sumner, Charley 1969–72
Dudley, Bill 1956	McLaughlin, Leon 1966–68	Taylor, Hugh 1966–68
Dungy, Tony 1981–88	McPeak, Bill 1956–58	Taylor, Lionel 1970–76
Erhardt, Ron 1992–95	Meyers, Bill 1984	Torgeson, LaVerne 1962–68
Evans, Walt 1982–88	Michelosen, John 1946–47	Uram, Paul 1972–81
Fletcher, Tom 1966–68	Mitchell, John 1995	Valesente, Bob 1990–91
Fitzgerald, Dennis 1982–88	Moore, Tom 1977–89	Walls, Will 1962–63
Fox, John 1989–91	McNally, Johnny "Blood" 1936	Walker, Dick 1978–81
Fry, Bob 1969–73	Neale, Greasy ★1943	Walton, Frank 1947
Furness, Steve 1992–93	Nixon, Mike 1961–65	Walton, Joe 1990–91
Gailey, Chan 1994–95	Ormiston, Ken 1948–50	Widenhofer, Woody 1973–83
Gilmer, Harry 1957–60	Painter, Dwain 1988–91	Wray, Lud 1945
Greene, Joe 1987–91	Parilli, Babe 1971–73	
Guy, John 1992–93	Patrick, Frank 1948	★Kiesling and Neale were co–head coaches of Phil–Pitt in 1943
Hackett, Walter 1969–70	Perles, George 1972–81	
Handler, Phil ★1944	Perry, Lowell 1957	Kiesling and Handler were co–head coaches of Card–Pitt in 1944
Harrison, Bob 1992–93	Plasman, Dick 1958–61	
Hefferle, Ernie 1965	Radakovich, Dan 1971, 74–77	

ALL-TIME ROSTER

A

Abercrombie, Walter [RB], Baylor 1982–87
Adamchik, Ed [T], Pitt 1967
Adams, Bob [TE], Pacific 1969–71
Adams, Paul [C], Morehead Teachers......... 1947
Agajanian, Ben [K], New Mexico............. 1945
Alban, Dick [E], Northwestern........... 1956–59
Alberghini, Tom [G], Holy Cross 1945
Albrecht, Art [C/OT], Wisconsin 1942
Alderton, John [E], Maryland............... 1953
Allen, Chuck [LB], Washington 1970–71
Allen, Dwane [LB], Santa Ana 1965
Allen, Jim [DB], UCLA................. 1974–77
Allen, Lou [T], Duke.................... 1950–51
Alley, Don [WR], Adams State 1969
Alston, Lyneal [WR], Southern Mississippi .. 1987
Andabaker, Rudy [G], Pitt............. 1952, 54
Anderson, Anthony [RB], Temple 1979
Anderson, Art [T], Idaho.................. 1963
Anderson, Chet [E], Minnesota 1967
Anderson, Fred [DE], Prairie View A&M 1978
Anderson, Gary [K], Syracuse........... 1982–94
Anderson, Jesse [TE], Miss. State......... 1992
Anderson, Larry [DB], Louisiana Tech 1978–81
Anderson, Melvin [WR], Minnesota 1987
Anderson, Ralph [DB], W. Texas St....... 1971–72
Apke, Steve [LB], Pitt 1987
Arndt, Al [G], South Dakota State 1935
Arndt, Dick [T], Idaho 1967–70
Arnold, David [CB], Michigan 1989
Arnold, Jay [QB], Texas.................. 1941
Artman, Corwan [T], Stanford 1933
Asbury, Willie [B], Kent State........... 1966–68
Askson, Burt [DE], Texas Southern 1971
Atkinson, Frank [T], Stanford 1963
August, Steve [OT], Tulsa 1984
Augusterfer, Gene [B], Catholic U............ 1935
Austin, Ocie [DB], Utah State........... 1970–71
Avery, Steve [FB], Northern Michigan 1994–95
Aydelette, Buddy [OT/C], Alabama 1987

B

Badar, Rich [QB], North Carolina 1967
Bahr, Matt [K], Penn State 1979–80
Baker, Conway [T], Centenary 1944**
Baker, Ed [E], Washington State........... 1953
Baker, John [E], N. Carolina College 1963–67
Baldacci, Lou [B], Michigan 1956
Ballman, Gary [B], Michigan State....... 1962–66
Balog, Bob [C], Denver 1949–50
Banaszak, John [DE/DT], E. Michigan 1975–81
Bankston, Warren [RB], Tulane 1969–72
Barbolak, Pete [T], Purdue 1949
Barnes, Reggie [LB], Oklahoma............. 1993
Barnett, Tom [B], Purdue 1959–60
Barry, Fred [DB], Boston College 1970
Bartaanen, Jim [C], Michigan.............. 1938
Bartlett, Earl [B], Centre 1939
Basrak, Mike [C], Duquesne 1937–38
Bassi, Dick [G], Santa Clara 1941
Beams, Byron [T], Notre Dame 1959–60
Beasley, Tom [DE/DT], Virginia Tech 1978–83
Beatty, Charles [DB], N. Texas St....... 1969–72
Beatty, Ed [C], Mississippi............. 1957–61
Becker, Wayland [E], Marquette............. 1939
Behning, Mark [OT], Nebraska 1986
Bell, Myron [S], Michigan State........... 1994–95
Bell, Richard [RB], Nebraska 1990
Bell, Theo [WR], Arizona 1976, 78–80

Bentley, Albert [RB], Miami (Fla.)........... 1992
Bernet, Ed [E], SMU 1955
Best, Greg [S], Kansas State 1983
Bettis, Tom [LB], Purdue 1962
Billock, Frank [G], St. Mary's of Minn....... 1937
Bingham, Craig [LB], Syracuse........ 1982–84, 87
Binotto, John [B], Duquesne 1942
Bishop, Don [B], Los Angeles Col........ 1958–59
Bivins, Charles [B], Morris Brown 1967
Blackledge, Todd [QB], Penn State........ 1988–89
Blankenship, Brian [G], Nebraska 1987–91
Blankenship, Greg [LB], Cal. St. (Hay.) 1976
Bleier, Rocky [RB], Notre Dame..... 1968, 1970–80
Blount, Mel [CB], Southern 1970–83
Bohannon, Fred [S/CB], Mass. Val. St........ 1982
Bolkovac, Nick [T], Pitt................. 1953–54
Bond, Randall [QB], Washington............. 1939
Bonelli, Ernie [B], Pitt.................... 1946
Bono, Steve [QB], UCLA................. 1987–88
Booth, Clarence [B], SMU................1944**
Boures, Emil [C/G], Pitt 1982–86
Bova, Tony [E], St. Francis... 1942, 43*, 44**, 45–47
Bowman, Bill [B], William & Mary 1957
Boyd, Sam [E], Baylor 1939–40
Boyle, Jim [OT], Tulane................. 1987–88
Boyle, Shorty [E] 1934
Bradley, Ed [LB], Wake Forest 1972–75
Bradshaw, Charles [T], Baylor 1961–66
Bradshaw, Jim [B], Chattanooga 1963–67
Bradshaw, Terry [QB], La. Tech 1970–83
Brady, Jeff [LB], Kentucky 1991
Brady, Pat [B], Nevada................ 1952–54
Brandau, Art [C], Tennessee 1945–46
Brandt, Jim [B], St. Thomas 1952–54
Bray, Maurice [T], SMU 1935–36
Breedlove, Rod [LB], Maryland 1965–68
Breedon, Bill [B], Oklahoma................. 1937
Breen, Gene [LB], Virginia Tech 1965–66
Brett, Ed [E], Washington State 1936–37
Brewster, Pete [E], Purdue.............. 1959–60
Brister, Bubby [QB], Northeast La. 1986–92
Britt, Jessie [WR], North Carolina A&T 1986
Britt, Ralph [TE], North Carolina State 1987
Broussard, Fed [C], Texas A & M 1955
Brovelli, Angelo [QB], St. Mary's (Cal.)..... 1933–34
Brown, Chad [LB], Colorado 1993–95
Brown, Chris [CB/S], Notre Dame 1984–85
Brown, Dave [DB], Michigan 1975
Brown, Ed [QB], San Francisco 1962–65
Brown, John [T], Syracuse 1967–72
Brown, Larry [TE/OT], Kansas 1971–84
Brown, Tom [E], William & Mary 1942
Brown, William [QB], Texas Tech 1945
Browning, Greg [E], Denver 1947
Bruder, Henry [QB], Northwestern 1940
Bruener, Mark [TE], Washington 1995
Brumbaugh, Boyd [B], Duquesne.......... 1939–41
Brumfield, Jim [RB], Ind. St. (Ind.)......... 1971
Brundage, Dewey [E], Brigham Young 1954
Bruney, Fred [B], Ohio State.......... 1956–57
Bruno, John [P], Penn State 1987
Bryant, Hubie [WR], Minnesota........... 1970
Bucek, Felix [G], Texas A & M 1946
Buckner, Brentson [DE], Clemson 1994–95
Buda, Carl [G], Tulsa 1945
Bukich, Rudy [QB], Southern Cal......... 1960–61
Bulger, Chester [T], Auburn 1944**
Bullocks, Amos [B], Southern Illinois 1966
Burleson, John [G], SMU 1933
Burnett, Len [DB], Oregon 1961

Burnette, Tom [B], North Carolina........... 1938
Burrell, John [E], Rice.................. 1962–64
Butler, Bill [DB/KR], Chattanooga........... 1961
Butler, Jack [B], St. Bonaventure 1951–59
Butler, Jim [B], Edward Waters........... 1965–67
Butler, John [B], Tennessee 1943–44
Bykowski, Frank [G], Purdue............... 1940

C

Cabrelli, Larry [E], Colgate................. 1943*
Calcagni, Ralph [T], Pennsylvania 1947
Caliguire, Dean [G/C], Pittsburgh 1991–92
Call, John [B], Colgate 1959
Calland, Lee [DB], Louisville............. 1969–72
Calloway, Chris [WR], Michigan 1990–91
Calvin, Tom [B], Alabama 1952–54
Cameron, Paul [B], UCLA................ 1954
Campbell, Bob [RB], Penn State.......... 1969
Campbell, Don [T], Carnegie Tech....... 1939–41
Campbell, Glenn [E], Emporia State 1935
Campbell, John [LB], Minnesota 1965–69
Campbell, Leon [B], Arkansas 1955
Campbell, Ray [LB], Marquette 1958–60
Campbell, Russ [TE], Kansas State 1992
Campbell, Scott [QB], Purdue............. 1984–86
Canale, Rocco [G], Boston College 1943*
Capers, Wayne [WR], Kansas 1983–84
Capp, Dick [E], Boston College 1968
Cara, Dom [E], N. Carolina State 1937–38
Cardwell, Joe [T], Duke.............. 1937–38
Carpenter, Preston [E], Arkansas 1960–63
Carr, Gregg [LB], Auburn 1985–88
Carter, Rodney [RB], Purdue 1987–89
Cash, Keith [TE], Texas................. 1991
Casper, Charles [QB], TCU 1935
Catano, Mark [DE/DT], Valdosta State 1984–85
Cenci, John [C], Pitt................... 1956
Chamberlain, Garth [G], Brig. Young 1945
Chandnois, Lynn [B], Mich. State 1950–56
Cheatham, Ernest [T], Loyola............. 1954
Cherry, Edgar [B], Hardin–Simmons 1939
Cherundolo, Chuck [C], Penn State . 1941–42, 45–48
Christy, Dick [B], N. Carolina State........... 1958
Cibulas, Joe [T], Duquesne 1945
Ciccone, Ben [C], Duquesne 1934–35
Cichowski, Gene [B], Indiana............... 1957
Cifelli, Gus [T], Notre Dame 1954
Cifers, Bob [QB], Tennessee 1947–48
Clack, Jim [C/G], Wake Forest 1971–77
Clark, Jim [B], Pitt.................. 1933–34
Clark, Mike [K], Texas A & M 1964–67
Clark, Reggie [LB], North Carolina 1994
Clark, Spark [RB], Akron 1987
Clayton, Harvey [CB], Florida State........ 1983–86
Clement, Henry [E], North Carolina 1961
Clement, John [B], SMU 1946–48*
Cline, Jackie [DE], Alabama 1987
Clinkscales, Joey [WR], Tennessee 1987–88
Cobb, Marvin [DB], Southern Cal........... 1980
Cole, Robin [LB], New Mexico.......... 1977–87
Cole, Terry [B], Indiana 1970
Collier, Mike [RB], Morgan State 1975
Collier, Reggie [QB], So. Mississippi 1987
Colquitt, Craig [P], Tennessee....... 1978–81, 83–84
Compagno, Tony [B], St. Mary's of Calif.... 1946–48
Compton, Dick [E], McMurry 1967–68
Condit, Merlyn [B], Carnegie Tech........ 1940, 46
Conn, Dick [DB], Georgia................. 1974
Connelly, Mike [C], Utah State............. 1968

Conti, Enio [G], Bucknell 1943*
Coomer, Joe [T], Austin. 1941, 45–46
Cooper, Adrian [TE], Oklahoma. 1991–93
Cooper, Sam [T], Geneva. 1933
Cordileone, Lou [G], Clemson 1962–63
Corley, Anthony [RB], Nevada–Reno. 1984
Coronado, Bob [E], Pacific 1961
Cotton, Russell [B], Texas Mines 1942
Courson, Steve [G], South Carolina 1978–83
Cousino, Brad [LB], Miami (O.). 1977
Craft, Russ [B], Alabama 1954
Cregar, William [G], Holy Cross. 1947–48
Crennel, Carl [LB], W. Va. 1970
Critchfield, Larry [G], Grove City 1933
Croft, Winfield [G], Utah. 1936
Cropper, Marshall [E], Maryland 1967–69
Cunningham, Bennie [TE], Clemson. 1976–85
Currivan, Don [E], Boston College. 1944**
Curry, Roy [B], Jackson State 1963
Cuthbert, Randy [RB], Duke 1993–94

D

Daigle, Anthony [RB], Fresno State. 1994
Dailey, Ted [E], Pitt 1933
Daniel, Willie [B], Miss. State. 1961–66
Davenport, Charles [WR], N. C. State 1992–94
Davidson, Bill [B], Temple 1937–39
Davidson, Kenny [DE], Louisiana State 1990–93
Davis, Art [B], Mississippi State. 1956
Davis, Charlie [DT], TCU. 1974
Davis, Dave [WR], Tennessee State 1973
Davis, Henry [LB], Grambling. 1970–73
Davis, Lorenzo [WR], Youngstown State 1990
Davis, Paul [QB], Otterbein 1947–48
Davis, Robert [E], Penn State 1946–50
Davis, Russell [RB], Michigan 1980–83
Davis, Sam [G], Allen 1967–79
Davis, Steve [RB], Delaware State 1972–74
Dawkins, Tommy [DE], Appalachian State. 1987
Dawson, Dermontti [G/C], Kentucky 1988–95
Dawson, Len [QB], Purdue. 1957–59
DeCarbo, Nick [G], Duquesne 1933
DeCarlo, Art [B], Georgia 1953
Deloplaine, Jack [RB], Salem (W.Va.). 1976–79
Demko, George [T], Appalachian St. 1961
Dempsey, John [T], Bucknell 1934
DePascal, Carmine [E], Wichita 1945
DePaul, Henry [G], Duquesne 1945
Derby, Dean [B], Washington 1957–61
Dess, Darrell [G], N. Carolina State 1958
Dial, Buddy [E], Rice. 1959–63
Dickey, Charlie [G], Arizona. 1987
Dicus, Chuck [WR], Arkansas 1973
Didio, Mark [WR], Connecticut. 1992
Dirden, Johnnie [WR], Sam Houston St. 1981
Dockery, John [DB], Harvard 1972–73
Dodrill, Dale [G], Colorado A & M 1951–59
Dodson, Les [B], Mississippi 1941
Doehring, John [B]. 1935
Dolly, Dick [E], West Virginia 1941–45
Doloway, Cliff [E], Carnegie Tech. 1935
Donelli, Allan [B], Duquesne 1941–42
Donnalley, Rick [C–G], North Carolina. 1982–83
Dornbrook, Thom [G–C], Kentucky 1979
Douds, Forrest [T], W & J. 1933–35
Dougherty, Bob [LB], Kentucky. 1958
Douglas, Bob [B], Kansas State. 1938
Doyle, Dick [B], Ohio State 1955
Doyle, Ted [T], Nebraska. 1938–42, 43*, 44**
Drulis, Al [B], Temple 1947
Druschel, Rick [G–OT], No. Car. St. 1974
Dudley, Bill [B], Virginia. 1942, 45–46
Dugan, Len [C], Wichita 1939
Duggan, Gil [T], Oklahoma 1944**
Duhart, Paul [B], Florida. 1945
Dunaway, Craig [TE], Michigan. 1983
Dungy, Tony [DB], Minnesota 1977–78
Dunn, Gary [DT–NT], Miami (Fla.) 1977–87
Dutton, Bill [B], Pitt 1946

E

Eaton, Vic [QB], Missouri 1955
Echols, Terry [LB], Marshall. 1984
Edwards, Dave [S], Illinois 1985–87
Edwards, Glen [DB], Florida A & M 1971–77
Elder, Donnie [CB], Memphis State. 1986
Elliott, Jim [K], Presbyterian 1967
Ellstrom, Marv [B], Oklahoma 1935
Elter, Leo [B], Duq. and Villa. 1953–54, 58–59
Engebretsen, Paul [G], Northwestern 1933
Engles, Rick [P], Tulsa. 1977
Erenberg, Rich [RB], Colgate 1984–86
Evans, Donald [DE], Kentucky 1990–93
Evans, Jon [E], Oklahoma A & M 1958
Evans, Ray [QB], Kansas. 1948
Everett, Thomas [FS], Baylor 1987–91

F

Farrar, Venice [B], N. Carolina State 1938–39
Farrell, Ed [B], Muhlenberg 1938
Farroh, Shipley [GB], Iowa 1938
Faumui, Taase [DL], Hawaii. 1994–95
Feher, Nick [G], Georgia 1955
Feniello, Garry [G], Wake Forest 1947
Ferguson, Bob [B], Ohio State 1962–63
Ferry, Lou [T], Villanova. 1952–55
Fife, Ralph [C], Pitt 1946
Figures, Deon [CB], Colorado. 1993–95
Fike, Dan [OL], Florida 1993
Filchock, Frank [QB], Indiana 1938
Finks, Jim [QB], Tulsa. 1949–55
Finn, Mike [OT], Ark.–Pine Bluff 1993
Fisher, Doug [LB], San Diego State. 1969–70
Fisher, Everett [B], Santa Clara. 1940
Fisher, Ray [T], Eastern Illinois 1959
Fiske, Max [B], DePaul 1936–39
Flanagan, Dick [G], Ohio State 1953–55
Flowers, Lethon [DB], Georgia Tech 1995
Foggie, Fred [CB], Minnesota. 1994
Folkins, Lee [E], Washington 1965
Foltz, Vernon [C], St. Vincent. 1945
Ford, Darryl [LB], New Mexico State 1992
Ford, Henry [B], Pitt 1956
Ford, Moses [WR], Fayetteville State. 1987
Foruria, John [B], Idaho 1967–68
Foster, Barry [RB], Arkansas. 1990–94
Fournet, Sid [G], LSU 1957
Francis, Sam [B], Nebraska. 1939
Frank, Joe [T], Georgetown. 1943*
Freeman, Lorenzo [NT/DT], Pitt. 1987–90
French, Ernest [S], Alabama A&M 1982
Frketich, Len [T], Penn State. 1945
Fugler, Dick [T], Tulane 1952
Fuller, Randy, [DB], Tennessee State 1995
Fullerton, Ed [B], Maryland 1953
Fuqua, John [B], Morgan State. 1970–76
Furness, Steve [DT], Rhode Island 1972–80

G

Gage, Bob [B], Clemson. 1949–50
Gagner, Larry [G], Florida 1966–69
Gammon, Kendall [OL], Pittsburg State. . . . 1992–95
Gaona, Bob [T], Wake Forest 1953–56
Garnaas, Wilford [B], Minnesota 1946–48
Garrett, Reggie [WR], Eastern Michigan. . . . 1974–75
Garrity, Gregg [WR], Penn State 1983
Gary, Keith [DE], Oklahoma 1983–88
Gasparella, Joe [QB], Notre Dame 1948, 50–51
Gauer, Charles [E], Colgate 1943*
Gentry, Byron [G], Southern Cal. 1937–39
Gerela, Roy [PK], New Mexico State 1971–78
Geri, Joe [B], Georgia. 1949–51
Gibson, Oliver [DT], Notre Dame 1995
Gildea, John [QB], St. Bonaventure 1935–37
Gildon, Jason [LB], Oklahoma State 1994–95
Gillespie, Scoop [RB], William Jewell 1984
Gilliam, Joe [QB], Tennessee State. 1972–1975
Girard, Earl [B], Wisconsin. 1957
Glamp, Joe [B], LSU 1947–49
Glass, Glenn [B], Tennessee 1962–63
Glass, Park [C], Westminster. 1947
Glatz, Fred [E], Pitt 1956
Glick, Gary [B], Colorado A & M. 1956–59
Goff, Clark [T], Florida 1940
Goldsmith, Bill [C], Emporia Tchrs 1947
Gonda, George [B], Duquesne 1942
Goodman, John [DE/DT], Oklahoma 1981–85
Goodson, John [P], Texas. 1982
Gorinski, Walt [B], LSU 1946
Gothard, Preston [TE], Alabama 1985–88
Gowdy, Cornell [CB], Morgan State. 1987–88
Grabowski, Ted [C], Duquesne 1939–40
Graff, Neil [QB], Wisconsin 1976–77
Graham, Jeff [WR], Ohio State 1991–93
Graham, Ken [DB], Washington State. 1970
Gravelle, Gordon [OT], Brigham Young 1972–76
Graves, Ray [C], Tennessee 1943*
Graves, Tom [LB], Michigan State. 1979
Gray, Sam [E], Tulsa. 1946–47
Grebinski, Ted [C], Duquesne. 1939–40
Green, Bob [K], Florida. 1960–61
Green, Eric [TE], Liberty 1990–94
Greene, Joe [DT], N. Texas State 1969–81
Greene, Kevin [LB], Auburn 1993–95
Greene, Tracy [TE], Grambling 1995
Greeney, Norm [G], Notre Dame 1934–35
Greenwood, L.C. [DE], Ark. AM&N. 1969–81
Griffin, Larry [CB/S], North Carolina 1987–93
Grigas, John [B], Holy Cross. 1944**
Gros, Earl [B], LSU 1967–69
Grossman, Randy [TE], Temple 1974–81
Gunderman, Bob [B], Virginia 1957
Gunnels, Riley [T], Georgia 1956–66

H

Hackney, Elmer [B], Kansas State 1941
Haggerty, Mike [G], Miami. 1967–70
Haines, Byron [B], Washington 1937
Hairston, Russell [WR], Kentucky. 1987
Haley, Dick [B], Pitt. 1961–64
Hall, Delton [CB], Clemson 1987–91
Hall, Ron [B], Missouri Valley 1959
Haller, Alan [CB], Michigan State 1992, 93
Ham, Jack [LB], Penn State 1971–82
Hanlon, Bob [B], Loras 1949
Hanneman, Craig [DE], Oregon State 1972–73
Hanratty, Terry [QB], Notre Dame. 1969–75
Hanson, Tom [B], Temple 1938
Harkey, Lem [B], Emporia 1955
Harper, Maurice [C], Austin 1941
Harris, Bill [E], Hardin–Simmons 1937
Harris, Franco [RB], Penn State. 1972–83
Harris, Lou [B], Kent State. 1968
Harris, Tim [RB], Washington St. 1983
Harrison Reggie [RB], Cincinnati 1974–77
Harrison, Richard [E], Boston College. 1964
Harrison, Robert [LB], Oklahoma 1964
Hartley, Howard [B], Duke 1949–52
Haselrig, Carlton [G], Pitt–Johnstown. 1990–93
Hastings, Andre [WR], Georgia 1993–95
Hawthorne, Greg [RB], Baylor 1979–83
Hayduk, Henry [G], Wash. State 1935
Hayes, Dick [LB], Clemson. 1959–60, 62
Hayes, Jonathan [TE], Iowa 1994–95
Hays, George [E], St. Bonaventure. 1950–52
Hebert, Ken [E & K], Houston. 1968

Hegarty, Bill [T], Villanova 1953
Held, Paul [QB], San Jose State 1954
Heller, Warren [B], Pitt 1934–36
Henderson, Jon [B], Colorado State 1968–69
Hendley, Dick [QB], Clemson. 1951
Henry, Kevin [DE], Mississippi State 1993–95
Henry, Mike [LB], Southern Cal. 1959–61
Henry, Urban [T], Georgia Tech. 1964
Hensley, Dick [E], Kentucky 1952
Henson, Ken [C], TCU 1965
Henton, Anthony [LB], Troy State. 1986, 88
Hewitt, Bill [E], Michigan. 1943*
Hickey, Howard [E], Arkansas 1941
Hill, Derek [WR], Arizona 1989–90
Hill, Harlon [E], Florence State 1962
Hill, Jim [B], Tennessee. 1955
Hillebrand, Jerry [LB], Colorado 1968–70
Hilton, John [E], Richmond 1965–69
Hines, Glen Ray [OT], Arkansas 1973
Hinkle, Bryan [LB], Oregon 1982–93
Hinkle, John [B], Syracuse 1943*
Hinnant, Mike [TE], Temple 1988–89
Hinte, Hale [E], Pitt. 1942
Hinton, Chuck [T], N. Car. College 1964–71
Hipps, Claude [B], Georgia 1952–53
Hoague, Joe [B], Colgate 1941–42, 46
Hoak, Dick [B], Penn State 1961–70
Hoel, Bob [G], Minnesota 1935
Hoffmann, Dave [LB], Washington 1993
Hogan, Darrell [G], Trinity–Texas 1949–53
Hoge, Merril [RB], Idaho State. 1987–93
Hohn, Bob [B], Nebraska 1965–69
Holcomb, Bill [T], Texas Tech 1937
Holler, Ed [LB], South Carolina. 1964
Holliday, Corey [WR], North Carolina 1995
Hollingsworth, Joe [B], E. Kan. State 1949–51
Holm, Bernard [B], Alabama 1933
Holmer, Walt [B], Northwestern. 1933
Holmes, Ernie [DT], Texas Southern. 1972–77
Holmes, Mel [OT], N. Carolina A & T 1971–73
Hood, Frank [B], Pitt. 1933
Hornick, Bill [T], Tulane. 1947
Howe, Garry [NT], Colorado 1992
Howe, Glen [OT], So. Mississippi 1985
Hubbard, Cal [T], Geneva & Centenary. 1936
Hubka, Gene [B], Bucknell 1947
Huff, Alan [NT], Marshall 1987
Hughes, David [RB], Boise State 1986
Hughes, Dennis [TE], Georgia 1970–71
Hughes, Dick [B], Tulsa. 1957
Hughes, George [G], Wm. & Mary. 1950–54
Hunter, Art [C], Notre Dame 1965

I

Ilkin, Tunch [OT], Indiana State 1980–92
Itzel, John [B], Pitt. 1945
Ivy, Frank [E], Oklahoma 1940
Izo, George [QB], Notre Dame 1966

J

Jackson, Earnest [RB], Texas A&M 1986–88
Jackson, John [OT], Eastern Kentucky 1988–95
James, Dan [T], Ohio State 1960–66
Janecek, Clarence [G], Purdue 1933, 35
Jansante, Val [E], Duquesne 1946–51
Jarvi, Toimi [B], Northern Illinois 1945
Jecha, Ralph [G], Northwestern 1956
Jefferson, Roy [E], Utah. 1965–69
Jelley, Tom [E], Miami. 1951
Jenkins, A.J. [LB/DE], Cal State–Fullerton . 1989–90
Jenkins, Ralph [C], Clemson. 1947
Jeter, Tony [E], Nebraska. 1966, 68
Johnson, Bill [DE], Michigan State 1995
Johnson, Charles [WR], Colorado. 1994–95
Johnson, David [CB], Kentucky. 1989–93
Johnson, Jason [WR], Illinois State 1989
Johnson, John Henry [B], St. Mary's (Cal.) and Arizona State. 1960–65
Johnson, Norm [PK], UCLA 1995
Johnson, Ron [CB], Eastern Michigan. 1978–84
Johnson, Tim [DE/DT], Penn State. 1987–89
Johnson, Troy [WR], Southern 1988
Johnston, Chet [B], Elmhurst & Marquette . 1939–40
Johnston, Rex [B], Southern Cal. 1960
Jones, Aaron [DE/LB], E. Kentucky 1988–92
Jones, Art [B], Richmond 1941, 45
Jones, Bruce [SS], Northern Alabama 1987
Jones, Donta [LB], Nebraska 1995
Jones, Gary [S], Texas A&M 1990–91, 93–94
Jones, Victor [FB], Louisiana State 1993–94
Jordan, Darin [LB], Northeastern 1988
Jorden, Tim [TE], Indiana 1992–93

K

Kahler, Royal [T], Nebraska 1941
Kakasic, George [G], Duquesne 1936–39
Kalina, Dave [WR], Miami (Fla.). 1970
Kalis, Todd [G], Arizona State 1994
Kapele, John [T], Brigham Young 1960–62
Kaplan, Phil [G], Miami (Fla.) 1947
Karcis, John [B], Carnegie Tech 1936–38
Karets, Joe [], ...
Karpowich, Ed [T], Catholic U. 1936–39
Karras, Ted [T], Indiana 1958–59
Kase, George [G], Duquesne. 1939
Kavel, George [B], Carnegie Tech. 1934
Keating, Tom [DT], Michigan 1973
Keith, Craig [TE], Lenoir–Rhyne 1993–94
Kelley, Jim [E], Notre Dame. 1964
Kellum, Marv [LB], Wichita State. 1974–76
Kelsch, Mose [B], Christian 1933–34
Kemp, Jack [QB], Occidental 1957
Kemp, Ray [T], Duquesne. 1933
Kenerson, John [G], Kentucky State 1962
Kerkorian, Gary [QB], Stanford 1952
Keys, Brady [B], Colorado State 1961–67
Kichefski, Walt [E], Miami. 1940–42, 44**
Kielbasa, Max [B], Duquesne 1946
Kiesling, Walt [G], St. Thomas. 1937–38
Kiick, George [B], Bucknell 1940, 45
Killorin, Pat [C], Syracuse. 1966
Kilroy, Frank [T], Temple. 1943*
Kimble, Frank [E], West Virginia. 1945
King, Phil [B], Vanderbilt. 1964
Kirchner, Mark [OT], Baylor 1983
Kirk, Ken [LB], Mississippi 1960
Kirkland, Levon [LB], Clemson. 1992–95
Kish, Ben [B], Pitt 1943*
Kissell, Ed [B], Wake Forest 1952–54
Klapstein, Earl [T], Pacific 1946
Klein, Dick [T], Iowa. 1961
Klumb, John [E], Washington State. 1940
Knox, Darryl [LB], UNLV 1987
Kohrs, Bob [LB], Arizona State 1981–85
Kolb, Jon [OT], Oklahoma State 1969–81
Kolberg, Elmer [E], Oregon State. 1941
Kolodziejski, Chris [TE], Wyoming. 1984
Kondrla, John [T], St. Vincent 1945
Kortas, Ken [T], Louisville. 1965–68
Kosanovich, Bronco [C], Penn State 1947
Koshlap, Jules [B], Georgetown 1945
Kottite, Dick [TE], Wagner 1968
Kottler, Martin [B], Centre 1933
Kresky, Joe [G], Wisconsin 1935
Krisher, Bill [G], Oklahoma 1958
Kruczek, Mike [QB], Boston College. 1976–79
Krupa, Joe [OT], Purdue. 1956–64
Krutko, Larry [RB], West Virginia. 1958–60
Kurrasch, Roy [E], UCLA. 1948
Kvaternik, Cvonimir [G], Kansas. 1934

L

Lach, Steve [B], Duke 1946–47
LaCrosse, Dave [LB], Wake Forest. 1977
Ladygo, Pete [G], Maryland 1952, 54
Lajousky, Bill [G], Catholic U. 1936
Lake, Carnell [SS], UCLA. 1989–95
Lamas, Joe [G], Mount St. Mary's 1942
Lambert, Frank [K], Mississippi 1965–66
Lambert, Jack [LB], Kent State 1974–84
Lantz, Montgomery [C], Grove City 1933
Lanza, Chuck [C], Notre Dame 1988–89
Larose, Dan [T], Missouri. 1964
Lassann, Lou [E], Western Maryland 1938
Lasse, Dick [LB], Syracuse 1958–59
Lattner, John [B], Notre Dame. 1954
Laux, Ted [B], St. Joseph of Penna. 1943*
Law, Hubbard [C], Sam Houston 1942, 45
Lawrence, Ben [G], Indiana (Pa.) 1987
Layne, Bobby [QB], Texas. 1958–62
Lea, Paul [T], Tulane 1951
Leahy, Bob [QB], Emporia State. 1971
Leahy, Gerald [T], Colorado 1957
Lee, Bernard [B], Villanova. 1938
Lee, Danzell [TE], Lamar 1987
Lee, Greg [DB], Arkansas State 1988
Lee, Herman [T], Florida A & M. 1957
Lee, John [B], Carnegie Tech 1939
Leftridge, Dick [B], West Virginia 1966
Lemek, Ray [G], Notre Dame. 1962–65
Lester, Tim [FB], Eastern Kentucky 1995
Letsinger, Jim [G], Purdue 1933
Levanti, Lou [G], Illinois 1951–52
Levey, Jim [B] 1934–36
Lewis, Frank [WR], Grambling 1971–77
Lewis, Joe [T], Compton Junior 1958–60
Liddick, Dave [T], George Washington. 1957
Lind, Mike [B], Notre Dame. 1965–66
Lipps, Louis [WR/KR], So. Mississippi 1984–91
Lipscomb, Gene [T] 1961–62
Little, David [LB], Florida 1981–92
Littlefield, Carl [B], Wash. State. 1939
Lloyd, Greg [LB], Fort Valley State 1988–95
Lockett, Charles [WR], Long Beach St. 1987–88
Logan, Charles [E], Northwestern 1964
Long, Bill [E], Oklahoma A & M. 1949–50
Long, Terry [G], East Carolina 1984–91
Longnecker, Ken [T], Lebanon Val.. 1960
Looney, Don [E], TCU 1941–42
Lott, John [C/G], North Texas State. 1987
Love, Duval [G], UCLA 1992–94
Lowther, Russ [B], Detroit 1945
Lucas, Jeff [OT], West Virginia. 1987
Lucente, John [B], W. Virginia 1945
Luna, Bob [B], Alabama 1959
Lusteg, Booth [K], Connecticut 1968

M

Mack, Red [B], Notre Dame 1961–63, 65
Mack, Rico [LB], Appalachian State 1993
Mackrides, Bill [QB], Nevada 1953
Magac, Mike [G], Missouri 1965–66
Magulick, George [B], St. Francis. 1944**
Maher, Francis [B], Toledo 1941
Malkovich, Joe [C], Duquesne 1935
Mallick, Francis [T] 1965
Malone, Mark [QB], Arizona State. 1980–87
Mandich, Jim [TE], Michigan 1978
Mansfield, Ray [C], Washington. 1964–76
Manske, Edgar [E], Northwestern 1938
Maples, Bob [C], Baylor. 1971
Maras, Joe [C], Duquesne 1938–40
Marchi, Basilio [C], NYU 1934
Marchibroda, Ted [QB], St. Bonaventure & Det. 1953, 55–56
Marion, Jerry [B], Wyoming 1967

Marker, Henry [B], W. Virginia 1934
Markland, Jeff [TE], Illinois 1988
Marotti, Lou [G], Toledo 1944**
Martha, Paul [B], Pitt 1964–69
Martin, John [B], Oklahoma 1944
Martin, Vernon [B], Texas 1942, 44**
Masters, Bob [B], Baylor 1939, 43*
Masters, Walt [B], Penn 1944**
Mastrangelo, John [G], Notre Dame 1947–48
Matesic, Ed [B], Pitt 1936
Matesic, Joe [T], Arizona State 1954
Mathews, Ray [B], Clemson 1951–59
Mattioli, Fran [G], Pitt 1946
Matuszak, Marv [LB], Tulsa 1953, 55–56
Maxson, Alvin [RB], So. Methodist 1977–78
May, Ray [LB], Southern Cal 1967–69
Mayhew, Hayden [G], Tex. Mines 1936–38
Mays, Alvoid [CB], West Virginia 1995
Mazzanti, Jerry [E], Arkansas 1967
McAfee, Fred [RB], Mississippi 1994–95
McCabe, Richie [B], Pitt 1955, 1957–58
McCaffray, Art [T], Pacific 1946
McCall, Don [RB], Southern Cal 1969
McCarthy, John [B], St. Francis 1944**
McClairen, Jack [E], Bethune-Cookman 1955–60
McClung, Willie [T], Flor. A & M 1955–57
McConnell, Dewey [E], Wyoming 1954
McCullough, Hugh [B], Oklahoma 1939, 43*
McDade, Karl [C], Portland 1938
McDonald, Ed [B], Duquesne 1936
McDonough, Coley [QB], Day 1939–41, 44**
McDonough, Paul [E], Utah 1938
McFadden, Marv [G], Mich. St. 1953, 56
McGee, Ben [E], Jackson State 1964–72
McGovern, Rob [LB], Holy Cross 1991
McGriff, Tyrone [G], Florida A & M 1980–82
McKyer, Tim [CB], Texas–Arlington 1994
McMakin, John [TE], Clemson 1972–74
McNally, Johnny "Blood" [B], St. John of Minn. 1934, 37–39
McNamara, Ed [T], Holy Cross 1945
McPeak, Bill [E], Pitt 1949–57
McWilliams, Tom [B], Miss St. 1950
Meadows, Ed [E], Duke 1955
Meeks, Bryant [C], S. Carolina 1947–48
Mehelich, Chuck [E], Duquesne 1946–51
Meilinger, Steve [E], Kentucky 1961
Merkovsky, Elmer [T], Pitt 1944**, 45–46
Merriweather, Mike [LB], Pacific 1982–87
Messner, Max [LB], Cincinnati 1964–65
Meyer, Dennis [DB], Arkansas State 1973
Meyer, Ron [QB], S. Dakota State 1966
Michael, Bill [G], Ohio State 1957
Michaels, Ed [G], Villanova 1943*
Michaels, Lou [E], Kentucky 1961–63
Michalik, Art [G], St. Ambrose 1955–56
Middleton, Kelvin [SS], Wichita State 1987
Midler, Lou [G], Minnesota 1939
Miles, Eddie [LB], Minnesota 1990
Miller, Jim [QB], Michigan State 1995
Miller, Tom [E], Hampden Sydney 1943*
Mills, Ernie [WR], Florida 1991–95
Minarik, Henry [E], Michigan State 1951
Miner, Tom [E], Tulsa 1958
Mingo, Gene [K] 1969–70
Minni, Frank [B], San Jose State 1949
Minter, Michael [DT], North Texas St. 1987
Modzelewski, Dick [T], Maryland 1955
Modzelewski, Ed [B], Maryland 1952
Moegle, Dick [B], Rice 1960
Momsen, Tony [C], Michigan 1951
Moore, Bill [B], Loyola of New Orleans 1933
Moore, Red [G], Penn State 1947–49
Morales, Gonzales [B], St. Mary's of California 1947–48
Morgan, Bob [B], New Mexico 1967–68
Moriarty, Tom [S], Bowling Green 1980
Morrall, Earl [QB], Mich. State 1957–58
Morris, Byron "Bam" [RB], Texas Tech 1994–95
Morris, John [B], Oregon 1960
Morse, Steve [RB], Virginia 1985
Moser, Rick [RB], Rhode Island 1978–79, 81–82
Mosher, Clure [C], Louisville 1942
Mosley, Norm [B], Alabama 1948
Moss, Paul [E], Purdue 1933
Motley, Marion [B], Nevada 1955
Mott, Norm [B], Georgia 1934
Mularkey, Mike [TE], Florida 1989–91
Mulleneaux, Lee [C], Northern Arizona 1935–36
Mullins, Gerry [G/OT], Southern Calif. 1971–79
Murley, Dick [T], Purdue 1956
Murray, Earl [G], Purdue 1952
Musulin, George, Pitt 1938

N

Nagler, Gern [E], Santa Clara 1959
Naiota, John [B], St. Francis 1942, 45
Nardi, Dick [B], Ohio State 1939
Nelsen, Bill [QB], Southern Cal 1963–67
Nelson, Darrell [TE], Memphis State 1984–85
Nelson, Edmund [NT/DE], Auburn 1982–87
Nery, Carl [G], Duquesne 1940–41
Newberry, Tom [G], Wisconsin–La Crosse 1995
Newsome, Harry [P], Wake Forest 1985–89
Niccolai, Armand [T/K], Duquesne 1934–42
Nicholas, Allen [B], Temple 1945
Nicholas, Bob [T], Stanford 1965
Nickel, Elbie [E], Cincinnati 1947–57
Nickerson, Hardy [LB], California 1987–92
Nicksich, George [G], St. Bonaventure 1950
Nisby, John [G], Pacific 1957–61
Nix, Kent [QB], TCU 1967–69
Nixon, Mike [B], Pitt 1935
Nobile, Leo [G], Penn State 1948–49
Nofsinger, Terry [QB], Utah 1961–64
Noppenberg, John [B], Miami 1940–41
Nosich, John [T], Duquesne 1938
Nutter, "Buzz" [C], VPI 1961–64
Nuzum, Jerry [B], New Mex. A & M 1948–51

O

O'Brien, Fran [T], Mich. State 1966–67
O'Brien, John [E], Florida 1954–56
O'Delli, Mel [B], Duquesne 1944**, 45
Odom, Henry [RB], So. Carolina St. 1983
O'Donnell, Neil [QB], Maryland 1990–95
Oehler, John [C], Purdue 1933–34
Oelerich, John [B], St. Ambrose 1938
Oldham, Chris [CB], Oregon 1995
Oldham, Ray [DB], Middle Tennessee St. 1978
Olejniczak, Stan [T], Pitt 1935
Oliver, Clarence [DB], San Diego St. 1969–70
Olsavsky, Jerry [LB], Pittsburgh 1989–95
Olszewski, Al [E], Penn St. & Pitt 1945
O'Malley, Joe [E], Georgia 1955–56
O'Neil, Bob [G], Notre Dame 1956–57
Oniskey, Dick [G], Chattanooga 1955
Opfar, Dave [DE/NT], Penn State 1987
Orr, Jim [E], Georgia 1958–60
Ortmann, Chuck [QB], Michigan 1951
O'Shea, Terry [TE], California (Pa.) 1989–90
Oswald, Paul [C], Kansas 1987
Owens, Darrick [WR], Mississippi 1992

P

Palelei, Si'ulagi [G], Nevada–Las Vegas 1993
Palmer, Tom [T], Wake Forest 1953–54
Papach, George [B], Purdue 1948–49
Parker, Frank [DT], Oklahoma State 1968–69
Parrish, James [OL], Temple 1995
Paschell, Bill [B], ... 1940
Pascka, Gordon [G], Minnesota 1943
Pastin, Frank [G], Waynesburg 1942
Patrick, John [B], Penn State 1941, 45–46
Patterson, Bill [QB], Baylor 1940
Pavia, Ralph [G], Dayton 1947
Pavkov, Stonko [G], Idaho 1939–40
Peaks, Clarence [B], Mich. State 1964–65
Pearson, Barry [WR], Northwestern 1972–73
Pearson, Preston [B], Illinois 1970–74
Pegram, Erric [RB], North Texas State 1995
Pense, Leon [QB], Arkansas 1945
Perko, John [G], Duq. 1937–40, 44**, 45–47
Perry, Darren [FS], Penn State 1992–95
Perry, Lowell [B], Michigan 1956
Petchel, John [QB], Duquesne 1945
Petersen, Ted [OT/C], E. Illinois 1977–83, 87
Petrella, John [B], Penn State 1945
Piatukas, George [E], Duquesne 1938–41
Pierre, John [E], Pitt 1945
Pillath, Roger [T], Wisconsin 1966
Pine, Ed [LB], Utah 1965
Pinney, Ray [OT/G/C], Washington . 1976–78, 80–82, 85–87
Pirro, Rocco [G], Catholic U. 1940–41
Pittman, Mel [C], Hardin–Simmons 1935
Pokorny, Frank [WR], Youngstown St. 1985
Pollard, Frank [RB], Baylor 1980–88
Popovich, John [B], St. Vincent 1944**–45
Postus, Al [B], Villanova 1945
Pottios, Myron [LB], Notre Dame 1961–65
Potts, Bill [B], Villanova 1934
Pough, Ernest [WR], Texas Southern 1976–77
Powell, Tim [E], Northwestern 1966
Powers, John [E], Notre Dame 1962–66
Priatko, Bill [LB], Pitt 1957
Putzier, Rollin [DT], Oregon 1988

Q

Quatse, Jesse [T], Pitt 1933–34
Quick, Jerry [OT/G], Wichita State 1987

R

Raborn, Carroll [C], SMU 1936–37
Rado, Alex [B], New River State 1934–35
Rado, George [G], Duquesne 1935–37
Radosevich, George [C], Pitt 1953
Ragunas, Vince [B], VMI 1949
Rajkovich, Pete [B], Detroit 1934
Randour, Hub, Pitt 1935
Rankin, Walt [B], Texas Tech 1944**
Rasby, Walter [TE], Wake Forest 1994
Raskowski, Leo [T], Ohio State 1933
Rasmussen, Randy [C–G], Minnesota 1984–86
Ravotti, Eric [LB], Penn State 1994–95
Reavis, Dave [DT], Arkansas 1974–75
Rechichar, Bert [B], Tennessee 1960
Recutt, Ray [E], VMI 1943*
Reeder, Dan [RB], Delaware 1986, 87
Reese, Jerry [DE], Kentucky 1988
Reger, John [LB], Pitt 1955–63
Renfro, Will [G], Memphis State 1960
Repko, Joe [T], Boston College 1946–47
Reutershan, Randy [DB], Pitt 1978
Reynolds, Billy [B], Pitt 1958
Reynolds, Jim [B], Oklahoma A & M 1946
Rhodes, Don [T], W & J 1933
Ribble, Loran [G], Hardin–Simmons 1934–35
Richards, Perry [E], Detroit 1957
Richardson, Huey [LB/DE], Florida 1991
Richmond, Rock [DB], Oregon 1987
Ricketts, Tom [OT], Pittsburgh 1989–91
Rienstra, John [G], Temple 1986–90
Riffle, Dick [B], Albright 1941–42
Riley, Avon [LB], UCLA 1987

Riley, Cameron [DB], Missouri............. 1987
Rivera, Gabe [DT], Texas Tech.............. 1983
Rizzo, Tony, Duquesne..................... 1938
Roberts, John [B], Georgia 1934
Robinson, Ed [LB], Florida 1994
Robinson, Gil [E], Catawba 1933
Robinson, Jack [T], N.E. Mo. St. 1938
Robnett, Marshall [C], Texas A & M 1944**
Rodak, Mike [B], Western Reserve........... 1942
Rodgers, John [TE], La. Tech. 1982–84
Rogel, Fran [B], Penn State.............. 1950–57
Rogers, Cullen [B], Texas A & M 1946
Rorison, Jim [T], Southern Cal. 1938
Rosepink, Marty [G], Pitt 1947
Rostosky, Pete [OT], Connecticut......... 1984–86
Rowley, Bob [LB], Virginia 1963
Rowser, John [DB], Michigan........... 1970–73
Royals, Mark [P], Appalachian State 1992–94
Rozelle, Aubrey [LB], Delta State 1957
Rucinski, Ed [E], Indiana 1944**
Ruff, Guy [LB], Syracuse 1982
Ruple, Ernie [T], Arkansas 1968–69
Russell, Andy [LB], Missouri 1963, 1966–76
Ryan, Ed [E], St. Mary's (Cal.) 1948

S

Sader, Steve [B]....................... 1943*
Salata, Paul [E], Southern California 1950–51
Sample, John [B], Maryland St. 1961–62
Samuel, Don [B], Oregon State........... 1949–50
Samuelson, Carl [T], Nebraska 1948–51
Sanchez, Lupe [CB/KR], UCLA 1986–88
Sandberg, Sigurd [T], Iowa Wes. 1935–37
Sandefur, Wayne [B], Purdue 1936–37
Sanders, Chuck [RB], Slippery Rock 1986–87
Sanders, John [G], SMU 1940–42
Sandig, Curt [B], St. Mary of Tex........ 1942
Sandusky, Mike [G], Maryland......... 1957–65
Sapp, Theron [B], Georgia............. 1963–65
Saul, Bill [LB], Penn State 1964, 66–68
Saumer, Sylvester [B], St. Olaf 1934
Scales, Charles [B], Indiana............. 1960–61
Scarbath, Jack [QB], Maryland 1956
Scales, Charles [B], Indiana............. 1960–61
Scherer, Bernard [E], Nebraska.......... 1939
Schiechl, John [C], Santa Clara 1941–42
Schmidt, John [C], Carnegie Tech 1940
Schmitz, Bob [LB], Montana St.......... 1961–66
Schnelker, Bob [E], Bowling Green 1961
Schuelke, Karl [B], Wisconsin 1939
Schultz, Eberle [G], Oregon St. 1941–42
Schwartz, Elmer [B], Wash. St. 1933
Schweder, John [G], Penn 1951–55
Scolnik, Glenn [WR], Indiana 1973
Scot, Wilbert [LB], Indiana............... 1961
Scudero, Joe [B], San Francisco 1960
Seabaugh, Todd [LB], San Diego St. 1984
Seabright, Charles [QB], W. Virginia 1946–50
Seals, Ray [DE], none................... 1994–95
Searcy, Leon [OT], Miami (Fla.) 1992–95
Sears, Vic [T], Oregon State 1943*
Sebastian, Mike [B], Pitt 1935
Seitz, Warren [TE], Missouri 1986
Semes, Bernard [B], Duquesne 1944**
Seward, Dean [B],......................
Sexton, Brent [DB], Elon 1977
Shaffer, George [B], W & J................ 1933
Shanklin, Ron [WR], N. Tex. St. 1970–74
Sharp, Rick [T], Washington 1970–71
Sheffield, Chris [CB], Albany State 1986–87
Shell, Donnie [SS], So. Carolina St. 1974–87
Shelton, Richard [CB], Liberty.......... 1990–93
Shepard, Charles [B], N. Tex. St. 1956
Sheriff, Stan [LB], Cal. Polytech. 1954
Sherman, Alex [QB], Brooklyn.......... 1943*
Sherman, Bob [B], Iowa................ 1964–65

Shields, Burrell [B], John Carroll 1954
Shiner, Dick [QB], Maryland 1968–69
Shipkey, Jerry [B], UCLA 1948–52
Shorter, Jim [B], Detroit 1969
Shugarts, Bret [DE], Indiana (Pa.) 1987
Shurtz, Hubert [T], LSU 1948
Shy, Don [B], San Diego St. 1967–68
Simerson, John [T], Purdue 1958
Simien, Tracy [LB], Texas Christian 1989
Simington, Milt [B], Arkansas 1942
Simmons, Jerry [WR], Bethune–Cookman.. 1965–66
Simms, Bob [E], Rutgers 1962
Simpson, Jack [B], Florida 1961–62
Simpson, Tim [G/C], Illinois 1994
Sims, Darryl [DE], Wisconsin 1985–86
Sinkovitz, Frank [C], Duke............. 1947–52
Sirochman, George [G], Duquesne.......... 1942
Sites, Vince [E], Pitt................... 1936–37
Skansi, Paul [WR], Washington 1983
Skladany, Joe [E], Pitt.................. 1934
Skorich, Nick [G], Cincinnati.......... 1946–48
Skoronski, Ed [E], Purdue............. 1935–36
Skulos, Mike [G], W & J 1938
Slater, Walt [B], Tennessee............... 1947
Small, Fred [LB], Washington 1985
Smith, Ben [E], Alabama............... 1934–35
Smith, Billy Ray [T], Arkansas 1958–60
Smith, Bob [B], N. Texas State 1966
Smith, Dave [WR], Indiana (Pa.) 1970–72
Smith, Jim [WR], Michigan 1977–82
Smith, Kevin [S], Rhode Island 1991
Smith, Laverne [RB], Kansas 1977
Smith, Ron [QB], Richmond 1966
Smith, Steve [E], Michigan 1966
Smith, Stu [QB], Bucknell............. 1937–38
Smith, Truett [QB], Wyoming & Mississippi St.
1950–51
Smith, Warren [T], Kansas Wes........... 1948
Snell, Ray [OT], Wisconsin............. 1984–85
Snyder, Bill [G], Ohio U............... 1934–35
Sodaski, John [DB], Villanova 1970
Soleau, Bob [LB], Wm. & Mary 1964
Solomon, Ariel [G/OT], Colorado 1991–95
Somers, George [T], LaSalle 1941–42
Sorce, Ross [T], Georgetown.............. 1945
Sortet, Wilbur [E], West Virginia 1933–40
Souchak, Frank [E], Pitt 1939
Spencer, Todd [RB], So. Cal. 1984–85
Spinks, Jack [G], Alcorn A & M 1952
Spizak, Charley [QB], Carn. Tech. 1938
Staggers, Jon [WR], Missouri 1970–71
Stai, Brenden [G], Nebraska 1995
Stallworth, John [WR], Alabama A&M 1974–87
Stanton, John [B], N. Car. St. 1961
Stark, Rohn [P], Florida State.......... 1995
Starret, Ben [B], St. Mary's of Cal. 1941
Station, Larry [LB], Iowa 1986
Stautner, Ernie [T], Bost. Col. 1950–63
Steed, Joel [NT], Colorado 1992–95
Steele, Ernie [B], Washington 1943*
Stehouwer, Ron [B], Colorado State 1960–64
Stenger, Brian [LB], Notre Dame 1969–72
Stenn, Paul [T], Villanova 1947
Steward, Denn [B], Ursinus 1943*
Stewart, Kordell [QB/WR], Colorado 1995
Stock, John [E], Pitt................... 1956
Stock, Mark [WR], Virginia Military 1989
Stofko, Ed [B], St. Francis 1945
Stone, Dwight [WR/RB/KR], Middle Tennessee State
1987–94
Stoudt, Cliff [QB], Youngstown St....... 1977–83
Stough, Glen [T], Duke 1945
Stowe, Tyronne [LB], Rutgers 1987–90
Strand, Eli [G], Iowa State Coll. 1966
Strom, Rick [QB], Georgia Tech 1989–93
Strugar, George [T], Washington 1962

Strutt, Art [B], Duquesne 1935–36
Stryzinski, Dan [P], Indiana 1990–91
Strzelczyk, Justin [OT], Maine.......... 1990–95
Stule, Ernie [B],.........................
Suhey, Steve [G], Penn State 1948–49
Sulima, George [E], Boston U. 1952–54
Sullivan, Frank [C], Loyola (New Or.). 1940
Sullivan, Robert [B], Holy Cross Iowa 1947
Sutherin, Don [B], Ohio State......... 1959–60
Sutton, Ricky [DL], Auburn............... 1993
Swain, John [CB], Miami (Fla.) 1985–86
Swann, Lynn [WR], Southern Cal....... 1974–82
Sweeney, Calvin [WR], Southern Cal. 1980–87
Sydnor, Willie [WR/KR], Syracuse 1982
Szot, Walter [T], Bucknell................ 1949–50

T

Tanguay, Jim [B], NYU 1933
Tarasovic, George [E], LSU 1952–53, 56–63
Tatum, Jesse [E], N. Carolina State........... 1938
Taylor, Jim [LB], Baylor 1956
Taylor, Mike [T], Southern Cal. 1968–69
Tepe, Lou [C], Duke................. 1953–55
Terry, Nat [CB], Florida State 1978
Tesser, Ray [E], Carnegie Tech 1933–34
Thigpen, Yancey [WR], Winston–Salem State
1992–95
Thomas, Ben [DE/DT], Auburn............. 1988
Thomas, Clendon [B], Oklahoma........ 1962–68
Thomas, J.T. [CB/S], Florida St..... 1973–77, 79–81
Thompson, Clarence [B], Minnesota 1937–38
Thompson, Leroy [RB], Penn State 1991–93
Thompson, Tommy [QB], Tulsa 1940
Thompson, Weegie [WR], Florida St. 1984–89
Thornton, Sidney [RB], Northwestern La. . 1977–82
Thurbon, Bob [B], Pitt 1943*–44**
Tiller, Morgan [E], Denver 1945
Tinsley, Sid [B], Clemson 1945
Titus, George [C], Holy Cross 1946
Titus, Silas [E], Holy Cross 1945
Toews, Loren [LB], California 1973–83
Tomasetti, Lou [B], Bucknell 1939–40
Tomasic, Andy [B], Temple 1942–46
Tomczak, Mike [QB], Ohio State 1993–95
Tomlinson, Dick [G], Kansas 1950–51
Tommerson, Clarence [B], Wisconsin 1938–39
Tosi, John [B], Niagara.................. 1939
Tracy, Tom [B], Tennessee 1958–63
Trout, Dave [PK], Pitt 1981, 87
Tsoutsouvas, Lou [C], Stanford............ 1938
Tuggle, Anthony [CB/S], Nicholls St...... 1985, 87
Turk, Dan [C], Wisconsin 1985–86
Turley, John [QB], Ohio Wesleyan 1935–36
Tyrrell, Tim [RB], Northern Illinois 1989

V

Valentine, Zack [LB], East Carolina....... 1979–81
Van Dyke, Bruce [G], Missouri........... 1967–73
Varrichione, Frank [T], Notre Dame 1955–60
Vaughan, John [QB], Ind. St. (Pa.) 1933–34
Veals, Elton [RB], Tulane 1984
Veasey, Craig [DL], Houston........... 1990–91
Vidoni, Vic [E], Duquesne............. 1935–36
Vincent, Shawn [CB], Akron 1991
Voss, Lloyd [T], Nebraska............. 1966–71

W

Wade, Bob [DB], Morgan State............. 1968
Wade, Tom [QB], Texas 1964–65
Wager, Clint [E], St. Mary's Minn. 1944**
Wagner, Mike [S], Western Illinois 1971–80
Walden, Bob [P], Georgia 1968–77
Walker, Sammy [CB], Texas Tech 1991–92
Wallace, Ray [RB], Purdue 1989

Walsh, Bill [C], Notre Dame 1949–55
Warren, Busit [B], Tennessee. 1945
Warren, Xavier [DE/DT], Tulsa 1987
Washington, Anthony [CB], Fresno State . . . 1981–82
Washington, Clarence [DT], Arkansas AM & N . . . .
  1969–70
Washington, Robert [OT], Alcorn State 1987
Washington, Sam [CB], Miss. Val. St. 1982–85
Watkins, Tom [B], Iowa State 1968
Watson, Allen [K], Newport (Wales) 1970
Watson, Sid [B], Northwestern 1955–57
Webster, Elnardo [LB], Rutgers 1992
Webster, George [LB], Michigan State. 1972–73
Webster, Mike [C], Wisconsin. 1974–88
Weed, Thurlow [K], Ohio State 1955
Weinberg, Henry [G], Duquesne 1934
Weinstock, Izzy [B], Pitt 1937–38
Weisenbaugh, Henry [B], Pitt 1935
Wells, Billy [B], Mich. State 1957
Wendlick, Joe [E], Oregon State 1941
Wenzel, Ralph [E], Tulane. 1942
Wenzel, Ralph [G], San Diego St. 1966–70
Westfall, Ed [B], Ohio Wesleyan 1933
Wetzel, Damon [B], Ohio State. 1935
Wheeler, Ernie [B], N. Dakota State. 1939
Whelan, Tom [B], Catholic U. 1933
White, Byron [B], Colorado 1938
White, Dwight [DE], East Texas State 1971–80
White, Paul [B], Michigan. 1947
Wiehl, Joe [T], Duquesne 1935

Wilburn, J. R. [WR], S. Carolina. 1966–70
Wilcots, Solomon [S], Colorado 1992
Wiley, Jack [T], Waynesburg. 1946–50
Wilkerson, Eric [RB/WR], Kent State 1989
Williams, Albert [LB], UTEP. 1987
Williams, Dave [WR], Washington 1973
Williams, Don [G], Texas. 1941
Williams, Eric [S], N.C. State 1983–86
Williams, Erwin [WR], Maryland St. 1969
Williams, Gerald [NT/DE], Auburn. 1986–94
Williams, Jerrol [LB], Purdue. 1989–92
Williams, Joe [LB], Grambling. 1987
Williams, Joe [B], Ohio State 1939
Williams, John L. [FB], Florida 1994–95
Williams, Ray [CB], Rhode Island 1987
Williams, Robert [S], Eastern Illinois 1984
Williams, Sidney [LB], Southern 1969
Williams, Warren [RB], Miami (Fla.). 1988–92
Williams, Willie [CB], Western Carolina. . . . 1993–95
Williamson, Fred [B], Northwestern 1960
Willis, Keith [DE], Northeastern 1982–87, 89–91
Wilson, Bill [E], Gonzaga 1938
Wilson, Frank [TE], Rice 1982
Winfrey, Carl [LB], Wisconsin 1972
Wingle, Blake [G], UCLA 1983–85
Winston, Dennis [LB], Arkansas 1977–81, 85–86
Withycombe, Mike [C], Fresno State 1991
Wolf, Jim [DE], Prairie View. 1974
Wolfley, Craig [G/OT], Syracuse 1980–89
Womack, Joe [B], Los Angeles St. 1962

Woodard, Ken [LB], Tuskegee Institute 1987
Woodley, David [QB], Louisiana St. 1984–85
Woodruff, Dwayne [CB], Louisville . 1979–85, 87–90
Woods, Rick [S/CB], Boise State. 1982–86
Woodson, Marv [B], Indiana. 1964–69
Woodson, Rod [DB/KR], Purdue 1987–95
Worley, Tim [RB], Georgia 1989–91, 93
Woudenbeg, John [T], Denver 1940–42
Wren, Lowe [B], Missouri 1960
Wukits, Al [C], Duquesne 1943*–44*–45
Wydo, Frank [T], Cornell 1947–51

Y

Young, Al [WR], South Carolina St. 1971–72
Young, Dick [B], Chattanooga. 1957
Young, Theo [TE], Arkansas. 1987
Younger, Paul [B], Grambling. 1958
Yurchey, John [B], Duquesne 1940

Z

Zaninelli, Silvio [B], Duquesne 1934–37
Zgonina, Jeff [DL], Purdue. 1993–94
Zimmerman, Leroy [QB], San Jose St. 1943*
Zombek, Joe [E], Pitt. 1954
Zopetti, Frank [B], Duquesne 1941

* Steelers combined with Philadelphia Eagles
** Steelers combined with Chicago Cardinals.

PHOTO CREDITS

All photos provided courtesy of the Pittsburgh Steelers except the following:

Bill Amatucci: 66, 122, 131, 142, 147

The Cleveland Press Collection: 36 bottom, 37 left, 50 bottom, 53, 62

Michael F. Fabus: i, ii–iii, vi–vii, xi, xiii, xiv, 17, 61, 67, 70, 74, 76, 78, 79, 95, 121, 133, 149, 152, 154 left and top right, 156 top left and top right, 158 top left, top right, and bottom right, 161 top left and top right, 165, 167 right, 168 bottom, 169 bottom, 170 top left and bottom right, 171, 172 left and right, 173, 174 top, 175 left and right, 176, 178 top left, bottom right, and bottom left, 179 bottom, 181 bottom, 182 top and bottom, 183, 184-185, 188 top and bottom, 189 left and right, 190, 191, 192 bottom, 194, 196, 197, 198, 199, 201, 202 bottom, 203, 214 bottom, 224 bottom, 225 bottom

Harry H. Homa: 59 top

Dick Raphael: 127 top

Steve Yakub: 210